21st International Workshop on Treebanks and Linguistic Theories (TLT 2023)

Computational and Corpus Linguistics

Washington, DC, USA
9-12 March 2023

ISBN: 978-1-7138-9063-8

Printed from e-media with permission by:

Curran Associates, Inc.
57 Morehouse Lane
Red Hook, NY 12571

Some format issues inherent in the e-media version may also appear in this print version.

Printed with permission by Curran Associates, Inc. (2025)

For permission requests, please contact the Association for Computational Linguistics at the address below.

Association for Computational Linguistics
209 N. Eighth Street
Stroudsburg, Pennsylvania 18360

Phone: 1-570-476-8006
Fax: 1-570-476-0860

acl@aclweb.org

Additional copies of this publication are available from:

Curran Associates, Inc.
57 Morehouse Lane
Red Hook, NY 12571 USA
Phone: 845-758-0400
Fax: 845-758-2633
Email: curran@proceedings.com
Web: www.proceedings.com

TLT 2023

The 21st International Workshop on Treebanks and Linguistic Theories (TLT, GURT/SyntaxFest 2023)

Proceedings of the Conference

March 9-12, 2023

The TLT organizers gratefully acknowledge the support from the following sponsors.

The Georgetown College of Arts & Sciences, the Georgetown Faculty of Languages and Linguistics, and the Georgetown Department of Linguistics

Association for Computational Linguistics (ACL)
209 N. Eighth Street
Stroudsburg, PA 18360
USA
Tel: +1-570-476-8006
Fax: +1-570-476-0860
acl@aclweb.org

Introduction

The 21st International Workshop on Treebanks and Linguistic Theories (TLT 2023) follows an annual series that started in 2002 in Sozopol, Bulgaria. TLT addresses all aspects of treebank design, development, and use. "Treebank" is taken in a broad sense, comprising any spoken, signed, or written data augmented with computationally processable annotations of linguistic structure at various levels. For the first time, TLT is part of GURT2023, an annual linguistics conference held at Georgetown University, which this year co-locates four related but independent events:

- The Seventh International Conference on Dependency Linguistics (Depling 2023)
- The 21st International Workshop on Treebanks and Linguistic Theories (TLT 2023)
- The Sixth Workshop on Universal Dependencies (UDW 2023)
- The First International Workshop on Construction Grammars and NLP (CxGs+NLP 2023)

The Georgetown University Round Table on Linguistics (GURT) is a peer-reviewed annual linguistics conference held continuously since 1949 at Georgetown University in Washington DC, with topics and co-located events varying from year to year.

In 2023, under an overarching theme of 'Computational and Corpus Linguistics', GURT/SyntaxFest continues the tradition of SyntaxFest 2019 and SyntaxFest 2021/22 in bringing together multiple events that share a common interest in using corpora and treebanks for empirically validating syntactic theories, studying syntax from quantitative and theoretical points of view, and for training machine learning models for natural language processing. Much of this research is increasingly multilingual and cross-lingual and requires continued systematic analysis from various theoretical, applied, and practical perspectives. New this year, the CxGs+NLP workshop brings a usage-based perspective on how form and meaning interact in language.

For these reasons and encouraged by the success of the previous editions of SyntaxFest, we —the chairs of the four events— decided to facilitate another co-located event at GURT 2023 in Washington DC.

As in past co-located events involving several of the workshops, we organized a single reviewing process, with identical paper formats for all four events. Authors could indicate (multiple) venue preferences, but the ultimate assignment of papers to events for accepted papers was made by the program chairs.

33 long papers were submitted, 11 to Depling, 16 to TLT, 10 to UDW and 10 to CxGs+NLP. The program chairs accepted 27 (82%) and assigned 7 to Depling, 6 to TLT, 5 to UDW and 9 to CxGs+NLP.

16 short papers were submitted, 6 of which to Depling, 6 to TLT, 10 to UDW and 2 to CxGs+NLP. The program chairs accepted 9 (56%) and assigned 2 to Depling, 2 to TLT, 3 to UDW, and 2 to CxGs+NLP.

Our sincere thanks go to everyone who is making this event possible: everybody who submitted their papers; Georgetown University Linguistics Department students and staff—including Lauren Levine, Jessica Lin, Ke Lin, Mei-Ling Klein, and Conor Sinclair—for their organizational assistance; and of course, the reviewers for their time and their valuable comments and suggestions. Special thanks are due to Georgetown University, and specifically to the Georgetown College of Arts & Sciences and the Faculty of Languages and Linguistics for supporting the conference with generous funding. Finally, we would also like to thank ACL SIGPARSE for its endorsement and the ACL Anthology for publishing the proceedings.

Owen Rambow, François Lareau (Depling2023 Chairs)
Daniel Dakota, Kilian Evang, Sandra Kübler, Lori Levin (TLT2023 Chairs)
Loïc Grobol, Francis Tyers (UDW2023 chairs)
Claire Bonial Harish Tayyar Madabushi (CxG+NLP2023 Chairs)
Nathan Schneider, Amir Zeldes (GURT2023 Organizers)
March 2023

Organizing Committee

Depling2023 Chairs

Owen Rambow, Stony Brook University
François Lareau, Université de Montréal

TLT2023 Chairs

Daniel Dakota, Indiana University
Kilian Evang, Heinrich Heine University Düsseldorf
Sandra Kübler, Indiana University
Lori Levin, Carnegie Mellon University

UDW2023 Chairs

Loïc Grobol, Université Paris Nanterre
Francis Tyers, Indiana University

CxGs+NLP2023 Chairs

Claire Bonial, U.S. Army Research Lab
Harish Tayyar Madabushi, The University of Bath

GURT2023 Organizers

Amir Zeldes, Georgetown University
Nathan Schneider, Georgetown University

GURT2023 Student Assistants

Lauren Levine, Georgetown University
Ke Lin, Georgetown University
Jessica Lin, Georgetown University

Program Committee

Program Committee for the Whole of GURT2023

Lasha Abzianidze, Utrecht University
Patricia Amaral, Indiana University
Valerio Basile, University of Turin
Emily Bender, University of Washington
Bernd Bohnet, Google
Claire Bonial, Army Research Lab
Gosse Bouma, University of Groningen
Miriam Butt, Universität Konstanz
Marie Candito, Université de Paris
Giuseppe G. A. Celano, Universität Leipzig
Xinying Chen, Xi'an Jiaotong University
Silvie Cinkova, Charles University Prague
Cagri Coltekin, Universität Tübingen
Stefania Degaetano-Ortlieb, Universität des Saarlandes
Éric Villemonte de la Clergerie, INRIA
Miryam de Lhoneux, KU Leuven
Valeria de Paiva, Topos Institute
Lucia Donatelli, Saarland University
Timothy Dozat, Google
Kim Gerdes, Université Paris-Saclay
Koldo Gojenola, University of the Basque Country
Loïc Grobol, Université Paris Nanterre
Bruno Guillaume, INRIA
Dag Trygve Truslew Haug, University of Oslo
Jena Hwang, Allen Institute for Artificial Intelligence
András Imrényi, Eötvös Lorand University
Alessandro Lenci, University of Pisa
Lori Levin, Carnegie Mellon University
Markéta Lopatková, Charles University Prague
Sylvain Kahane, Université Paris Nanterre
Jordan Kodner, State University of New York, Stony Brook
Sandra Kübler, Indiana University
Jan Macutek, Mathematical Institute, Slovak Academy of Sciences
Harish Tayyar Madabushi, University of Sheffield
Nicolas Mazziotta, Université de Liège
Alexander Mehler, Johann Wolfgang Goethe Universität Frankfurt am Main
Simon Mille, Dublin City University
Pierre André Ménard, Computer research institute of Montréal
Yusuke Miyao, The University of Tokyo
Simonetta Montemagni, ILC-CNR
Alexis Nasr, Aix Marseille Univ
Joakim Nivre, Uppsala University
Pierre Nugues, Lund University
Timothy John Osborne, Zhejiang University
Petya Osenova, Bulgarian Academy of Sciences
Robert Östling, Stockholm University

Simon Petitjean, Heinrich-Heine Universität Düsseldorf
Dirk Pijpops, Université de Liège
Michael Regan, University of Colorado, Boulder
Mathilde Regnault, Universität Stuttgart
Laurence Romain, University of Birmingham
Rudolf Rosa, Charles University Prague
Haruko Sanada, Rissho University
Beatrice Santorini, University of Pennsylvania
Giorgio Satta, Università degli studi di Padova
Sebastian Schuster, Universität des Saarlandes
Olga Scrivner, Rose-Hulman Institute of Technology
Ashwini Vaidya, Indian Institute of Technology, Delhi
Remi van Trijp, Sony Computer Sciences Laboratories Paris
Giulia Venturi, Institute for Computational Linguistics "A. Zampolli" (ILC-CNR)
Nianwen Xue, Brandeis University
Eva Zehentner, University of Zurich
Amir Zeldes, Georgetown University
Daniel Zeman, Charles University Prague
Heike Zinsmeister, Universität Hamburg
Hongxin Zhang, Zhejiang University

Table of Contents

Corpus-Based Multilingual Event-type Ontology: Annotation Tools and Principles

Eva Fučíková, Jan Hajič, and Zdeňka Urešová
Institute of Formal and Applied Linguistics, Faculty of Mathematics and Physics
Charles University, Prague, Czech Republic
{fucikova,hajic,uresova}@ufal.mff.cuni.cz

Abstract

In the course of building a multilingual Event-type Ontology resource called SynSemClass, it was necessary to provide the maintainers and the annotators with a set of tools to facilitate their job, achieve data format consistency, and in general obtain high-quality data. We have adapted a previously existing tool (Urešová et al., 2018b), developed to assist the work in capturing bilingual synonymy. This tool needed to be both substantially expanded with some new features and fundamentally changed in the context of developing the resource for more languages, which necessarily is to be done in parallel. We are thus presenting here the tool, the new data structure design which had to change at the same time, and the associated workflow.

1 Introduction

This paper describes the tools and the associated annotation process used for building up a corpus-based multilingual event-type ontology, called SynSemClass (Urešová et al., 2022). Since the overall premise is based on working from data ("bottom-up", see esp. Urešová et al. (2018a)), the work starts from a parallel corpus (at least between English and the given language being processed/annotated). Similarly, the ontology classes are also built from the language side: there is no predefined ontology. The words included in the classes are translational counterparts and as such can be considered synonyms (and we will refer to them in such a way with all the caveats connected with such simplification). The language of original texts is English, the verb synonyms captured in the ontology are, at the moment, only English, Czech, German, and Spanish.

In order to allow for independent annotation of different languages, it was necessary to develop guidelines for an annotation procedure applicable to many languages, design a workflow of the annotation for new languages, and create a configurable annotation tool for adding such new languages. This involved, among other things, designing a general configuration, including e.g., URLs for external linking of language resources, a stand-off annotation scheme (each language needs to be annotated separately by, presumably, teams scattered all over the world), and an editor capable of working with just the relevant language(s). Here, we describe the principles of restructuring and reformatting the dataset to accommodate multilinguality as well as the description of the capabilities of the extended new tool.

2 Related Work

General editors over databases used for editing lexical resources are not suitable due to the amount of customization and overhead needed for the complex structure of SynSemClass ontology, as argued already by Urešová et al. (2018b).

Specific tools for building lexicons have been built and/or used since at least the 1980s, as described e.g., in (Teubert, 2007). *Lexicon Creator* is suitable for working with pre-extracted wordlists. *Lexicon Builder* is a web service (Parai et al., 2010) for compiling custom lexicons from BioPortal ontologies. *CoBaLT Editor* (Kenter et al., 2012) has been used for historical texts and lexica. *Dicet* (Gader et al., 2012) is aimed at lexical graphs (this one is closest to the needs of SynSemClass annotation).

A broad overview and a brief description of some available editors and environments that can be used for the building of ontologies is provided for example by Alatrish (2012). Others are, e.g., Apollo[1], OntoStudio[2], Protégé[3], Swoop[4] and Top-

[1] http://apollo.open.ac.uk/index.html
[2] https://www.semafora-systems.com/
[3] https://protege.stanford.edu/
[4] https://www.softpedia.com/get/Internet/Other-Internet-Related/MIND-lab-SWOOP.shtml1

Proceedings of the 21st International Workshop on Treebanks and Linguistic Theories (TLT, GURT/SyntaxFest 2023), pages 1 - 10
March 9-12, 2023 ©2023 Association for Computational Linguistics

Braid Composer Free Edition[5].

Also relevant for our work are the general Linguistic Linked Open Data (LLOD) editors, but the SynSemClass data are still to be (re)defined as LLOD.[6]

SynSemClass is linked to a number of existing resources having their own specific editors so we tested also the suitability of their editors for our purposes but we found them not readily adaptable to the SynSemClass annotation scheme, since it requires more tasks to be covered than e.g., FrameNet editor (Fillmore, 2002) or Propbank frameset editor (Choi et al., 2010) can provide.[7]

3 Starting Point

As described in (Urešová et al., 2018a) and especially in (Urešová et al., 2018b), the previous version of the SynSemClass ontology was aimed at building the core, bilingual event-type ontology. It has been done in a specific situation - when advanced, manually annotated resources existed for both Czech and English, which had (indeed) been used to get an efficient workflow and accurate, richly annotated resource. The complexity of the definition of the then-called CzEngClass resource - with its syntactic-semantic mappings of valency slots to the newly developed semantic roles (associated with every class), linking to 9 external resources, and examples from a parallel corpus - has led to the development of the SynEd annotation tool with its functions tailored to the resources at hand. While the the semantic roles resemble FrameNet (Baker et al., 1998a) "Frame Elements", and sometimes borrow their names from there, it should be pointed out that there is one fundamental difference: the semantic roles used in SynSemClass aim at being defined across the ontology and not per class (as they would be if we follow the "per frame" approach used in FrameNet). In addition, the existence of the parallel treebank (the Prague Czech-English Dependency Treebank, (Hajič et al., 2012)) with its rich annotation scheme, exactly matching the task at hand in that it contained the necessary sense distinctions as recorded in the valency frames of the Czech and English valency lexicons, was taken advantage of in the design. The associated workflow was then very efficient, including complete double annotation and adjudication to arrive at high-quality resource.

The resources used come from the following datasets:

- Prague Czech-English Dependency Treebank (PCEDT) (Hajič et al., 2012),
- PDT-Vallex (Urešová et al., 2021),
- CzEngVallex lexicon (Urešová et al., 2015),
- EngVallex lexicon (Cinková et al., 2014),
- VALLEX lexicon (Czech) (Lopatková et al., 2020),
- FrameNet (Baker et al., 1998b; Fontenelle, 2003)[8],
- VerbNet (Schuler, 2006)[9],
- PropBank (Palmer et al., 2005)[10],
- OntoNotes Groups (Pradhan and Xue, 2009)[11], and
- WordNet 3.1(Fellbaum, 1998)[12].

The result of the previous efforts to create CzEngClass and subsequently extend it as SynSemClass is publicly available as a dataset[13] and for browsing as a web interface and service.[14] This latest version contains 883 classes; 63 of them already contain German verbs (while still being added using the original workflow and editor). Of the original 67,401 class member candidates, approx. 8,000 class members remained in this SynSemClass version, i.e., approx. 3,595 English, 464 German, and 4,110 Czech class members.[15] Adding German (and then Spanish) brought many new issues that needed to be addressed, and eventually it led to the development of the new data structure, editor and workflow that we are presenting in this paper.

We summarize briefly the design of the lexicon (Fig. 1) and the main points of its composition and structure.[16] Each class in SynSemClass is assigned a common set of semantic roles, called a "roleset",

[5] `https://franz.com/agraph/tbc/`

[6] Under the HumanE AI Net Micro-Project called Multilingual LLOD for the Semantic Web, still under construction.

[7] VerbNet uses the XML structure supplied in the associated DTD file.

[8] `https://framenet.icsi.berkeley.edu`

[9] `https://verbs.colorado.edu/verbnet`

[10] `https://propbank.github.io/v3.4.0/frames/index.html`

[11] `https://doi.org/10.35111/xmhb-2b84`

[12] `https://wordnet.princeton.edu`

[13] `https://hdl.handle.net/11234/1-4746`

[14] `https://lindat.cz/services/SynSemClass.`

[15] Currently, there are approx. 70 Spanish classes annotated with about 5,200 class members.

[16] Described in detail in (Urešová et al., 2020).

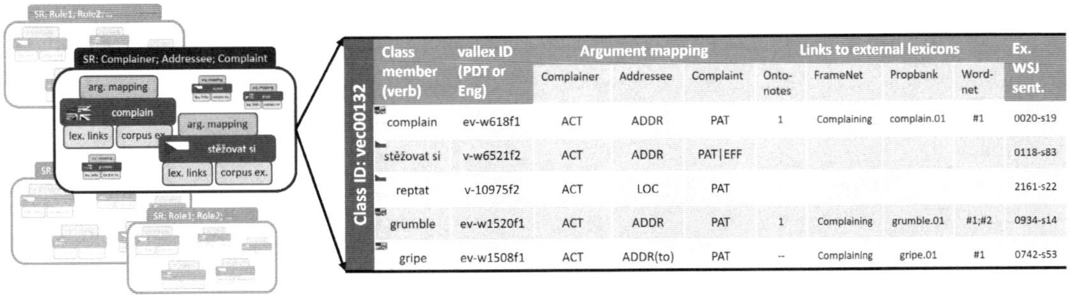

Figure 1: Example entry in SynSemClass ("complain-stěžovat si")

indicating the prototypical meaning of the given class. A roleset contains the core "situational participants" labelled as "semantic roles" common for all the multilingual class members (the individual multilingual verb senses) in one class. Each class in SynSemClass is viewed as a substitute for an ontology unit, similar to the treatment of WordNet synsets. Class members are (for the time being) verbs (in different languages). It is essential that these verbs are sense-distinguished; more precisely, each "class member" is meant to be a verb sense. These senses must be predefined (or defined on-the-fly and assigned a particular sense ID). For Czech end English, they have been taken from the existing valency lexicons PDT-Vallex and EngVallex, where the individual valency frames are already sense-disambiguated (and IDs assigned to them).

Class members are linked to both internal and external resources. The Czech class members are linked to the following Czech valency lexicons: PDT-Vallex, CzEngVallex (both internal, linked by means of their ID's), and VALLEX (external).[17] The English class members are linked to the internal lexicons EngVallex and CzEngVallex and to external sources, i.e., FrameNet, VerbNet, PropBank, OntoNotes Groups and WordNet.

4 Towards Multilingual Lexicon Design

The work on adding German and now Spanish (Fernández-Alcaina et al., 2023) made it clear that a refactorization of both the data structure of SynSemClass and corresponding changes in the SynEd and the associated workflow are necessary in order to be able to concurrently work on more languages. We are testing the new, more "universal" approach on Spanish. In the future, we would like to engage external teams (anyone who wants to contribute their language). In such a case, the design, datasets, suggested workflow and tools provided must be easy to use and understandable. However, this has not changed the original idea nor the overall design of SynSemClass - it is still an event-type ontology with classes as the main units representing event-type concepts, associated with a fixed set of semantic roles, and the class members are word senses representing the expression of that event-type concept in a particular language. This schema will not change even if other parts of speech (nouns, adjectives, etc.) are added.

But still, some assumptions providing a basis for the creation of the original structure and tools have to be scaled down. For example, a parallel (deeply and richly annotated) corpus exists only for a handful of language pairs and only some of them have associated valency (or predicate-argument, or word-sense-disambiguated, or similar) lexicons linked to the corpus. Word (or even just verb) senses are sometimes available (e.g., in multilingual WordNets), but generally not in referred to as such from an annotated corpus. Each language has a different set of available semantic lexicons to which the class members in that particular language can be linked.

4.1 The Overall Design

The main reason for the new design of the SynSemClass resource as a whole comes from the following basic requirements:

- work on different languages will be carried out in parallel by different teams, without the need for continuous access to the main repository,
- versions of the lexicon will integrate various versions of the language-dependent parts,
- common data (such as the set of semantic roles) cannot be amended independently.

[17] https://ufal.mff.cuni.cz/vallex/4.0

In addition, there are other constraints, like the size of the language-dependent part and the whole resource, time needed to copy the whole resource or its parts over the internet when editing and committing changes, etc.

A natural question arises regarding a comparison to the massively parallel and massively multilingual effort of building the Universal Dependencies treebanks (Nivre et al., 2016), which looks similar, and which uses a simple GitHub repository[18] that contains everything from the documentation and guidelines to the validation scripts. The SynSemClass annotation is similar but differs in one important point: while in the UD case, the only thing that is shared across the languages is the CoNLL-U format and the sets of base (or core) labels used for annotating POS, morphological features, and dependency relations that allow only for some language-specific flexibility, in the SynSemClass case, the common set of classes (event-type concepts) of the ontology, to which all the language-dependent data point to, will certainly undergo much more frequent changes than the shared UD "tagsets" did.[19] This factor has to be reflected in the data structure design, the workflow, and the editor as well.

Based on these requirements, the data structures and the editor have been designed as follows:

- the structure of the resource is implemented in a stand-off mode, i.e., the common part will be shared by the language-dependent parts (i.e., by the dataset containing words expressing the classes (event-type concepts) in the particular language),
- the editor remains a desktop application working on locally available data (possibly versioned in github or svn or similar system),
- the central repository will be a GitHub repository, with a "read-only" part containing the common data (i.e., the set of current classes with definitions, set of semantic roles and their distribution across classes as the main contents),
- the minimal requirement for existing resources to work on a new language will be the existence of a parallel corpus[20] between a language already covered by SynSemClass (preferably English that will, presumably, always have the highest coverage) and the language being added.

The design is such that there are no redundancies - all the common data are in the centrally maintained dataset (a single file) while all the language-dependent data are separate, making the parallel work possible and independent of the changes made in other languages.

Of course, the very existence of the dynamically changing common dataset is a complication that cannot be circumvented by technical means. However, it is unavoidable in all such multilingual projects - as known from, e.g., medicine (MESH databases, the ICD classification of diseases, etc.). It implies continued commitment on the maintainers side and also some commitment on the side of the authors of the individual language datasets, even if many amendments caused by changes in the central common datasets are either "non-breaking", such as adding a class and related semantic roles, or can be done automatically, e.g., renaming a role.

The workflow is then as follows:

1. based on the required parallel corpus, candidates are determined for each class in the current SynSemClass version,
2. an initial stand-off style language-dependent file is created with the correct format, annotators allowed to edit, etc., properly linking to the central common file classes and semantic roles,
3. annotators, following the guidelines for editing individual classes, work on pruning the language-dependent file from wrongly suggested class member candidates, assign roles mapped to syntactic arguments, add links to external resources, and select examples, using the SynEd editor and described in Sect. 4.3),
4. the annotators suggest changes by creating GitHub issues, or emailing the central maintainers to change or add classes and/or roles, edit role definitions, etc.; the maintainers will have to decide which changes to implement to the common dataset that will not break the

[18] `https://universaldependencies.org/`

[19] They have only changed between version 1 and 2, and were extended in a central way for the "Enhanced dependencies" available now for several treebanks.

[20] This could be, in the future, further relieved to assume just an existence of a monolingual corpus, depending on the progress in the way initial assignment to classes can be done, e.g., by multilingual embeddings, the results of current experiments with multilingual BERT(s), transfer learning, etc.

other language-dependent datasets, or batch-edit them to validate against the common (amended) dataset,

5. after adjusting for these changes, the language-dependent file will be committed and validated, iteratively and in cooperation with the annotators, until an error-free version can be declared publishable.

In this paper, we further elaborate and demonstrate the editor (point 3 of the above workflow) in Sect. 4.3. However, before presenting the main features of the editor, we describe also the new structure of the datasets in more detail in Sect. 4.2 below.

4.2 Structure of the Datasets

The datasets are the files the new editor works with, in a configurable way. We distinguish:

1. the common dataset and
2. the language-dependent dataset.

4.2.1 Common Dataset

The common dataset is a single file with the following structure:

```
<synsemclass_main owner="EF">
```

... (header with main users and roles [only])

```
<body>
<veclass id="vec00001">
 <commonroles>
  <role idref="vecroleAgent" />
  <role idref="vecroleComponents" />
  <role idref="vecroleCreated_Entity" />
  <role idref="vecroleAssets_currency" />
 </commonroles>
 <classnote/>
 <local_history><local_event
                time_stamp="..." .../>
                ...</local_history>
</veclass>
<veclass ...>
...
</veclass>
```

... (more classes of synonyms, using the veclass element)

```
</body> </synsemclass_main>
```

As seen from the above extract from the common (main) file, it only contains the definitions of semantic roles (which are common to the whole SynSemClass ontology) and a list of classes, with only the list of roles assigned to that particular class. For each class, this list of roles is fixed and common for all languages that are part of the SynSemClass ontology but which are contained in separate files, one file per language (see Sect. 4.2.2).

4.2.2 The Language-dependent Dataset

The language-dependent dataset has the following structure (German examples shown, simplified):

```
<synsemclass_DE>
 <header>
```

... (The first part of header with edition, version and description info)

```
  <list_of_users>
   <user id="2" annotator="yes" name=.../>
   <user .../>
  </list_of_users>
  <reflexicons>
   <lexicon id="\ssclass{}" name=.../>
```

... (default predicate-argument IDs for verbs with no entry in existing valency lexicons for German)

```
   </lexicon>
   <lexicon id="gup" name="gup">
    <lexref>http://alanakbik...
     </lexref>
    <lexbrowsing>http://alanakbik...
     </lexbrowsing>
    <lexsearching>http://alanakbik...
     </lexsearching>
    <argumentsused>
     <argdesc id="vecargA0">
      <comesfrom lexicon="gup"/>
      <label>Arg0</label>
      <shortlabel>A0</shortlabel>
     </argdesc>
     <argdesc id="vecargA1">
      ...
     </argdesc>
     ...
    </argumentsused>
   </lexicon>
   <lexicon>
    ...
   </lexicon>
  </reflexicons>
 </header>
 <body>
  <veclass id="vec00201"
   lemma="einwenden
   (\ssclass{}-ID-vec00201-de-cm00026)">
   <classmembers>
    <classmember id="vec00201-de-cm00016"
      idref="GUP-ID-argumentieren-01"
      lang="de" status="yes"
      lexidref="gup"
      lemma="argumentieren">
     <maparg>
      <argpair>
```

Argument-Role mapping here: A0 → Arguer

```
       <argfrom idref="vecargA0">
        <form/>
        <spec/>
       </argfrom>
       <argto idref="vecroleArguer"/>
      </argpair>
```

... (other argument to semantic roles mappings)

```
     </maparg>
     <restrict/>
     <cmnote/>
```

```
<extlex idref="gup" no_mapping="0">
 <links>
```

Links to external lexicon
here: the German UPB ("gup")

```
  <link predicate="argumentieren"
    rolesetid="01"
    filename="argumentieren"
    divid="argue.01"/>
 </links>
</extlex>
<extlex idref="fnd" no_mapping="0">
 <links>
```

Links to external lexicon
here: the German FrameNet ("fnd")

```
  <link frameid="937"
    framename="Begründen"/>
 </links>
</extlex>
```

... (more links to external German lexicons, such as E-VALBU or Woxikon[21])

```
<examples>
  <example corpref="paracrawl_ge"
  frpair="argue.argumentieren"
  nodeid="G-vec00060-001-s040"/>
</examples>
</classmember>
<classmember id="vec00201-de-cm00017"
  ...
  lemma="argumentieren">
 ...
</classmember>
```

... (more German classmembers)

```
  </classmembers>
 </veclass>
```

... (more classes)

```
</body> </synsemclass_DE>
```

In the above simplified example of the language-dependent file structure, the header contains some versioning information, list of allowed users (= annotators and maintainers), and list of pre-existing lexicons for the particular language (German in this case) to which the individual class members are being linked. Some of these pre-existing lexicons contain predicate-argument structure information to which the semantic roles of the class are mapped (in the above example, it is GUP[22] and E-VALBU (Kubczak, 2014; Schumacher et al., 2018)[23] for German).

The body element of the file contains the class members as assigned to the classes defined in the main file, by means of reference (e.g., `vec00201`), stating also the class name and ID of the references lemma in German. The individual class member entries contain the usual parts - the lemma and reference ID to one of the defining predicate-argument structure lexicons, then argument mapping(s) to semantic roles of the referenced class, links to external lexicons (the `extlex/link` element(s)), notes, and links to example sentences (here, from the ParaCrawl English-German corpus).

4.3 The SynEd Editor

The SynEd editor (Fig. 2) - in its "stand-off" version capable of working with one or (only) a few languages - has the following features:

- It can be customized to work with external lexicons (lexical resources) for the given language(s).
- It works with any number of language-specific files; these are typically two: English or some other already included language (in a "read-only" mode), and the language being added and worked on.
- It allows for marking the pre-extracted class members as OK (yes, to be kept) or as "no" meaning "to be deleted" (in fact, it allows for even more fine-grained distinctions, on a five-value scale: both "yes" and "no" have a weaker version ("rather yes/no") and there is also the possibility of marking the word as "undecided"; all decisions undergo a review by the maintainer).
- It allows for creating and editing the mapping of the semantic roles defined for the given class to syntactic arguments of the word (verb) in question (if some lexical resource describing these arguments exists).
- It allows for adding links (Fig. 3) to existing external lexical resources, such as WordNet or any other resource available on the web.
- It allows searching by lemma (cs, en, de) (Fig. 4), by semantic role to find classes that contain it (Fig. 5) or by class ID (Fig. 6).
- It allows for selecting textual examples from a user-defined language-specific corpus (if available, a parallel one), to exemplify the particular word sense or use of the word being assigned to the class as a class member.

[21] https://synonyme.woxikon.de

[22] GUP stands for [German] Universal Propositions Bank (Akbik et al., 2016), see https://github.com/UniversalPropositions/UP-1.0/tree/master/UP_German

[23] E-VALBU stands for Elektronisches Valenzlexikon des Deutschen, see https>//https://grammis.ids-mannheim.de/verbvalenz

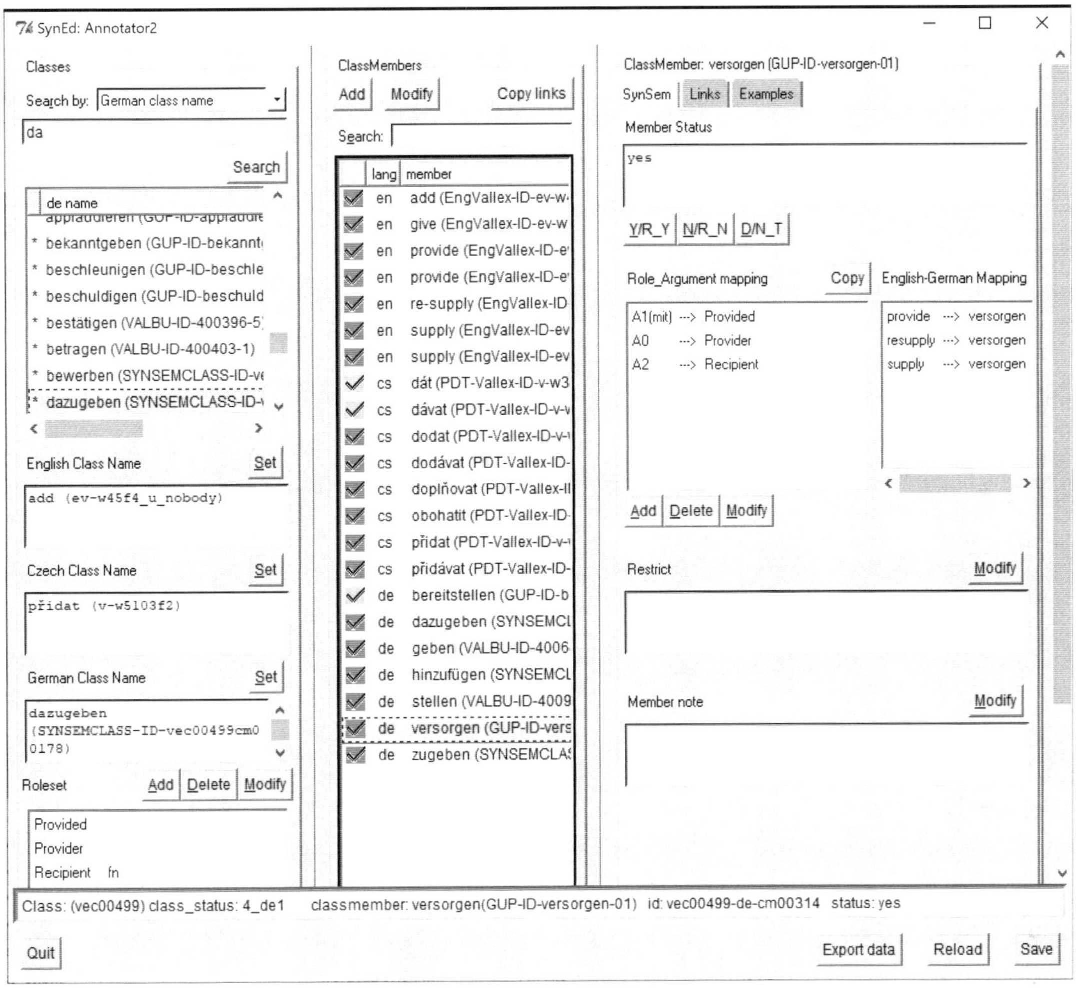

Figure 2: The "add" class with cs/en/de entries; "versorgen" (German) is highlighted to show mapping to roles

The editor allows to **edit the class members** for classes referred to in the language-specific file (Sect. 4.2). The typical workflow, as specified in the common guidelines (Urešová et al., 2019), asks for first pruning the pre-fetched class member candidates (middle column in Fig. 2), using the corresponding examples from the input parallel or monolingual corpus.

After filtering out unsuitable class members, the annotator proceeds via the editor **to map the semantic roles to the arguments** of the predicates represented by the class members (in the SynSem tab with the Role_Argument mapping window). The arguments are taken from the external valency or similar resources (defined for each language in the language-dependent file) if they exists; if not, special IDs are generated.

Next, in the Link tab, the editor allows to **edit links to other external semantic resources** (Fig. 3).

Finally, the editor allows to **select examples**; typically, 5 to 10 examples from the corpora used for pre-selection are marked and stored with the class member (in the Examples tab).

Language-specific annotators are not allowed to edit the main file or its parts, but they can suggest changes by means of GitHub issues, by emailing the central maintainers, or (if trained) by creating pull requests for the main file. It has to be stressed again that it is then the responsibility of the central maintainers to implement these changes carefully, since some changes may require that all languages be updated. This update might not be readily feasible, might need the cooperation (read: manual edits, or at least a check) by the maintainers of all language-dependent files, and must be scheduled and possibly discussed carefully in some form of, e.g., maintainers forum.

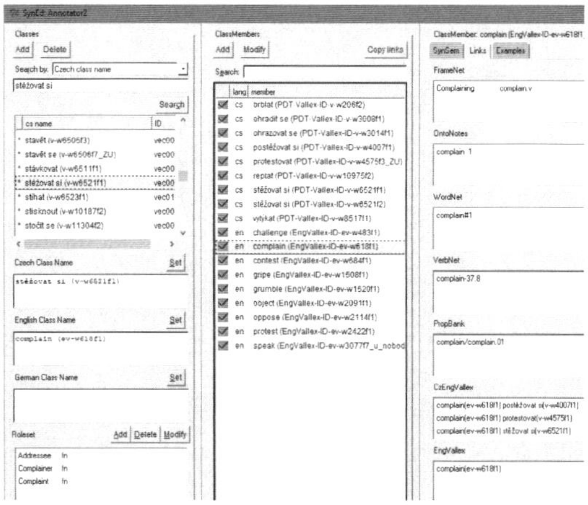

Figure 3: The "stěžovat si/complain" class with external "Links" for CM "complain" (on the right-hand side)

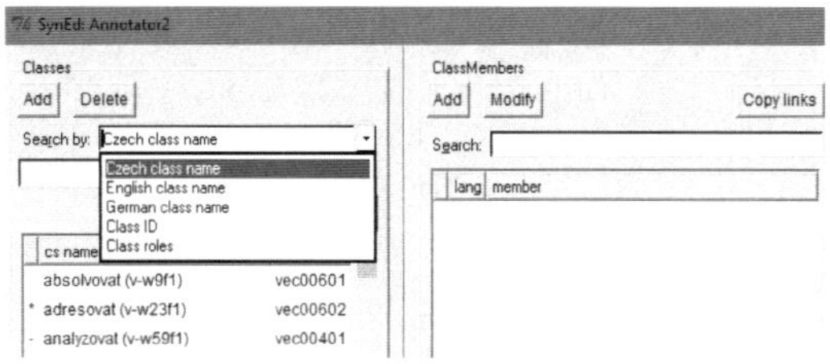

Figure 4: The search possibilities in the editor

5 The Current State of SynSemClass and SynEd

The latest release of SynSemClass ontology (SynSemClass 4.0)[24] is already in a stand-off format; it underwent both a detailed and intensive annotation check and contains new features, such as semantic role definitions, semantic role hierarchy, aspect verb pairs replenishing, search, etc.

The alignment within the input parallel corpus has been done by MGIZA++ (Gao and Vogel, 2008) and then from there, the initial language-specific file is created by a specific script that will be also released as part of the language-specific setup guidelines.

SynEd is available currently in an experimental version,[25] which allows for editing selected language-dependent files, and for the administrator and main maintainer also to edit the language-independent part in the main file. Classes can be searched for in the editor by a name in any language (of those selected for editing). The mappings to

[24] `http://hdl.handle.net/11234/1-4746`

[25] `http://github.com/fucikova/SynSemClass_multi`

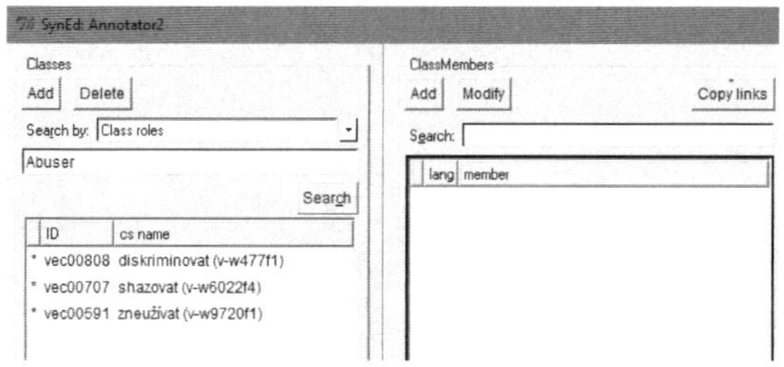

Figure 5: The results of searching the role "Abuser"

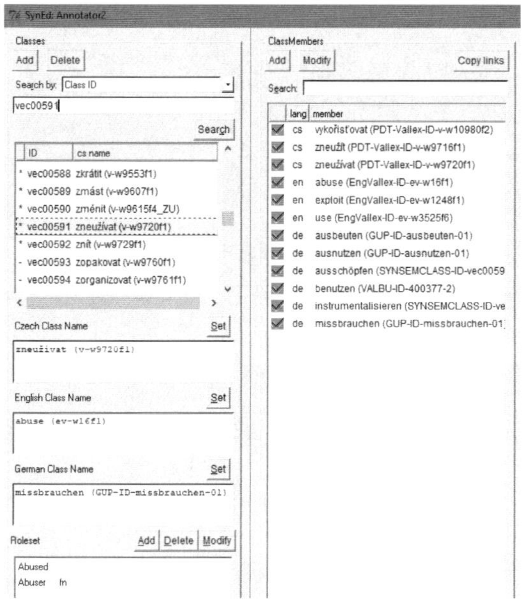

Figure 6: The results of searching by class ID - the class vec00591 "zneužívat"

syntactic properties of the individual class members, which are also language-dependent, can be created to multiple sources (a feature added while working on German, which does not have one large coverage valency dictionary, and therefore several of them had to be used). The external links and examples are shown and amended or added again only for the class member in "its" language, as configured in the language-dependent file. The editor, once fully tested on at least one more language will be also released publicly.[26]

6 Conclusions and Future Work

We have demonstrated a gradual approach to adapting a data specification and an annotation tool and the associated workflow to a multi-language, or in other words, partly language independent

[26] The editor will be available under Mozilla Public License 2.0 (MPL-2.0), presumably with SynSemClass version 5.

model, allowing concurrent annotation by independent teams working on the individual languages. Each new version of all the components is based on a practical experience with the previous version. While inspired very much by the UD approach to adding, maintaining, validating and publishing new datasets and languages. However, work on a multilingual ontology has one substantial difference: the amount of data that are language independent, but which are heavily being linked to from the language-dependent parts is much larger and will be changing often.

The experimental version of SynEd described herein is now being used for adding Spanish (Fernández-Alcaina et al., 2023).[27] Both the Spanish data and the editor will be publicly released as version 5.0 of SynSemClass.

Part of future work - once the components are in place - will be to open the development to the community, interested in similar resources, and also to develop tools that would allow possible (semi-)automatic "conversions" of those resources to the SynSemClass set.

The web application that shows the then-current version of SynSemClass is in place.[28] It is automatically generated from the dataset. However, at the moment it lacks more advanced search features that would serve possible more complex research tasks on this resource - another future work item.

Acknowledgements

The work described herein has been supported by the Grant Agency of the Czech Republic under the EXPRO program as project "LUSyD" (project No. GX20-16819X) and uses resources hosted by the LINDAT/CLARIAH-CZ Research Infrastructure (project No. LM2018101, supported by the Ministry of Education of the Czech Republic).

References

Alan Akbik, Xinyu Guan, and Yunyao Li. 2016. Multilingual aliasing for auto-generating proposition Banks. In *Proceedings of COLING 2016, the 26th International Conference on Computational Linguistics: Technical Papers*, pages 3466–3474, Osaka, Japan. The COLING 2016 Organizing Committee.

Emhimed Alatrish. 2012. Comparison of ontology editors. *ERAF Journal on Computing*, 4:23–38.

[27]This paper also discusses issues related to use of the editor, e.g., how long it takes to annotate an entry, etc.

[28]`https://lindat.cz/services/SynSemClass`

Collin F. Baker, Charles J. Fillmore, and John B. Lowe. 1998a. The Berkeley FrameNet Project. In *Proceedings of the 36th Annual Meeting of the Association for Computational Linguistics and 17th International Conference on Computational Linguistics - Volume 1*, ACL '98, pages 86–90, Stroudsburg, PA, USA. Association for Computational Linguistics.

Collin F. Baker, Charles J. Fillmore, and John B. Lowe. 1998b. The Berkeley FrameNet Project. In *Proceedings of the 36th Annual Meeting of the Association for Computational Linguistics and 17th International Conference on Computational Linguistics - Volume 1*, ACL '98, pages 86–90, Stroudsburg, PA, USA. Association for Computational Linguistics.

Jinho D. Choi, Claire Bonial, and Martha Palmer. 2010. Propbank Frameset Annotation Guidelines Using a Dedicated Editor, Cornerstone. In *International Conference on Language Resources and Evaluation*.

Silvie Cinková, Eva Fučíková, Jana Šindlerová, and Jan Hajič. 2014. EngVallex - English Valency Lexicon. `http://hdl.handle.net/11858/00-097C-0000-0023-4337-2`, LINDAT/CLARIN digital library at the Institute of Formal and Applied Linguistics, Charles University.

Christiane Fellbaum. 1998. *WordNet: An Electronic Lexical Database*. Language, Speech, and Communication. MIT Press, Cambridge, MA.

Cristina Fernández-Alcaina, Eva Fučíková, and Zdeňka Urešová. 2023. Spanish verbal synonyms in the synsemclass ontology. In *Proceedings of the 21st TLT conference*, pages 1–12. Georgetown University in Washington D.C.

Charles J. Fillmore. 2002. Linking sense to syntax in FrameNet. In *Proceedings of 19th International Conference on Computational Linguistics*, Taipei. COLING, COLING.

Thierry Fontenelle. 2003. FrameNet and Frame Semantics. *International Journal of Lexicography*, 16(3):231–231.

Nabil Gader, Veronika Lux-Pogodalla, and Alain Polguère. 2012. Hand-crafting a lexical network with a knowledge-based graph editor. In *Proceedings of the 3rd Workshop on Cognitive Aspects of the Lexicon*, pages 109–126, Mumbai, India. The COLING 2012 Organizing Committee.

Qin Gao and Stephan Vogel. 2008. Parallel implementations of word alignment tool. In *Software Engineering, Testing, and Quality Assurance for Natural Language Processing*, pages 49–57, Columbus, Ohio. Association for Computational Linguistics.

Jan Hajič, Eva Hajičová, Jarmila Panevová, Petr Sgall, Silvie Cinková, Eva Fučíková, Marie Mikulová, Petr Pajas, Jan Popelka, Jiří Semecký, Jana Šindlerová, Jan Štěpánek, Josef Toman, Zdeňka Urešová, and Zdeněk Žabokrtský. 2012. Prague Czech-English Dependency Treebank 2.0. `https://hdl.handle.`

net/11858/00-097C-0000-0015-8DAF-4, LINDAT/CLARIAH-CZ digital library at the Institute of Formal and Applied Linguistics (ÚFAL), Faculty of Mathematics and Physics, Charles University.

Tom Kenter, Tomaž Erjavec, Maja Žorga Dulmin, and Darja Fišer. 2012. Lexicon construction and corpus annotation of historical language with the CoBaLT editor. In *Proceedings of the 6th Workshop on Language Technology for Cultural Heritage, Social Sciences, and Humanities*, pages 1–6, Avignon, France. Association for Computational Linguistics.

Jacqueline Kubczak. 2014. Valenzwörterbuch e-VALBU. LINDAT/CLARIAH-CZ digital library at the Institute of Formal and Applied Linguistics (ÚFAL), Faculty of Mathematics and Physics, Charles University.

Markéta Lopatková, Václava Kettnerová, Anna Vernerová, Eduard Bejček, and Zdeněk Žabokrtský. 2020. VALLEX 4.0. https://hdl.handle.net/11234/1-3524, LINDAT/CLARIAH-CZ digital library at the Institute of Formal and Applied Linguistics (ÚFAL), Faculty of Mathematics and Physics, Charles University.

Joakim Nivre, Marie-Catherine de Marneffe, Filip Ginter, Yoav Goldberg, Jan Hajič, Christopher Manning, Ryan McDonald, Slav Petrov, Sampo Pyysalo, Natalia Silveira, Reut Tsarfaty, and Daniel Zeman. 2016. Universal dependencies v1: A multilingual treebank collection. In *Proceedings of the 10th International Conference on Language Resources and Evaluation (LREC 2016)*, pages 1659–1666, Paris, France. European Language Resources Association.

Martha Palmer, Daniel Gildea, and Paul Kingsbury. 2005. The Proposition Bank: An Annotated Corpus of Semantic Roles. *Computational Linguistics*, 31(1):71–106.

Gautam K. Parai, Clement Jonquet, Rong Xu, Mark A. Musen, and Nigam H. Shah. 2010. The Lexicon Builder Web service: Building Custom Lexicons from two hundred Biomedical Ontologies. In *American Medical Informatics Association Annual Symposium, AMIA'10*.

Sameer S. Pradhan and Nianwen Xue. 2009. OntoNotes: The 90% solution. In *Proceedings of Human Language Technologies: The 2009 Annual Conference of the North American Chapter of the Association for Computational Linguistics, Companion Volume: Tutorial Abstracts*, pages 11–12, Boulder, Colorado. Association for Computational Linguistics.

Karin Kipper Schuler. 2006. *VerbNet: A Broad-Coverage, Comprehensive Verb Lexicon*. Ph.D. thesis, University of Pennsylvania.

Helmut Schumacher, Jacqueline Kubczak, Renate Schmidt, and Vera de Ruiter. 2018. *VALBU - Valenzwörterbuch deutscher Verben*. Narr, Tübingen.

Wolfgang Teubert. 2007. *Text Corpora and Multilingual Lexicography*. John Benjamins Publishing Company.

Zdeňka Urešová, Alevtina Bémová, Eva Fučíková, Jan Hajič, Veronika Kolářová, Marie Mikulová, Petr Pajas, Jarmila Panevová, and Jan Štěpánek. 2021. PDT-vallex: Czech Valency lexicon linked to treebanks 4.0 (PDT-Vallex 4.0). https://hdl.handle.net/11234/1-3499, LINDAT/CLARIAH-CZ digital library at the Institute of Formal and Applied Linguistics (ÚFAL), Faculty of Mathematics and Physics, Charles University.

Zdeňka Urešová, Eva Fučíková, Jan Hajič, and Jana Šindlerová. 2015. CzEngVallex - Czech English Valency Lexicon. LINDAT/CLARIAH-CZ digital library at the Institute of Formal and Applied Linguistics, Charles University, http://hdl.handle.net/11234/1-1512.

Zdeňka Urešová, Eva Fučíková, and Eva Hajičová. 2019. Czengclass: Contextually-based synonymy and valency of verbs in a bilingual setting. Technical Report 62, ÚFAL MFF UK, Prague, Czechia.

Zdeňka Urešová, Eva Fučíková, Eva Hajičová, and Jan Hajič. 2018a. Creating a verb synonym lexicon based on a parallel corpus. In *Proceedings of the 11th International Conference on Language Resources and Evaluation (LREC 2018)*, pages 1432–1437, Paris, France. European Language Resources Association.

Zdeňka Urešová, Eva Fučíková, Eva Hajičová, and Jan Hajič. 2018b. Tools for Building an Interlinked Synonym Lexicon Network. In *Proceedings of the 11th International Conference on Language Resources and Evaluation (LREC'18)*, Miyazaki, Japan. European Language Resources Association (ELRA).

Zdeňka Urešová, Karolina Zaczynska, Peter Bourgonje, Eva Fučíková, Georg Rehm, and Jan Hajič. 2022. Making a semantic event-type ontology multilingual. In *Proceedings of the 13th Conference on Language Resources and Evaluation (LREC 2022)*, pages 1332–1334, Marseille, France. European Language Resources Association.

Zdeňka Urešová, Eva Fučíková, Eva Hajičová, and Jan Hajič. 2020. SynSemClass linked lexicon: Mapping synonymy between languages. In *Proceedings of the 2020 Globalex Workshop on Linked Lexicography*, pages 10–19, Marseille, France. European Language Resources Association.

Spanish Verbal Synonyms in the SynSemClass Ontology

Cristina Fernández-Alcaina, Eva Fučíková, Jan Hajič and Zdeňka Urešová
Institute of Formal and Applied Linguistics, Faculty of Mathematics and Physics
Charles University, Prague, Czech Republic
{alcaina,fucikova,hajic,uresova}@ufal.mff.cuni.cz

Abstract

This paper presents ongoing work in the expansion of the multilingual semantic event-type ontology SynSemClass (Czech-English-German) to include Spanish. As in previous versions of the lexicon, Spanish verbal synonyms have been collected from a sentence-aligned parallel corpus and classified into classes based on their syntactic-semantic properties. Each class member is linked to a number of syntactic and/or semantic resources specific to each language, thus enriching the annotation and enabling interoperability. This paper describes the procedure for the data extraction and annotation of Spanish verbal synonyms in the lexicon.

1 Introduction

The work presented in this paper is part of a larger project aiming at building an event-type multilingual ontology. SynSemClass (SSC) (Urešová et al., 2020) is a multilingual verbal lexicon where contextually-based synonymous verbs are classified into classes based on the semantic and syntactic properties they display. Synonymy here is understood in terms of contextually-based synonymy: a verb considered a member of a class must reflect the same (or similar) meaning expressed by the class in the same context (i.e., it has a similar "semantic behavior" as the other verbs) both monolingually and cross-lingually. Apart from providing fine-grained syntactic-semantic multilingual annotation, SynSemClass also contributes to research by building a database that links several resources in different languages (Czech, English and German). The information gathered in the lexicon allows for a comparison across languages relevant for linguistic research at the same it provides curated data for Natural Language Processing tasks, such cross-lingual synonyms or synonymy discovery.

This paper presents ongoing work on the extension of SynSemClass to include a fourth language, Spanish. Specifically, section 2 introduces the SynSemClass lexicon and section 3 describes the set of Spanish resources linked to SynSemClass. The method for data extraction and annotation of Spanish verbal synonyms is presented in section 4. The results obtained and the limitations encountered during the process are summarized in section 5. The paper closes (section 6) with a summary of the main findings and with some hints for future work.

2 SynSemClass

SynSemClass (Urešová et al., 2020) attempts to create specifications and definitions of a hierarchical event-type ontology while focusing on contextually-based synonymy (both monolingually and cross-lingually) and verb valency in a multilingual setting. The notion of synonymy is regarded in a broad sense based on definitions such as "near-synonyms", "partial synonyms" or "plesionyms" (Lyons, 1968; Jackson, 1988; Lyons, 1995; Cruse, 2000, 1986). The approach to valency used in SynSemClass is based on the linguistic descriptive framework Functional Generative Description (FGD) (Sgall et al., 1986) and its application in the Prague Dependency Treebanks (Hajič et al., 2006; Hajič et al., 2012, 2020; Hajič et al., 2020).

Entries in the lexicon are grouped into individual multilingual (for now, English, Czech, and German) *verbal synonym classes.* Each class is considered similar to an ontological unit and it is assigned a specific set of roles (i.e. *Roleset*), which expresses the prototypical meaning of the class (Urešová et al., 2022). The most important criterion for inclusion of a particular verb (sense) into a given class is the mapping of each of the semantic roles specified in the class Roleset to the verb valency slots (represented by a syntactic-semantic functor[1]) captured in the valency frame (*Role* ↔

[1]The syntactic-semantic (tectogrammatical) functor is used in the FGD valency theory as a label for valency frame members.

Proceedings of the 21st International Workshop on Treebanks and Linguistic Theories (TLT, GURT/SyntaxFest 2023), pages 11 - 20
March 9-12, 2023 ©2023 Association for Computational Linguistics

Argument mapping). While sharing the same set of roles is a requirement for a verb to be included in a class, roles can be expressed by different morphosyntactic realizations and be subject to additional restrictions (Urešová et al., 2018a). Another criterion for verb sense inclusion is a functionally adequate relationship (i.e., in terms of translation, the verb senses are considered synonymous in the given context(s) if the translated verb in the target language adequately expresses the functional intent of the original language) between the meanings of all class members in one synonym class.

The SynSemClass class members (individual multilingual synonym verb senses, CMs) are linked to entries in similar language-specific syntactic and/or semantic databases (Urešová et al., 2020). The English entries are linked to FrameNet (Baker et al., 1998), Princeton WordNet (Fellbaum, 1998), VerbNet (Schuler and Palmer, 2005) and PropBank (Palmer et al., 2005), the German entries to FrameNet des Deutschen (FdD)[2], the Universal Proposition Bank (UPB) (Akbik et al., 2016)[3], the Elektronisches Valenzlexikon des Deutschen[4] (Electronic German Valency Lexicon, in short E-VALBU) (Kubczak, 2014; Schumacher et al., 2018), and Woxikon[5], and the Czech entries to PDT-Vallex (Hajič et al., 2003), which was used for building the Czech part of the PCEDT, to the lexicon of Czech and English translation equivalents called CzEngVallex (Urešová et al., 2015) and to VALLEX (Lopatková et al., 2017; Lopatková et al., 2020).

The latest release, SynSemClass4.0 (Figure 1), is dated June 2022 and contains 883 classes with approx. 6,000 CMs.[6] As shown in Figure 1, each class in the lexicon is named using the most prototypical verb in each language (*allow*, *dovolit*, *erlauben*). For each class, the online version of the lexicon displays the information related to the Roleset assigned to the class (*Authority*, *Permitted*, *Affected*), the list of class members in each language, their valency frame (e.g., for English *allow*, the valency frame is ACT, EFF, PAT) and the related senses in the external resources used for each language (e.g., for English, English VerbNet (EV), FrameNet (FN) or OntoNotes (ON), among others). It is also possible to display the corpus examples selected to illustrate the class members.

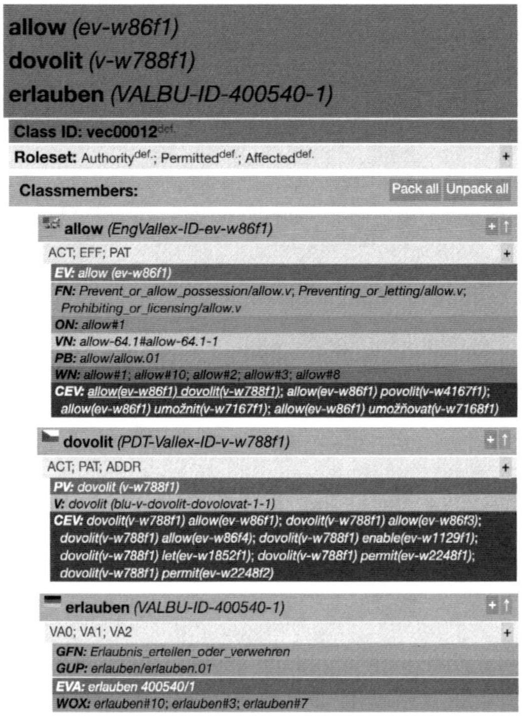

Figure 1: Simplified version of an entry in SynSemClass 4.0 (class *allow/dovolit/erlauben*).

The work on German has thus been moved to this version (from the previous version 3.5); the fourth version of the lexicon is more complete and it has additional corrections (such as some classes having been merged, etc.) Also, it adds the integration of class and roles definitions. The next release of SynSemClass (presumably version 5, planned for early spring 2023) will be enriched by Spanish synonymous verbs as described here.

3 Resources

Following (Urešová et al., 2022), the minimal set of resources required to add a language to SynSemClass is: (i) a parallel corpus and (ii) (at least) one lexical resource containing syntactic and semantic information. This section describes the corpus and the lexical resources used for Spanish.

[2] https://gsw.phil.hhu.de/framenet/

[3] https://github.com/System-T/UniversalPropositions

[4] https://grammis.ids-mannheim.de/verbvalenz

[5] https://synonyme.woxikon.de

[6] Available online at https://lindat.cz/services/SynSemClass and for download at http://hdl.handle.net/11234/1-4746. The lexicon can be also now accessed through the Unified Verb Index developed by the University of Colorado Boulder (https://uvi.colorado.edu/).

3.1 Corpus

Verbal synonyms in SynSemClass have been collected from two different parallel corpora, the Prague Czech-English Dependency Treebank Corpus (PCEDT) (Hajič et al., 2012) for Czech-English and the ParaCrawl (Chen et al., 2020) corpus for German-English. For Spanish, for which no corpus richly annotated for syntactic-semantic information is available, the corpus selected for the extraction of Spanish verbal synonyms was the X-SRL dataset (Daza and Frank, 2020). The choice of a parallel corpus is justified based on the assumption that if two words are semantically similar in a given language, their translations would also be similar in another language, both in meaning and in the translation context they share (Urešová et al., 2018b).

The X-SRL dataset is a sentence-aligned parallel corpus containing approx. three million words for the English-Spanish part. The texts are tokenized, lemmatized and POS-tagged.[7] Despite the existence of larger-sized corpora (such as the ParaCrawl corpus), the X-SRL dataset proved to provide enough data for the Spanish part, at least for its initial steps. Furthermore, the X-SRL dataset has the advantage of being composed by English texts extracted from the Wall Street Journal section of the Penn Treebank, on which the PCEDT is based, thus given consistency and cross-coverage of the annotation. In fact, it is possible to find some verbal synonyms for which the examples selected are the same for the Czech-English and Spanish-English parts, as illustrated by verbs *vybuchnout/erupt/hacer erupción*:

Na slavném bulváru Strip ***vybuchne*** *příští měsíc sopka: 60 stop vysoká hora chrlící každých pět minut kouř a oheň.*

A volcano ***will erupt*** *next month on the fabled Strip: a 60-foot mountain spewing smoke and flame every five minutes.*

Un volcán ***hará erupción*** *el próximo mes en la legendaria Franja: una montaña de 60 pies que arroja humo y llamas cada cinco minutos.*

3.2 Lexical resources

Spanish verbal synonyms in SynSemClass are linked to five resources. The resources are of two types: (i) a monolingual valency lexicon which serves as the sense identification source (AnCora) and (ii) four resources that provide extra information; specifically, three monolingual lexicons (SenSem, ADDESE and Spanish FrameNet) and a multilingual resource (Spanish WordNet). What follows is a description of the main features of each of the lexical resources used:

- AnCora[8] is a lexicon based on the corpus AnCora-ES, which is built on texts from Spanish newspapers. The corpus contains 500,000 words and it is annotated at different levels, including syntactic and semantic properties. The resulting lexicon consists of 2,820 lemmas (amounting to 3,938 senses and 5,117 frames). For each verb sense, AnCora provides the argument structure and the thematic roles defined. Each sense in AnCora is also linked (if available) to its English counterpart in VerbNet, PropBank, FrameNet, WordNet 3.0 and OntoNotes, to which the English class members in SynSemClass are also linked. Having links to the same resources in AnCora and SynSemClass is an advantage as it allows for the extraction of only those AnCora senses that are linked to the same English sense contained in a particular class in the lexicon, thus restricting the list of candidate verbs and facilitating their annotation (see section 4.1).

- Spanish SenSem[9] (Alonso et al., 2007) is a monolingual verbal lexicon containing the most frequent 250 verbs. The lexicon is based on the SenSem corpus (Fernández-Montraveta and Vázquez, 2014), which contains approx. 700,000 words from the Spanish newspaper 'El Periódico' and, to a lesser degree, from literary sources. For each sense, SenSem provides a definition, the argument structure and the set of semantic roles. Each sense is also linked to its equivalent in WordNet.

- ADESSE[10] (García-Miguel et al., 2005) is a monolingual verbal lexicon containing 3,400 lemmas and 4,000 verbal entries based on the ARTHUS corpus (1.5 million words), built using texts from European Spanish (78.77%)

[7]The corpus contains information regarding argument labels projected from the original English corpus, but we decided not to use this information as the annotation of arguments other than A0 and A1 is not as fine-grained as our purposes require.

[8]http://clic.ub.edu/corpus/en/ancoraverb_es

[9]http://grial.edu.es/sensem/lexico?idioma=en

[10]http://adesse.uvigo.es

and American Spanish (21.23%)[11]. The lexicon provides information regarding argument structure and semantic roles. Arguments are ordered according to their frequency in the corpus. ADESSE also provides information regarding the argument structure of alternations and examples for each alternation.

- Spanish WordNet 3.0 is integrated within the Multilingual Central Repository (MCR)[12] (Gonzalez-Agirre et al., 2012). The MCR contains wordnets for six languages: English, Basque, Galicia, Catalan, Portuguese and Spanish (including senses from varieties other than European Spanish although without specification). Cross-linguistic synonyms are connected through the Inter-Lingual-Index (ILI). The MCR is also enriched with semantically tagged glosses and contains ontology information from WordNet Domains, Top Ontology and AdimenSUMO.
- Spanish FrameNet[13] (Subirats, 2009) is the Spanish version of the FrameNet project and it is built on a corpus under construction that includes both 'New World and European Spanish'.[14] The online lexical resource is based on frame semantics and supported by corpus data. The resource contains more than 1,000 lexical items (including verbs, but also other parts of speech) from a variety of semantic domains. It provides syntactic and semantic information for each sense automatically annotated and validated by human annotators.

The representation of Spanish varieties in the lexical resources listed above is uneven since most resources are built exclusively (AnCora, SenSem) or mainly on European Spanish (ADESSE). However, in these resources, there is no specific information on this aspect and some characteristics of the senses of a variety other than European Spanish appear without any explicit reference, e.g., *manejar* is included in ADESSE as 'drive' (more frequently used in American Spanish) without further specification regarding variety. To overcome this drawback and whenever possible, annotators have used the information provided by the *Diccionario de la lengua española*[15] and the *Diccionario de americanismos*.[16] For now, the information regarding variety is specified as a 'Member note', as specified in the guidelines provided to annotators (Fernández-Alcaina et al., 2022).

4 Extending SynSemClass by Spanish

This section describes two phases of the annotation of Spanish verbal synonyms: (i) automatic data extraction (section 4.1) and (ii) manual data annotation (section 4.2).

4.1 Data extraction

The data extraction and preparation process consists of two phases: (i) automatic extraction of English-Spanish pairs from the corpus and (ii) data filtering.

In the first phase, candidate synonyms were extracted from the sentence-aligned corpus X-SRL (section 3.1). Pairs of Spanish-English were automatically extracted using the existing English Class Members as input. That is, for each English verb contained in SynSemClass, the Spanish counterpart attested in the corpus was extracted.

The dataset contained 39,279 sentences for each language. As an initial step, the extraction of synonym pairs was restricted to sentences containing the same number of verbs in both languages. The final dataset amounted to 21,551 sentences, i.e., 40,408 verbs. The number of different verbal types (after discarding wrongly-tagged elements) amounted to 1,715. For each sentence in each language, verbs were extracted as a list and paired to their translation counterparts according to index (e.g., $\text{Verb1}_{\text{en}} \rightarrow \text{Verb1}_{\text{spa}}$, $\text{Verb2}_{\text{en}} \rightarrow \text{Verb2}_{\text{spa}}$).

The second phase consists of two steps: (i) manual filtering of verbs and (ii) automatic filtering of the argument structures imported from AnCora (used as the source of valency frames).

Step 1: Manual filtering

The list of automatically paired verbs for each class was presented to annotators, who were asked to discard the verbs that did not belong to the class where they were automatically included. Discarded verbs were of two types:

- Wrongly-paired verbs during the automatic

[11] http://adesse.uvigo.es/data/corpus.php

[12] https://adimen.si.ehu.es/cgi-bin/wei/public/wei.consult.perl

[13] http://sfn.spanishfn.org/SFNreports.php

[14] http://spanishfn.org/corpus

[15] https://dle.rae.es/

[16] https://www.asale.org/damer/

extraction process (e.g., *seek-declarar*) due to mismatches in POS tagging or in word order.

- Verbs that were translation counterparts of a certain verb but that did not reflect the same meaning in that particular class (e.g., *solicitar* can be translated as *seek* but this is not the sense represented by class *hledat/search*, defined as 'A Seeker looks for a Sought entity'[17]).

Apart from labelling entries as belonging (or not) to a particular class, annotators were also asked to specify any restrictions applying to the inclusion of a verb in that particular class, e.g., if the verb is part of an idiomatic construction (e.g., *hacer erupción* 'erupt'). In this phase, annotators could also add any comments relevant for the annotation.

Based on a sample of 59 classes (51 verbs per class on average), it took approx. 30 minutes (on average) to filter one class. Out of the 3,016 lemmas initially included in the 59 classes, only 990 lemmas were kept (32% of the initial list). Inclusion of a verb by one annotator was enough to consider a verb a potential CM of a particular class. After annotating the first ten classes of the set, even if the initial list was considerably reduced, it was clear that the list obtained still contained a large number of verbs that did not belong to the class in which they had been included, thus slowing down the process of annotation.

Step 2: Automatic filtering of AnCora senses

As described in section 3.2, the AnCora lexicon links senses to several English resources, such as PropBank and VerbNet, two resources that are used in the English part of our lexicon. Using the links provided by AnCora, the list of potential CMs manually filtered in the previous step was filtered again to retrieve Spanish potential CMs for which:

- AnCora senses were linked to the same PropBank and VerbNet entries that the English CMs already contained in our lexicon, and

- no links were available in AnCora because the sense represented is not available in any of the English resources used.

The data annotation workflow is illustrated in Figure 2.

[17]https://lindat.cz/services/SynSemClass40/SynSemClass40.html

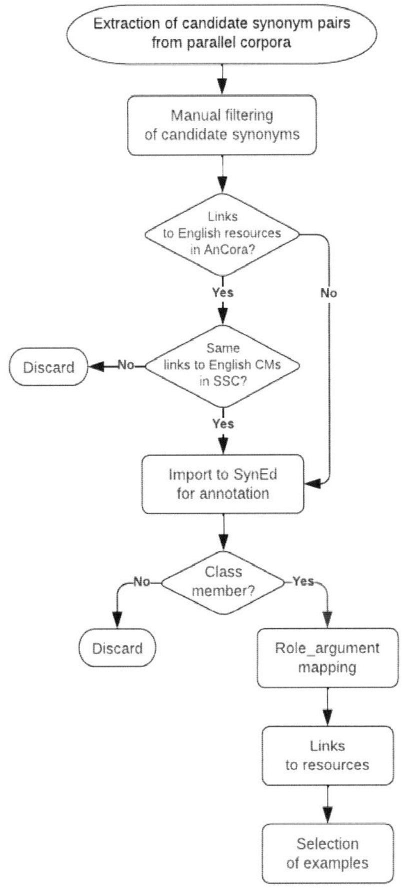

Figure 2: Data extraction and annotation workflow.

4.2 Data annotation

Data were annotated by three native Peninsular Spanish speakers fluent in English with similar backgrounds and previous experience working on a bilingual dictionary (English-Spanish). The three annotators also had a basic knowledge of German, which they can use to cross-check meanings. Annotators were given instructions on how to proceed before and during the process of annotation and they were also provided with annotation guidelines specifically designed for Spanish verbal synonyms (Fernández-Alcaina et al., 2022). The quality of annotators' work was tested on an initial set in which they were asked to annotate four classes.

After the first 40 classes, which were annotated by the three annotators, each set of classes is assigned to two annotators. Annotations are systematically monitored by one of the authors of this paper and unclear cases are discussed whenever necessary (section 4.2.2).

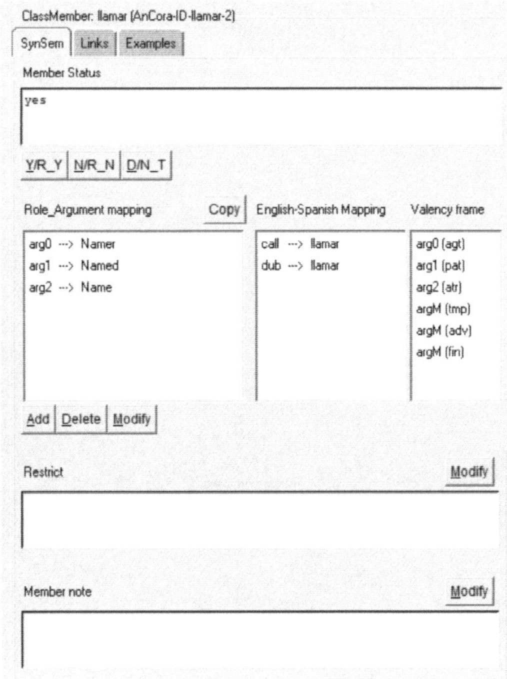

Figure 3: Role-Argument mapping for *llamar (AnCora-ID-llamar-2)* (class *call/nazvat/llamar*, ID vec00043).

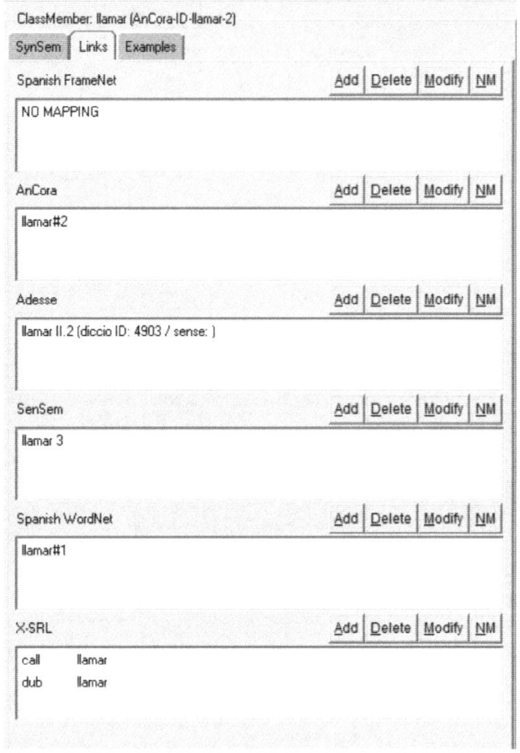

Figure 4: Selection of links to external resources for *llamar (AnCora-ID-llamar-2)* (class *call/nazvat/llamar*, ID vec00043).

The final complex annotation (role to argument mapping, external links, example selection, etc.) has been done using the SynEd editor (Urešová et al., 2018; Fučíková et al., 2023) available from the SynSemClass maintainers. However, as part of the task of adding Spanish, the data structure and the editor have been refactored to allow for more convenient and modular annotation for any number of languages. The technical details of these, however substantial, modifications are out of scope of this paper; please see (Fučíková et al., 2023) for the description of the modifications made to the SynEd editor.

For the candidate verbs retained after the filtering phase (section 4.1) and imported to SynEd, annotators were asked to provide fine-grained syntactic and semantic annotation by mapping the Roleset of the class with the valency frame of each verb, add links to external resources and select a set of representative examples from the corpus. To facilitate the work of annotators, SynEd provides both roles and class definitions in Czech, English, German and now also Spanish.

The process of annotation is divided into several interlinked steps (Figures 3, 4 and 5). In the first step, the task of annotators is to decide whether a candidate member matched the syntactic and semantic properties of the class. The annotation of Spanish synonyms–built upon existing synonym classes with Czech, English and in part German verbs–used semantic roles already defined for each class. The task of the annotators is thus to map the valency frame of the verb with each role in the existing Roleset associated with the given class (Figure 3). For example, based on the valency frame described for *llamar (AnCora-ID-llamar-2)* in AnCora and on the roles defined for class vec00043, the mapping is as follows: arg0→*Namer*, arg1→*Named* and arg2→*Name*. If a candidate verb is not included in AnCora, then it is imported to the editor using the label "SynSemClass-ID", as described in (Urešová et al., 2022) for German.

Since synonyms in SynSemClass are linked to external lexical resources (described in more detail in section 3.2), the second task in the annotation process consists in adding links to Spanish lexical resources (Figure 4). This is considered to be an essential step of the annotation process as linking the verbs in SynSemClass with other resources provides rich and comparable syntactic and semantic

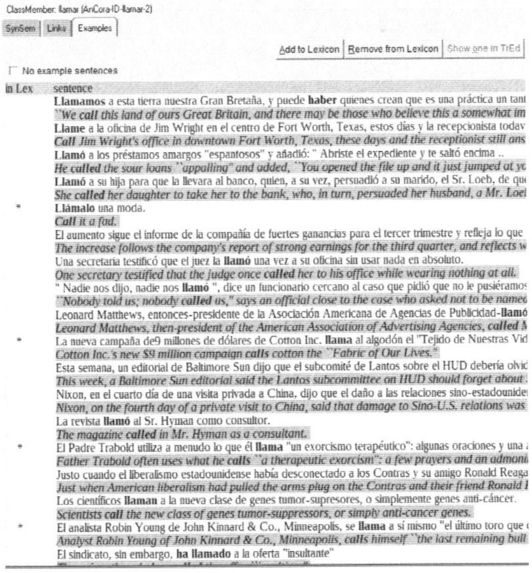

Figure 5: Selection of examples for *llamar (AnCora-ID-llamar-2)* (class *call/nazvat/llamar*, ID vec00043).

information about class members. Furthermore, linked data supports interoperability, thus adding value to the lexicon and enabling its use in Computational Linguistics.

In the last step of the annotation, annotators select a set of examples for Spanish and their English counterparts extracted from the corpus, if available (Figure 5).

4.2.1 Special cases

The annotation of certain cases demands special attention and requires a specific procedure:

- *Light Verb Constructions* (LVCs) (e.g., *hacer erupción*, 'erupt'). For LVCs, the nominal complement is considered to be part of the predicate and thus it is not mapped to any functor in the Role-Argument mapping but it is included as a restriction and a note specifying 'LVC' is added for easier identification. For example, the Roleset defined for the class *erupt/explodovat* (vec00018) contains only one Role (*Explosive*). The LVC *hacer erupción* has been included in the class by mapping A0 to the role *Explosive*, adding the noun complement ('erupción') as a restriction.

- Prepositional complements (e.g., *remontarse a*, 'date back'). Whenever necessary, the obligatory preposition introducing a prepositional complements is specified in the Role-Argument mapping. For the example above, the Role-Argument mapping is the following: arg0→*Entity*, arg1(**a**)→*Origin*.

4.2.2 Annotation monitoring

This section presents the criteria for the monitoring of the annotation in each step of the annotation. In cases of disagreement between annotators regarding the class membership, the verb is discarded from the class if:

- It expresses a general meaning that is better captured by a different class.

- There is a pattern in the inclusion of similar verbs whose meaning is deemed to be better captured by another class.

If there is a disagreement in the links to external resources, the rule of thumb is to reach a consensus between annotators so that only those links that are selected by the two annotators remain in the final annotation. Exceptions to this rule may occur, especially in the case of WordNet, where the selection of a sense is not as straightforward as in the rest of the resources and more variation is observed. It is up to the researcher then to decide if a sense must be included or not in the final annotation, for which the English equivalents provided may be of help.

In case of disagreement in the selection of examples, if no examples selected by the two annotators are available, the criteria are the following: (i) explicit argument realization (as much as possible), (ii) avoidance of highly specific or technical vocabulary, and (iii) preference for shorter sentences.

5 Results and limitations

The Spanish part of the SynSemClass lexicon is still in its early stages, but results have been encouraging so far even if the number of classes annotated represents a small part of the lexicon (72 classes, 5,200 verbs).[18]

The results obtained are especially relevant from a methodological perspective. While some changes in the tools used and/or in the annotation process can be expected as more data is processed, the results obtained so far set the basis for future work on Spanish. Since the addition of Spanish to SynSemClass was devised as an opportunity to "simulate" a scenario where a team works almost independently (that is, only with central support), the results obtained are also relevant for the future extension of the lexicon.

[18] As of January 2023.

Apart from the methodological aspects mentioned, adding a new language from a different linguistic subfamily enriches the existing lexicon by providing more linguistic evidence (including special cases, such as LVCs or prepositional complements) that led to a refinement of synonym classes. In order to accommodate new data, new classes will be added to the lexicon and it will be necessary to split or merged existing classes as more verbs are added to the lexicon.

Regarding Spanish and to the best of our knowledge, SynSemClass has become the first multilingual richly annotated resource of a general ontology type that includes Spanish. It is also the first one in linking various existing Spanish lexical resources, in line with other initiatives such as the UVI for English.

Even if theoretically feasible, including a new language in SynSemClass inevitably leads to certain issues that need to be addressed regarding technical, organizational and resource-related aspects, some of them being already tackled in (Urešová et al., 2022). In particular for Spanish, the main issues arising concern the limitations related to the resources available. While the Czech-English part of the lexicon relies on an annotated human-translated parallel dependency corpus with semantic information and on rich lexical resources, the comprehensiveness of the resources for Spanish is more limited as, to the best of our knowledge, no deeply syntactically annotated parallel corpus (similar to the PCEDT corpus) or bilingual verbal valency lexicon are available.

Another limitation is the scarce representation of dialectal varieties other than European Spanish. Although some of the resources (e.g., ADESSE or Spanish FrameNet) are not restricted to European Spanish, its coverage is uneven and entries do not contain specific information in this respect. To avoid this limitation where possible, verb senses from varieties other than European Spanish are included in SSC and specified in the lexicon based on the information provided by two dictionaries (with the limitations lexicographic resources entail).

6 Conclusions and future work

This paper has described the process of data processing and annotation and the initial results of adding Spanish to SynSemClass. Based on the method used for adding German class members to the resource, Spanish synonymous verbs have been extracted from a parallel corpus and linked to a set of lexical resources available. While part of the methodology for adding Spanish to the lexicon built on previous work on German, the specific features of the resources used for Spanish have required to make changes (some quite substantial, at least from the technological point of view) in the process of data extraction and adapt the tool used for annotation.

Spanish is one step more towards the creation of a collaborative multilingual event-type ontology. For the time being, plans in the near future include extending the lexicon to cover Korean. While the addition of German and Spanish in the lexicon will certainly provide the basis for the addition of more languages, it is assumed that both the lexicon and the tools will continually evolve to adapt to the intricacies of new languages.

From a more global perspective, this project is part of a larger early-stage project aimed at multilingual knowledge representation. SynSemClass classes will serve as the grounding for the events and states included in such representation, connecting (relating) all other entities in the resulting representation which will also be grounded (by other means). While some verb annotation experiments have been done so far, a detailed specification of the process is still to be developed.

Acknowledgements

The work described herein has been supported by the Grant Agency of the Czech Republic under the EXPRO program as project "LUSyD" (project No. GX20-16819X) and uses resources hosted by the LINDAT/CLARIAH-CZ Research Infrastructure (project No. LM2018101, supported by the Ministry of Education of the Czech Republic). The German part of the lexicon is partly supported by the grant Humane AI Network, funded by the EC by award No. 952026. We would like to thank the reviewers for their insightful comments and the annotators Cristina Lara-Clares and Alba E. Ruz for their work and invaluable input.

References

Alan Akbik, Xinyu Guan, and Yunyao Li. 2016. Multilingual aliasing for auto-generating proposition Banks. In *Proceedings of COLING 2016, the 26th International Conference on Computational Linguistics: Technical Papers*, pages 3466–3474, Osaka, Japan. The COLING 2016 Organizing Committee.

Laura Alonso, Joan Antoni Capilla, Irene Castellón, Ana Fernández-Montraveta, and Gloria Vázquez. 2007. The SenSem project: Syntactico-semantic annotation of sentences in Spanish. *Recent Advances in Natural Language Processing IV*, pages 89–98.

Collin F. Baker, Charles J. Fillmore, and John B. Lowe. 1998. The Berkeley FrameNet Project. In *Proceedings of the 36th Annual Meeting of the Association for Computational Linguistics and 17th International Conference on Computational Linguistics - Volume 1*, ACL '98, pages 86–90, Stroudsburg, PA, USA. Association for Computational Linguistics.

Pinzhen Chen, Barry Haddow, Kenneth Heafield, Hieu Hoang, Miquel Esplà-Gomis, Mikel Forcada, Amir Kamran, Faheem Kirefu, Philipp Koehn, Sergio Ortiz, Leopoldo Sempere, Gema Ramírez-Sánchez, Elsa Sarrías, Marek Strelec, Brian Thompson, William Waites, Dion Wiggins, and Jaume Zaragoza. 2020. Paracrawl: Web-scale acquisition of parallel corpora. In *Proceedings of ACL'2020*, pages 4555–4567.

Alan Cruse. 2000. *Meaning in Language. An Introduction to Semantics and Pragmatics*. Oxford University Press. Oxford, UK.

D.Alan Cruse. 1986. *Lexical Semantics*. Cambridge University Press, UK.

Angel Daza and Anette Frank. 2020. X-SRL: A parallel cross-lingual semantic role labeling dataset. *arXiv preprint arXiv:2010.01998*.

Christiane Fellbaum, editor. 1998. *WordNet: An Electronic Lexical Database*. MIT Press, Cambridge, MA and London.

Cristina Fernández-Alcaina, Eva Fučíková, and Zdeňka Urešová. 2022. Annotation guidelines for Spanish verbal synonyms in the SynSemClass lexicon. Technical Report 72, UFAL MFF UK.

Ana Fernández-Montraveta and Gloria Vázquez. 2014. The SenSem corpus: An annotated corpus for Spanish and Catalan with information about aspectuality, modality, polarity and factuality. *Corpus Linguistics and Linguistic Theory*, 10(2):273–288.

Eva Fučíková, Jan Hajič, and Zdeňka Urešová. 2023. Corpus-based multilingual event-type ontology: annotation tools and principles. Note = To be published at GURT/TLT, Wash., D.C,.

José M García-Miguel, Lourdes Costas, and Susana Martínez. 2005. Diátesis verbales y esquemas construccionales. Verbos, clases semánticas y esquemas sintáctico-semánticos en el proyecto ADESSE. *Entre semántica léxica, teoría del léxico y sintaxis*, pages 373–384.

Aitor Gonzalez-Agirre, Egoitz Laparra, and German Rigau. 2012. Multilingual central repository version 3.0. In *Proceedings of the Eighth International Conference on Language Resources and Evaluation (LREC'12)*, pages 2525–2529, Istanbul, Turkey. European Language Resources Association (ELRA).

Jan Hajič, Eduard Bejček, Alevtina Bémová, Eva Buráňová, Eva Fučíková, Eva Hajičová, Jiří Havelka, Jaroslava Hlaváčová, Petr Homola, Pavel Ircing, Jiří Kárník, Václava Kettnerová, Natalia Klyueva, Veronika Kolářová, Lucie Kučová, Markéta Lopatková, David Mareček, Marie Mikulová, Jiří Mírovský, Anna Nedoluzhko, Michal Novák, Petr Pajas, Jarmila Panevová, Nino Peterek, Lucie Poláková, Martin Popel, Jan Popelka, Jan Romportl, Magdaléna Rysová, Jiří Semecký, Petr Sgall, Johanka Spoustová, Milan Straka, Pavel Straňák, Pavlína Synková, Magda Ševčíková, Jana Šindlerová, Jan Štěpánek, Barbora Štěpánková, Josef Toman, Zdeňka Urešová, Barbora Vidová Hladká, Daniel Zeman, Šárka Zikánová, and Zdeněk Žabokrtský. 2020. Prague dependency treebank - consolidated 1.0 (PDT-c 1.0). LINDAT/CLARIAH-CZ digital library at the Institute of Formal and Applied Linguistics (ÚFAL), Faculty of Mathematics and Physics, Charles University.

Jan Hajič, Eduard Bejček, Jaroslava Hlavacova, Marie Mikulová, Milan Straka, Jan Štěpánek, and Barbora Štěpánková. 2020. Prague dependency treebank - consolidated 1.0. In *Proceedings of the 12th Language Resources and Evaluation Conference*, pages 5208–5218, Marseille, France. European Language Resources Association.

Jan Hajič, Eva Hajičová, Jarmila Panevová, Petr Sgall, Ondřej Bojar, Silvie Cinková, Eva Fučíková, Marie Mikulová, Petr Pajas, Jan Popelka, Jiří Semecký, Jana Šindlerová, Jan Štěpánek, Josef Toman, Zdeňka Urešová, and Zdeněk Žabokrtský. 2012. Announcing Prague Czech-English Dependency Treebank 2.0. In *Proceedings of the 8th International Conference on Language Resources and Evaluation (LREC 2012)*, pages 3153–3160, İstanbul, Turkey. ELRA, European Language Resources Association.

Jan Hajič, Jarmila Panevová, Eva Hajičová, Petr Sgall, Petr Pajas, Jan Štěpánek, Jiří Havelka, Marie Mikulová, Zdeněk Žabokrtský, Magda Ševčíková Razímová, and Zdeňka Urešová. 2006. *Prague Dependency Treebank 2.0*. LDC2006T01. LDC, Philadelphia, PA, USA.

Jan Hajič, Jarmila Panevová, Zdeňka Urešová, Alevtina Bémová, Veronika Kolářová, and Petr Pajas. 2003. PDT-VALLEX: creating a large-coverage valency lexicon for treebank annotation. In *Proceedings of the 2nd Workshop on Treebanks and Linguistic Theories*, volume 9, page 57–68.

Howard Jackson. 1988. *Words and Their Meaning*. Routledge.

Jacqueline Kubczak. 2014. Valenzwörterbuch e-VALBU. LINDAT/CLARIAH-CZ digital library at the Institute of Formal and Applied Linguistics (ÚFAL), Faculty of Mathematics and Physics, Charles University.

Markéta Lopatková, Václava Kettnerová, Eduard Bejček, Anna Vernerová, and Zdeněk Žabokrtský. 2017.

Valenční slovník českých sloves VALLEX. Nakladatelství Karolinum, Praha.

Markéta Lopatková, Václava Kettnerová, Anna Vernerová, Eduard Bejček, and Zdeněk Žabokrtský. 2020. VALLEX 4.0 (2021-02-12). LINDAT/CLARIAH-CZ digital library at the Institute of Formal and Applied Linguistics (ÚFAL), Faculty of Mathematics and Physics, Charles University, http://hdl.handle.net/11234/1-3524 and https://ufal.mff.cuni.cz/vallex/4.0.

John Lyons. 1968. *Introduction to Theoretical Linguistics*. Cambridge University Press.

John Lyons. 1995. *Linguistic Semantics*. Cambridge University Press.

Martha Palmer, Daniel Gildea, and Paul Kingsbury. 2005. The proposition bank: An annotated corpus of semantic roles. *Comput. Linguist.*, 31(1):71–106.

Karin Kipper Schuler and Martha S. Palmer. 2005. *Verbnet: A Broad-Coverage, Comprehensive Verb Lexicon*. Ph.D. thesis, University of Pennsylvania, USA. AAI3179808.

Helmut Schumacher, Jacqueline Kubczak, Renate Schmidt, and Vera de Ruiter. 2018. *VALBU - Valenzwörterbuch deutscher Verben*. Narr, Tübingen.

Petr Sgall, Eva Hajičová, and Jarmila Panevová. 1986. *The Meaning of the Sentence in its Semantic and Pragmatic Aspects*. D. Reidel, Dordrecht.

Carlos Subirats. 2009. Spanish FrameNet: A frame-semantic analysis of the Spanish lexicon. In *Multilingual FrameNets in Computational Lexicography*, pages 135–162. De Gruyter Mouton.

Zdeňka Urešová, Eva Fučíková, Jan Hajič, and Jana Šindlerová. 2015. CzEngVallez – Czech–English Valency Lexicon.

Zdeňka Urešová, Eva Fučíková, Eva Hajičová, and Jan Hajič. 2018a. Creating a verb synonym lexicon based on a parallel corpus. In *Proceedings of the 11th International Conference on Language Resources and Evaluation (LREC 2018)*, pages 1432–1437, Paris, France. European Language Resources Association.

Zdeňka Urešová, Eva Fučíková, Eva Hajičová, and Jan Hajič. 2018b. Synonymy in bilingual context: The CzEngClass Lexicon. In *Proceedings of The 27th International Conference on Computational Linguistics*, pages 2456–2469, Sheffield, GB. ICCL, ICCL.

Zdeňka Urešová, Eva Fučíková, Eva Hajičová, and Jan Hajič. 2018. Tools for building an interlinked synonym lexicon network. In *Proceedings of the Eleventh International Conference on Language Resources and Evaluation (LREC 2018)*, Miyazaki, Japan. European Language Resources Association (ELRA).

Zdeňka Urešová, Eva Fučíková, Eva Hajičová, and Jan Hajič. 2020. SynSemClass Linked Lexicon: Mapping Synonymy between Languages. In *Proceedings of the 2020 Globalex Workshop on Linked Lexicography (LREC 2020)*, pages 10–19, Marseille, France. European Language Resources Association.

Zdeňka Urešová, Karolina Zaczynska, Peter Bourgonje, Eva Fučíková, Georg Rehm, and Jan Hajič. 2022. Making a semantic event-type ontology multilingual. In *Proceedings of the Thirteenth Language Resources and Evaluation Conference*, pages 1332–1343, Marseille, France. European Language Resources Association.

Hedging in diachrony: the case of Vedic Sanskrit *iva*

Erica Biagetti
Department of Humanities
Section of Linguistics
University of Pavia
erica.biagetti@unipv.it

Oliver Hellwig
Institute for Linguistics,
H.-Heine-Univ. Düsseldorf
Dep. of Comp. Lang. Science,
University of Zurich
Oliver.Hellwig@hhu.de

Sven Sellmer
Institute for Linguistics,
H.-Heine-Univ. Düsseldorf
Institute of Oriental Studies,
A. Mickiewicz Univ. Poznań
sellmer@hhu.de

Abstract

The rhetoric strategy of hedging serves to attenuate speech acts and their semantic content, as in English 'kind of' or 'somehow'. While hedging has recently met with increasing interest in linguistic research, most studies deal with modern languages, preferably English, and take a synchronic approach. This paper complements this research by tracing the diachronic syntactic flexibilization of the Vedic Sanskrit particle *iva* from a marker of comparison ('like') to a full-fledged adaptor. We discuss the outcomes of a diachronic Bayesian framework applied to *iva* constructions in a Universal Dependencies treebank, and supplement these results with a qualitative discussion of relevant text passages.

1 Introduction

Hedging is a rhetorical strategy by which a speaker can attenuate either the full semantic membership of an expression, as in example (1a) (propositional hedging), or the force of a speech act, as in (1b) (speech act hedging; Fraser, 2010, 22).

(1) a. *The pool has* ***sort of*** *a L-shaped design.*

b. ***I guess*** *I should leave now.*

Until recently,[1] hedges were considered to be marginal items that contribute little to communication, but their crucial role both in spoken and in written speech is now generally acknowledged by various linguistic disciplines (Kaltenböck et al., 2010, 1).

From the point of view of grammaticalization and/or pragmaticalization studies, hedges are interesting because they have been proven to emerge from different sources both intra- and cross-linguistically (Mihatsch, 2010). Furthermore, although the distinction between propositional and speech act hedges is commonly accepted, we often witness the emergence of speech act hedging as implicature of propositional hedging and vice versa (Mihatsch, 2010, 94; Kaltenböck et al., 2010).

Despite the abundance of studies on hedging in modern languages, the phenomenon has still been little studied in ancient languages, one exception being an in-depth analysis of the use of the approximation marker *hōs épos eipeîn* 'so to say' in Plato's *Gorgias* (Caffi, 2010). However, ancient languages that enjoy centuries of attestation and that have been handed down to us in sufficiently large corpora provide a privileged point of view for the study of hedging, because they allow us to trace the emergence of new hedges as well as the successive development of new functions. With centuries of attestation and an extant corpus of over three million tokens, Vedic Sanskrit (henceforth Vedic) is one such language. In this paper, we investigate the development of the particle *iva*, which in Vedic functions both as a comparison and an approximation marker. After summarizing the grammaticalization process that in the earliest texts lead to the development of the approximative function from the comparative one, we perform a quantitative analysis of the occurrences of *iva* in Vedic texts, in order to assess whether the particle underwent further syntactic and pragmatic developments.

Given the pragmatic nature of the phenomenon, corpus-based approaches are most suited for the study of hedging, because they allow to investigate genuinely attested language data rather than just invented sample sentences. In the case of an ancient language like Vedic, for which we can only make use of the available texts, a corpus-based approach to the study of *iva*'s approximating function is still a desideratum, as the only existing study (Brereton, 1982) is based on a handful of passages. In our study we employ a corpus

[1] Lakoff (1972) is the first study on hedges in English.

Proceedings of the 21st International Workshop on Treebanks and Linguistic Theories (TLT, GURT/SyntaxFest 2023), pages 21 - 31

with manually validated syntactic annotations, the Vedic Treebank (VTB, see Hellwig et al., 2020), which allows us to investigate the syntactic functions taken by the particle and to detect changes in the syntactic contexts in which it occurs. Since the occurrences of approximating *iva* are sparse in the VTB, we extend our data set with silver annotations obtained by an unsupervised parse of all Vedic texts contained in the Digital Corpus of Sanskrit (DCS, Hellwig, 2010–2022).

Section 2 of this paper gives a summary of previous research on approximators, including an overview of the current understanding in Vedic Studies. Sections 3 and 4 introduce the data set and describe the probabilistic model used to assess diachronic trends in the data, with a special focus on how to use data obtained in an unsupervised manner (Sec. 4.2). A more detailed qualitative evaluation is presented in Sec. 5. – Data and scripts are available at `https://github.com/OliverHellwig/sanskrit/tree/master/papers/2023tlt`.

2 The diachronic development of approximation markers

2.1 Cross-linguistic evidence

Adaptors are propositional hedges (approximators in Prince et al., 1982) that trigger loose readings of a lexical expression: in other words, they signal a loose correspondence between the referents or intended concepts and the lexemes employed, as in example (2) (see also *somewhat*, *some*, *a little bit*, etc.).

(2) a. *He's* ***sort of*** *nice.*

b. *He's really* ***like a geek****.*

As explained in Mihatsch (2010), a well-attested source for adaptors are markers of similative constructions that serve to compare two entities either globally, as in (3a), or with respect to some quality, as in 3b (Haspelmath and Buchholz, 1998, 278).

(3) a. *She is* ***like*** *her grandmother.*

b. *He sings* ***like*** *a nightingale.*

Semantically, the passage from markers of similative constructions to adaptors is triggered by the very idea of similative comparison which, unlike equative comparison of quantity, always implies an approximation; compare the above similatives with the equative *Robert is* ***as tall as*** *Maria* (Haspelmath and Buchholz, 1998, 278).

Syntactically, similative markers that turn into adaptors lose their function of situating the object of comparison in relation to a standard and become modifiers of noun phrases, signaling their semantically loose use (Mihatsch, 2010). See examples (4a) and (4b) from French (Mihatsch, 2009, 72):[2]

(4) a. *[Q]ui a fait passer* ***quelque chose comme un frisson*** *dans le dos des supporters français*
'Who sent **something like a shiver** down the back of the French supporters'

b. *[I]l a eu comme une étrange secousse, Ø* ***comme un frisson****...*
'He had like a strange spasm, **like a shiver**...'

Adaptors often develop new functions. For instance, they can be employed to signal figurative speech, as in example (5) from Italian (Mihatsch, 2010, 111); this function of adaptors derives from the fact that metaphors, like similative constructions, are also based on similarity, although across two conceptual domains.

(5) *[I] francesi hanno voluto* ***come*** *pagare un debito verso il loro poverissimo ciclismo*
'**It was as if** the French wanted to pay a debt toward their poor cyclism.' (Lit. 'The French wanted to **like** pay a debt toward their poor cyclism.')

As mentioned in the introduction, speech act hedging often arises as implicature of propositional hedging. For instance, adaptors may be used as shields for pragmatic mitigation as in French *Y'a* ***comme*** *un problème* 'there is like a problem' (Mihatsch, 2009, 84). The employment of adaptors as pragmatic shields leads to their syntactic flexibilization, allowing them to occur with parts of speech other than nouns. For instance, in languages such as Spanish and Portuguese, the same

[2] For similar developments in other Romance languages as well as Germanic languages, see Mihatsch (2009) and Mihatsch (2010); on languages outside of Europe, see Ziv (1998) and Fleischman (1999).

adaptors that have developed shield functions are also employed as rounders, i.e. as expressions that indicate imprecise numerical values (e.g., *Peter's house is* ***almost*** *100 feet wide*; see also Spanish and Portuguese *como* 'like'; Mihatsch, 2010, 112).

2.2 The Vedic approximation marker *iva*

The Vedic corpus, whose texts cover a period ranging from the 2nd millenium BCE to around 500-300 BCE (Witzel, 1997, 2009), provides further evidence for the development of comparative markers into adaptors. In the *Rigveda* (= RV), the oldest layer of Vedic literature, the particle *iva* primarily functions as a marker of similative constructions, as in example (6). In such constructions, *iva* always follows the standard of comparison or, when this standard is a complex noun phrase, the first element of the standard (see *pitā iva sūnave* 'like a father for a son' in 6):

(6) *saḥ* *naḥ* *pitā* ***iva***
3SG.NOM 1PL.DAT father:NOM like
sūnave *agne* *sūpāyanaḥ*
son:DAT Agni:VOC of-easy-approach:NOM
bhava
be:IMPV.2SG

'**Like** a father for a son, be of easy approach for us, o Agni.' (RV 1.1.9ab; trans. Jamison and Brereton, 2014)[3]

In more recent layers of the Vedic corpus, besides retaining its function of marking similative comparison, *iva* performs other functions that correspond to those attested cross-linguistically for adaptors, as in example (7):

(7) a. *saḥ* *avet* *pāpmānam*
3SG.NOM know:IMPF.3SG evil:ACC
vā *asṛkṣi* *yasmai* *me*
PTC cast:AOR.1SG REL.DAT 1SG.DAT
sasṛjānāya ***tamaḥ*** ***iva***
create:ABS darkness:NOM APPROX
abhūd
come-to-be:AOR.3SG

'He knew, "Verily, I have created evil for myself since, after creating (the Asuras), there has come to be **a kind of darkness** for me."' (*Śatapatha-Brāhmaṇa* [M] 11.1.6.9; trans. adapted from Eggeling, 1900)

b. *tasmāt* *api* *etarhi* ***bhūyān***
therefore even today big.NOM
iva *naktam* *saḥ* ***yāvat***
APPROX at-night 3SG.NOM as-far-as
mātram ***iva*** *apakramya*
just APPROX travel:ABS
bibheti
be-afraid:3SG

'Therefore, even today, (although) **quite big**, he who travels even a **quite short** distance at night becomes afraid.' (*Gopatha-Brāhmaṇa* 2.5.1; trans. Brereton, 1982)

Brereton (1982) describes the different functions performed by *iva* in Vedic prose, but he does not engage in a diachronic analysis of the particle nor does he address the relation between its comparative and approximating functions. The fact that *iva*'s approximative function is already attested in some Rigvedic passages led Pinault (2004) to hypothesize that this was the original function of the particle, which only later developed a comparative function. Based on comparative and textual evidence, Biagetti (2022) makes a case for the opposite development of *iva*, namely from a marker of similative constructions into an adaptor. Through a manual scrutiny of some Rigvedic passages listed in Pinault (2004), Biagetti identifies different ambiguous contexts that may have led to the emergence of the new function and to its progressive conventionalization. In particular, *iva*'s adaptor function seems to have emerged from similative constructions whose object of comparison consists in (a) null referential argument(s), as in example (8).[4] Among such cases, those in which neither the linguistic context nor the discourse universe provide referents for a null comparee (as likely in the first half of example 9) trigger a reanalysis of the standard of comparison as the argument of the verb and of *iva* as its modifier.

[4]In example 8, the subscripts *i* and *j* indicate that *indraḥ* 'Indra' and *rathāya* 'for (his) chariot' can be interpreted as referents respectively of the null subject ($\emptyset_i$) and null object ($\emptyset_j$) of *unoti* 'urges' in the following sentence

(8)

indraḥ$_i$	***rathāya***$_j$	*pravatam*
Indra:NOM	chariot:DAT	easy-slope:ACC

kr̥ṇoti	…	*yūthā*	***iva***
make:3SG	...	flock:ACC.PL	like/APPROX

paśavaḥ	$\emptyset_i$	$\emptyset_j$	*vi*	*unoti*
livestock:GEN	Ø	Ø	PTC	urge:3SG

gopāḥ	*ariṣṭaḥ*
herdsman:NOM	invulnerable:NOM

yāti	*prathamaḥ*	*siṣāsan*
drive:3SG	first:NOM	win:DES.PTCP.NOM

1. Comparative reading: 'Indra makes an easy slope for his chariot [. . .]. Like a herdsman the flocks of livestock, he (Indra, *indraḥ* in *pāda* a) urges (his chariot, *rathāya* in *pāda* a). Invulnerable, he drives as the first to seek winnings.' (RV 5.31.1a-c; trans. adapted from Jamison and Brereton, 2014)
2. Approximative reading: (*pāda* c) 'The herdsman urges the flocks of livestock, as it were.'

(9)

cittiḥ	*apām*	*dame*
bright:NOM	water:GEN.PL	house:LOC

viśvāyuḥ	***sádma***	***iva***
whole-lifetime	seat:ACC	like/APPROX

dhīrāḥ	*sammāya*	*cakruḥ*
clever:NOM.PL	measure:ABS	make:PF.3PL

1. Comparative reading (unlikely): '(He is) the bright apparition in the house of the waters through his whole lifetime. Like clever men an abode, the wise have made a seat (for him), having measured it out completely.' (RV 1.67.10ab; trans. Jamison and Brereton, 2014)
2. Approximative reading: 'The clever ones made (for him, Agni) **some kind of seat** by building together.' (trans. Pinault, 2004)

Since in similative constructions *iva* always follows a noun (phrase), the adaptor function must first have developed with nouns (see example 7a) and then have spread to other parts of speech (see, e.g., example 7b with adjectives). In the following sections, we aim to trace this syntactic flexibilization of *iva* throughout different diachronic layers of Vedic literature.

3 Data

Our diachronic analysis of *iva* as an approximator is based on the dependency annotations collected in the Vedic Treebank (Hellwig et al., 2020), which is annotated using Universal Dependencies.[5] As is shown in Table 1, *iva* occurs in several syntactic functions; `discourse`, the label on which we focus in this paper, is only the third most frequent annotation of this particle. The two most frequent labels, `case` and `mark`, are employed when *iva* functions as a marker of similative comparison; in particular, the particle takes the relation `case` when it introduces a single standard of comparison (e.g. ***gaúḥ iva*** *śākináḥ* 'strong like an ox'), whereas it is labeled as `mark` when it introduces a complex standard resulting in a gapping construction (e.g. *tam tvā vayam* ***sudughām iva goduhaḥ*** *juhūmasi śravasyavaḥ* 'we call to you, as milkers [call] on a cow who gives good milk').

The alternation between the main functions of *iva* becomes much clearer when we add a chronological component to the data. Dating Vedic texts is notoriously difficult because text-internal and external chronological clues are largely missing (see e.g. Witzel, 1995). The VTB therefore assigns each Vedic text to one of five successive chronological layers, based on a general consensus in Vedic studies (details in Hellwig and Sellmer, 2021): the oldest part of the Rigveda (1-RV, ca. 15th–11th c. BCE), the metrical texts of the Mantra period (2-MA, 10th–8th c. BCE), old (3-PO ca. 8th–7th c. BCE) and late prose (4-P, ca. 7th–6th c. BCE), and the prose texts of the Sūtra period (5-SU, ca. 4th c. BCE – 3th c. CE). Rows 2ff. of Table 1 show how the syntactic functions of *iva* are distributed over these five chronological layers. We observe a clear break in the usage of *iva* between the two early metrical layers (1-RV, 2-MA) and the later prose layers: in the former, the `case` and `mark` relations are frequent, while `discourse` is virtually unattested; on the contrary, `case` and `mark` decrease in later prose layers, while `discourse` becomes more frequent. A reason for the high frequency of comparative *iva* may be found in the fact that layers 1-RV and 2-MA include metrical texts composed

[5] The current version of the VTB, which is available at `https://github.com/OliverHellwig/sanskrit/tree/master/papers/2020lrec/treebank`, contains 140,442 words in 18,958 sentences.

Time	case	mark	discourse	other
Global	397	132	126	5
1-RV	135	53	1	1
2-MA	183	72	7	1
3-PO	31	2	49	0
4-PL	33	3	65	3
5-SU	15	2	4	0

Table 1: Gold labels for *iva*. First row: global counts; following rows: counts per time slot in the VTB. See p. 4 for the chronological labels in the first column.

in a highly formulaic diction which is characterized, among other figures of speech, by the extensive use of similes introduced by *iva*.[6] Moreover, `discourse` is employed so rarely in 1-RV and 2-MA because at this diachronic stage *iva*'s approximative function has not yet fully developed (see Sect. 2.2 and below). At this point it should be added that the ambiguous nature of the function of *iva* in examples such as (8) is not explicitly reflected in our data, as the annotation software used did not allow to assign two or more alternative labels. As far as the annotation guidelines are concerned, they did not contain any specific rules as to the treatment of these two functions of *iva*.

4 Quantitative evaluation

4.1 Gold data from the VTB

In this section, we focus on the data in column four of Table 1. For this study, the counts of these words are further split by the word class of the head of *iva*. This view of the gold annotations is presented in the first two rows of Table 2, along with the proportion of noun constructions in each time slot. The first three rows of Table 2 suggest that the diachronic distribution of *iva* with nouns is influenced not only by chronology but also by the register of the texts (metrical vs. prose). First, only one construction of this type is found in the first two layers of the VTB which contain the early metrical texts (1-RV, 2-MA) although there are seven cases in which *iva* is labeled as discourse marker here.[7] Second, the proportion of this construction (see row 3 of Table 2) decreases in the three layers that contain middle and late Vedic prose texts (3-PO, 4-PL, 5-SU). The two factors of time and register are not easy to disentangle because the metrical texts constitute all of the two oldest strata. In order to test how these factors influence the frequency of *iva* with nouns, we fit a binomial logistic regression to the gold data in the upper half of Table 2. Such a model generates the observed counts of *iva* with nouns in a time slot given the total number of instances in this slot and the values of the covariates (predictors). As the data set is small, we use a Bayesian approach that restricts the values of the inferred coefficients. We develop models that test the plausibility of the following three scenarios:

1 Time alone is responsible for the distribution in Table 2. Let t_i denote the time slot, scaled to the range $[-1, +1]$,[8] n_i the number of cases in which the head of *iva* is a noun in time slot i (row 1 of Table 2), N_i the total number of occurrences of *iva* in slot i (sum of rows 1 and 2 of Table 2), and $\sigma(\ldots)$ the logistic link function. After placing standard Normal priors on the coefficients a, b, the observed frequencies of *iva* (n_i) are generated in the following way:

$$n_i \sim \text{Binomial}(N_i, \sigma(a + bt_i)) \quad (1)$$

2 The distribution in Table 2 is solely caused by register, i.e. the opposition between (early) metrical and (late) prose texts. The link function in Eq. 1 changes to $\sigma(a + cr_i)$, with r_i denoting the register of layer i encoded as a binary factor.

3 Each row in Table 2 is generated by jointly considering register and time. If $t_i \in (1, 2)$, p_i is generated as in model 2; else as in Eq. 1.

We implement all models in `RStan` (Stan Development Team, 2022) and compare them using the

[6]On the formulaic nature of Rigvedic similes, see Pinault (1985) and Pinault (1997), among others.

[7]This may partly be due to the fact that, as explained in Sect. 5, in the first two layers *iva*'s adaptor function has not yet become conventionalized. While cases where *iva* follows another part of speech are easy for annotators to interpret, some cases where *iva* follows a noun can be ambiguous between comparative and adaptor reading (see example 8): since the former reading is by far the most frequent in the RV and mantra language, annotators in these cases are likely to chose the label `case` or `mark`, and therefore approximative *iva* with a noun as head may be slightly under-represented in these two layers.

[8]This implies that an ordinal variable is transformed into a scalar. Such an approach is problematic (see e.g. McKelvey and Zavoina 1975 for the case of ordinal predicted variables), and it would be more meaningful to model time either with an ordered factor or to estimate at least the widths of the time slots before performing the transformation. The data set studied here is, however, not large enough to obtain reliable estimates of the additional parameters.

		1-RV	2-MA	3-PO	4-PL	5-SU
VTB (gold)	noun	0	1	24	28	0
	other	1	6	25	37	4
	Prop.	0	14.3	49	43.1	0
DCS (silver)	noun	1	3	84	128	4
	other	3	12	91	240	23
	Prop.	25	20	48	34.8	14.8
	correct/wrong	0/0	1/1	11/1	19/2	2/0

Table 2: POS tag of the syntactic head of *iva* used as discourse marker, conditioned on the time slot (columns). Gold data in the upper half is from the VTB. Rows with 'noun': The head of *iva* is a noun; 'other': The head has any other POS. For the silver data in the lower half of the table, refer to Sec. 4.2 of this paper.

expected log pointwise predictive density (elpd) in a leave-one-out setting (Vehtari et al., 2017). Each model is trained for 5,000 iterations and with four parallel chains. Model diagnostics ($\hat{R}$, ESS) show no problems in the sampling process.

The results in Table 3 show that the elpd of model 1, which only considers time, is more than one standard error (column 'SE') lower than that of the two other models which include the register split. This outcome suggests that time alone cannot explain the distribution of *iva* with nouns, and register information is relevant for modeling the data in Table 2. This conclusion finds further support by a posterior predictive check the results of which are given in the column labeled 'β' in Table 3. To calculate β, we sample values of n_i (counts of *iva* with nouns) from the posterior distributions of the three models at each post-burn-in iteration of the sampler. The five sampled values n' (one for each time slot) are compared with the observed distribution of n (row 1 of Table 2) using the exact Fisher test for quantifying the goodness of fit. β in Table 3 is the proportion of these tests in which the null hypothesis (n and n' come from the same distribution, i.e. the model generates "naturally looking" samples) was rejected at an error level of 5%. β can thus be interpreted as an approximation of the type II error of wrongly accepting the null hypothesis. The chance of making such an error is clearly higher (0.0192, i.e. 1.9%) for the model that only considers time than for those that integrate register as well (0.63% and 0.44%). As the values of β and elpd show, the best fit of the data is achieved by the third model which combines time and register. This outcome is not surprising. While model 2 (register only) adapts to the observed counts using two estimates that remain constant over slots 1-2 and 3-5, model 3 has the chance to capture the temporal dynamics in the three later slots of Vedic and thus achieves a better fit.

Model	elpd	SE	β
Time	-12.4	2.43	0.0192
Register	-9.92	2.34	0.0063
Time/register	-9.92	2.6	0.0044
Time/reg., silver	-320.76	29.47	0.0297

Table 3: Summary evaluation of the models applied to the data in Table 2. 'elpd' and 'SE' quantify the predictive power and its standard error. 'β' reports the results of a posterior predictive check. Higher values of elpd and lower ones of β are better. elpd and SE of the fourth model are not comparable with the values of the other three models and are only given for reference.

4.2 Exploring silver annotations

While the results discussed so far are in favor of a diachronic scenario that explains NOUN + *iva* constructions with a combination of the Vedic register split and a chronological model, one should keep in mind that the data set on which this conclusion is built consists of only 125 observations and is therefore tiny. As the DCS, on top of which the Vedic Treebank is built, is much larger than the VTB and a parser for Vedic is available,[9] it is obvious to extend the data set with silver annotations made by this parser. We therefore extract all occurrences of *iva* from an up-to-date unsupervised parse of the DCS[10] and merge gold and silver an-

[9] This parser uses a biaffine architecture (see Dozat and Manning, 2017) with the addition of a character based CNN (see Rotman and Reichart, 2019; Zhang et al., 2015), and reaches a performance of 87.61 UAS and 81.84 LAS. For further details see Hellwig et al. (Forthcoming).

[10] The Con-LLU data are available at `https://github.com/OliverHellwig/sanskrit/tree/master/dcs/data/conllu`. Silver parses are contained in the `conllu_parsed` files.

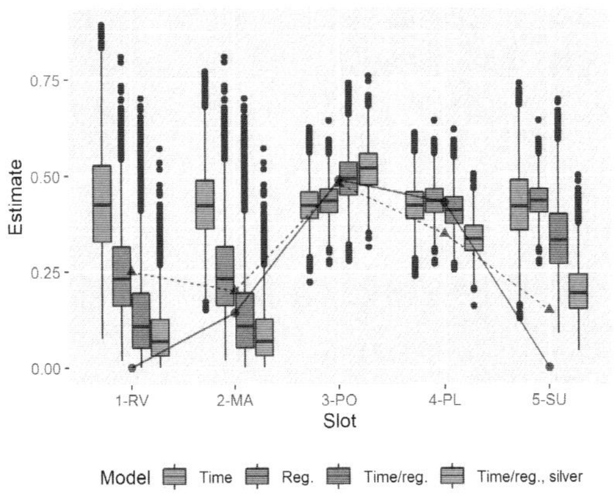

Figure 1: Temporal dynamics predicted by the four models. The y-values are parameters of binomial distributions that predict the presence of *iva* with nominal heads. Dots and lines give the observed proportions in the gold (circles; Sec. 4.1) and silver data (triangles; Sec. 4.2).

notations; statistics of the silver data are presented in the lower half of Table 2. While the gold data used in Sec. 4.1 only contain instances of *iva* labeled as discourse, the merged data set contains all gold and silver annotations of *iva* regardless of their syntactic labels, because we want to recover instances of *iva* as discourse particle that were mislabeled by the parser.

Instead of the plain GLM of Eq. 1, we now use a hierarchical model that integrates a mechanism for error detection. At the first level, this model decides if, in a given record k, the true label of *iva* is `discourse`. The corresponding binary variable z_k (1 = record k is an instance of *iva* as discourse, 0 = it is not) is only partly observed. Somewhat over-confidently, we assume that all gold annotations are labeled correctly. To get an estimate of the error level in the silver data, one author of this paper manually annotated the correct label of 100 randomly chosen silver records, marking those cases in which a wrong head was chosen for *iva*. z_k is predicted using the following covariates: time; the label; the distance between *iva* and its head; the POS and label of the head; interactions between time and position difference and time and head POS. At the second level, the model proceeds with model 3 (Time/register) from Sec. 4.1 if z_k has the value 1, i.e. is correct according to the first level of the model. The only difference is that the binomial is replaced with a Bernoulli distribution because individual records are inspected. More formally, let $\mathbf{x}_k$ denote the vector of covariates for the Bernoulli logistic model at level 1, and $\mathbf{d}$ the vector of the corresponding coefficients to be estimated. After placing standard normal priors on the coefficients, z_k is drawn from a Bernoulli distribution Bern$(\sigma(\mathbf{x}^T\mathbf{d}))$. If $z_k = 1$, model 3 from Sec. 4.1 is used for describing the diachronic distribution.

Figure 1 provides a graphical comparison of the results produced by the four models discussed in Sections 4.1 and 4.2. Here, the values on the y-axis are the estimated proportion parameters that model the occurrence of *iva* with nominal heads. In addition, Fig. 1 also shows the proportions observed in the gold and silver data as points connected with lines. As could already be deduced from the β values in Table 3, neither the time-only nor the register-only models fit the observed gold data well. The outcome is much better for the two models that combine register and time. Both predict low values for the early metrical texts (1-RV, 2-MA), and they appropriately describe the decreasing trend in the three prose levels. Note that neither 'Register' nor 'Time or register' fully capture the low frequencies in the last chronological layer (5-SU). This suggests that further, probably domain or genre specific, factors are in effect here. One possible explanation may be that the language of the late Vedic Sūtra texts differs markedly from that of the earlier Vedic literature (see e.g. Renou, 1957, 15-16).

5 Qualitative analysis

The data presented in Section 4 confirms the syntactic flexibilization of *iva* hypothesized in Section 2: as the proportion of NOUN + *iva* constructions decreases, the particle starts occurring with other parts of speech; furthermore, the analysis in Section 4 suggests that this development is to be attributed to both register and time. In this section, we provide a more detailed qualitative evaluation of the data showing that the extension of *iva*'s scope to other parts of speech co-occurs with the development of new functions for this particle.

The grammaticalization process described in Section 2 first results in the employment of *iva* with nouns (see example 7a). Other parts of speech occurring with *iva* in layers 3-PO and 4-PL belong either to open classes, such as verbs (example 10) and adjectives (11), or to closed classes such as conjunctions (12) and particles (13). In example (10), king Janaka asks the sage Yājñavalkya about the possible substitutes for the *agnihotra*, a meal offering usually consisting of milk. The conversation comes to an end when Yājñavalkya states that, even in the absence of water, the *agnihotra* can be celebrated by offering, 'in some way' (*iva)*, 'truth in faith' (*satyam śraddhāyām*). Similarly, in (11), the author explains that, during the Soma sacrifice, the sacrificial post is anointed from its base upwards because it is for heaven that it is anointed and heaven is 'in some way' (*iva*) 'upwards' (*parāṅ*).

(10) *yat āpaḥ na syuḥ*
if water:NOM.PL NEG be:OPT.3SG
kena juhuyāḥ iti.
what:INST offer:OPT.2SG QUOT
saḥ ha uvāca na vai iha
3SG.NOM PTC say:PF.3SG NEG PTC here
tarhi kiṃcana āsīt atha etat
then nothing be:IMPF.3SG but here
u ***hūyate iva*** *satyam*
PTC offer:PASS.3SG APPROX truth:NOM
śraddhāyām iti
faith:ACC QUOT

'If there would be no water, with what would you perform the offering?' He said: 'Then, indeed, there would be nothing at all here, and yet **there would be offered in some way** here, namely, truth in faith.' (*Jaiminīya-Brāhmaṇa* 1.19.23.1; trans. adapted from Bodewitz, 1973)

(11) *parāñcam prokṣati.* ***parāṅ***
upwards:ACC anoint:3SG upwards:NOM
iva *hi suvargaḥ lokaḥ*
APPROX for heavenly:NOM world:NOM

'He anoints (he sacrificial post) from the foot upwards, for **upwards as it were** is the world of heaven.' (*Taittirīya-Saṃhitā* 6.3.4.1)

In examples (12) and (13), where *iva* follows the conjunctions *uta* 'and' and the causal expression *tasmāt vā* 'therefore', the particle seems to have scope not only on the preceding lexical item, but on the whole proposition. In (12), Ajātaśatru explains to Gārgya that, when one is asleep, one gathers the cognitive power of the vital functions into the space within one's heart. The dream then consists of the perceptions that the sleeping person experiences in her heart, rather than in the external world. In this example, the sequence of *uta iva* marks the fictive nature of the events experienced in the dream.

(12) *saḥ yatra etat svapnyayā*
3SG.NOM wherever thus in-dream
carati ... tat ***uta iva***
go:3SG ... then CONJ APPROX
mahārājaḥ bhavati ***uta***
great-king:NOM become:3SG CONJ
iva *mahābrāhmaṇaḥ* ***uta***
APPROX great-Brahmin:NOM CONJ
iva *uccāvacam*
APPROX high-and-low(-region):ACC
nigacchati
enter:3SG

'Wherever he may travel in his dream [...] He may appear to become a great king or an eminent Brahmin, or to visit the highest and the lowest regions.' (*Bṛhadāraṇyaka-Upaniṣad* 2.1.18.3; trans. Olivelle, 1998)

Example (13) is concerned with explaining the creation of the universe by pointing out similarities between words. At the beginning there was nothing but seven vital airs; they were turned into seven persons and these, in turn, into body parts of Prajāpati, the 'lord of generation'. In this process, the best part (*śrī-*) of each person was concentrated and became Prajāpati's head (*śiras-*; note the phonetic similarity of the words *śrī* and *śiras*). In the example, the sequence ***tasmāt vā iva*** *etat śiraḥ* seems to present the preceding clause ('It was thereto that the vital airs resorted'), which involves the verb *śri-* 'rest on', as a further possible explanation of the word *śiras* 'head' to which, however, the author does not fully commit.

(13) *tasmin* *etasmin* *prāṇāḥ*
3SG.LOC DEM.LOC vital-air:NOM.PL
aśrayanta. ***tasmāt vā iva***
resort:IMPF.3PL therefore PTC APPROX
etat *śiraḥ*
3SG.NOM head:NOM

'{And because (in it) they concentrated the excellence (*śriyaṃ* < *śrī*), therefore it is (called) the head (*śiras*).} It was thereto (in the head) that the vital airs resorted (*aśrayanta* < *śri-*): possibly therefore it is the head (*śiras*). (*Śatapatha-Brāhmaṇa* [M] 6.1.1.4.4; trans. adapted from Eggeling, 1894)

The source for the syntactic flexibilization of *iva* may also be found in the very sort of texts contained in layers 3-PO and 4-PL. In the *Brāhmaṇas*, ancillary texts providing detailed explanations of rituals, *iva* is often employed in order to point out correspondences among elements of the ritual realm, of the cosmic realm, or of daily life. In such cases, the sequence NOUN + *iva* co-occurs with a causal particle or adverb such as *hi* 'for, because' or *tasmāt* therefore': see example (14), where the phrase *vājinam iva* 'some sort of steed' is followed by the particle *hi* (see also example 11):

(14) *paryagnaye kriyamāṇāya anubrūhi iti āha adhvaryuḥ [...]*
'Recite for the carrying round of fire' the Adhvaryu (priest) says [...]'
vājī *san* *pari*
steed:NOM be:PTCP.NOM around
nīyate *iti* ***vājinam***
carry:PASS.3SG QUOT steed:ACC
iva ***hi*** *enam* *santam*
APPROX for DEM.ACC be:PTCP.ACC
pariṇayanti
around-carry:3PL

'Being a steed he (the fire, god Agni) is carried round' (the Adhvaryu says), **for him being as it were a steed** they carry round.' (*Aitareya-Brāhmaṇa* 2.5.3.2; trans. Keith, 1920)

In example (14), for instance, *iva* does not signal a loose reading of the noun *vājinam* 'steed' alone, but rather the metaphorical nature of the correspondence between the fire (god Agni) and a steed. The frequency of structures such as (14) in the *Brāhmaṇas* may have caused an interpretation of *iva* as having scope not only on the preceding lexical item, but on the whole proposition, and may eventually have caused the emergence of sequences such as *tasmāt vā iva* in (13), where the particle directly follows the causal adverb and the disjunctive particle.

6 Summary and conclusion

Originally a marker of phrasal comparison, the Vedic particle *iva* grammaticalized into an approximation marker signaling the semantically loose use of the preceding noun (Sect. 2.2). This grammaticalization process can already be traced in the oldest texts (layers 1-RV and 2-MA) by manual scrutiny (Biagetti, 2022), but is not captured by the syntactic annotation contained in the VTB; this is because, in ambiguous contexts that may have been responsible for the reanalysis of *iva* into an adaptor, the particle was usually annotated as a marker of comparison (deprels `case` or `mark`) by the annotators, as this is by far its most common function in the RV.

In this paper we have focused on the further syntactic flexibilization of *iva* in later Vedic texts. Bayesian analysis (Sect. 4) has shown that the proportion of NOUN + *iva* constructions, in which the particle has scope on the immediately preceding lexical item, decreases in layers 3-PO, 4-PL and 5-SU and that this break is to be attributed to both time and register. Accordingly, *iva* starts occurring with parts of speech other than noun and, as shown by the qualitative analysis of Sect. 5, gradually develops new functions. First, the frequent occurrence of *iva* with other particles or conjunctions leads to an extension of its scope to the whole proposition (see examples 11 to 14); second, in some such cases *iva* seems to mark the metaphorical meaning of the expression (example 14) or seems to function as a speech-act edge, signaling lack of commitment in the statement being uttered (example 13).

Ultimately, the quantitative and qualitative analyses of *iva* in Vedic prose seems to mirror the diachrony of adaptors as attested cross-linguistically and thus provides further evidence for the development of the particle from a marker of comparison to an approximation marker, and not vice versa.

7 Acknowledgments

We would like to thank three anonymous reviewers for their remarks and suggestions.
Oliver Hellwig and Sven Sellmer were funded by the German Federal Ministry of Education and Research, FKZ 01UG2121, while doing research for this paper.

References

Erica Biagetti. 2022. From standard marker to adaptor: The case of Vedic *iva*. *Bhasha. Journal of South Asian Linguistics, Philology and Grammatical Traditions*, 1(2).

Henk Bodewitz. 1973. *Jaiminīya Brāhmaṇa I, 1-65: Translation [from the Sanskrit] and commentary*. Number v. 17 in Orientalia Rheno-Traiectina. Brill, Leiden.

Joel P. Brereton. 1982. The particle *iva* in Vedic prose. *Journal of the American Oriental Society*, 102(3):443–450.

Claudia Caffi. 2010. Weakening or strengthening? A case of enantiosemy in Plato's *Gorgias*. In Gunther Kaltenböck, Wiltrud Mihatsch, and Stefan Schneider, editors, *New Approaches to Hedging*, pages 181–202. Emerald Group Publishing Limited, Bingley.

Timothy Dozat and Christopher D. Manning. 2017. Deep biaffine attention for neural dependency parsing. In *5th International Conference on Learning Representations*, pages 1–8.

Julius Eggeling. 1894. *The Śatapatha-Brāhmaṇa. According to the text of the Mādhyandina School. Translated. Part III, Books V, VI and VII*, volume 3. Clarendon Press, Oxford.

Julius Eggeling. 1900. *The Śatapatha-Brāhmaṇa. According to the text of the Mādhyandina School. Translated. Part V, Books XI, XII, XIII andXIV*, volume 5. Clarendon Press, Oxford.

Suzanne Fleischman. 1999. Pragmatic markers in comparative perspective. In *Paper presented at PRAGMA 99, Tel Aviv, Israel.*

Bruce Fraser. 2010. Pragmatic competence: The case of hedging. In Gunther Kaltenböck, Wiltrud Mihatsch, and Stefan Schneider, editors, *New approaches to hedging*, pages 15–35. Emerald Group Publishing Limited, Bingley.

Martin Haspelmath and Olga Buchholz. 1998. Equative and similative constructions in the languages of Europe. In Johan Van der Auwera, editor, *Adverbial Constructions in the Languages of Europe*, pages 277—334. Mouton de Gruyter, Berlin.

Oliver Hellwig. 2010–2022. DCS - The Digital Corpus of Sanskrit.

Oliver Hellwig, Sebastian Nehrdich, and Sven Sellmer. Forthcoming. Data-driven dependency parsing of Vedic Sanskrit. *Language Resources and Evaluation*.

Oliver Hellwig, Salvatore Scarlata, Elia Ackermann, and Paul Widmer. 2020. The treebank of Vedic Sanskrit. In *Proceedings of the 12th Language Resources and Evaluation Conference*, pages 5137–5146, Marseille, France. European Language Resources Association.

Oliver Hellwig and Sven Sellmer. 2021. The Vedic treebank. In Erica Biagetti, Chiara Zanchi, and Silvia Luraghi, editors, *Building New Resources for Historical Linguistics*, pages 31–40. Pavia University Press, Pavia.

Stephanie W. Jamison and Joel P. Brereton. 2014. *The Rigveda: the earliest religious poetry of India. 3 volumes*. Oxford University Press, New York.

Gunther Kaltenböck, Wiltrud Mihatsch, and Stefan Schneider. 2010. Introduction. In Gunther Kaltenböck, Wiltrud Mihatsch, and Stefan Schneider, editors, *New approaches to hedging*, pages 1–14. Emerald Group Publishing Limited, Bingley.

Arthur Berriedale Keith. 1920. *Rigveda Brahmanas: The Aitareya and Kausītaki Brāhmanas of the Rigveda*, volume 25 of *The Harvard Oriental Series*. Harvard University Press, Cambridge, Massachusetts.

George Lakoff. 1972. Hedges: A study in meaning criteria and the logic of fuzzy concepts. In J.N. Levi Deborah James, Paul M. Peranteau and G.C. Phares, editors, *Papers from the Eighth Regional Meeting of the Chicago Linguistic Society*, pages 183–228. Pavia University Press, Chicago.

Richard D McKelvey and William Zavoina. 1975. A statistical model for the analysis of ordinal level dependent variables. *Journal of Mathematical Sociology*, 4(1):103–120.

Wiltrud Mihatsch. 2009. The approximators French comme, Italian come, Portuguese como and Spanish como from a grammaticalization perspective. In Corinne Rossari, Claudia Ricci, and Adriana Spiridon, editors, *Grammaticalization and pragmatics: facts, approaches, theoretical issues*, pages 65–91. Brill, Leiden.

Wiltrud Mihatsch. 2010. The diachrony of rounders and adaptors: approximation and unidirectional change. In Gunther Kaltenböck, Wiltrud Mihatsch, and Stefan Schneider, editors, *New approaches to hedging*, pages 93–122. Emerald Group Publishing Limited, Bingley.

Patrick Olivelle. 1998. *The Early Upaniṣads. Annotated text and translation*. Oxford University Press, Oxford.

Georges Pinault. 1985. Négation et comparaison en védique. *Bulletin de la Société de linguistique de Paris*, 80(1):103–144.

Georges Pinault. 1997. Distribution des particules comparatives dans la *Rik-Samhitā*. *Bulletin d'Études Indiennes*, 13-14:307–367.

Georges Pinault. 2004. On the usages of the particle *iva* in the Rigvedic hymns. In *The Vedas. Texts, languages and ritual. Proceedings of the Third International Vedic Workshop (Leiden, May 29-June 2, 2002)*, pages 285–306, Groningen. Groningen Oriental Studies.

Ellen F. Prince, Charles L. Bosk, and Joel E. Frader. 1982. On hedging in physician-physician discourse. In Robert J. di Pietro, editor, *Linguistics and the professions*, pages 83–97. Ablex, Norwood, NJ.

Louis Renou. 1957. *Altindische Grammatik, Introduction Générale*. Vandenhoeck & Ruprecht, Göttingen.

Guy Rotman and Roi Reichart. 2019. Deep contextualized self-training for low resource dependency parsing. *Transactions of the Association for Computational Linguistics*, 7:695–713.

Stan Development Team. 2022. RStan: the R interface to Stan. R package version 2.21.5.

Aki Vehtari, Andrew Gelman, and Jonah Gabry. 2017. Practical Bayesian model evaluation using leave-one-out cross-validation and WAIC. *Statistics and Computing*, 27(5):1413–1432.

Michael Witzel. 1995. Early Indian history: Linguistic and textual parametres. In George Erdosy, editor, *The Indo-Aryans of Ancient South Asia. Language, material Culture and ethnicity*, volume 1, pages 85–125. Walter de Gruyter, Berlin, New York.

Michael Witzel. 1997. The development of the Vedic canon and its schools: the social and political milieu (Materials on Vedic Sakhas, 8). In Michael Witzel, editor, *Inside the texts, beyond the texts. New approaches to the study of the Vedas*, pages 258–348. Harvard Oriental Series, Cambridge.

Michael Witzel. 2009. Moving targets? Texts, language, archaeology and history in the late Vedic and early Buddhist periods. *Indo-Iranian Journal*, 52(2/3):287–310.

Xiang Zhang, Junbo Zhao, and Yann LeCun. 2015. Character-level convolutional networks for text classification. In *Advances in Neural Information Processing Systems*, volume 28, pages 649–657. Curran Associates, Inc.

Yael Ziv. 1998. Hebrew *kaze* as a discourse marker and lexical hedge: conceptual and procedural properties. In Andreas H. Jucker and Yael Ziv, editors, *Discourse markers: descriptions and theory*, pages 203–221. Benjamins, Leiden.

Is Japanese CCGBank empirically correct?
A case study of passive and causative constructions

Daisuke Bekki
Ochanomizu University
bekki@is.ocha.ac.jp

Hitomi Yanaka
The University of Tokyo
hyanaka@is.s.u-tokyo.ac.jp

Abstract

The Japanese CCGBank serves as training and evaluation data for developing Japanese CCG parsers. However, since it is automatically generated from the Kyoto Corpus, a dependency treebank, its linguistic validity still needs to be sufficiently verified. In this paper, we focus on the analysis of passive/causative constructions in the Japanese CCGBank and show that, together with the compositional semantics of ccg2lambda, a semantic parsing system, it yields empirically wrong predictions for the nested construction of passives and causatives.

1 Introduction

The process of generating wide-coverage syntactic parsers from treebanks was established in the era of probabilistic context-free grammar (CFG) parsers in the 1990s. However, it was believed at that time that such an approach did not apply to linguistically-oriented formal syntactic theories. The reason was that formal syntactic theories were believed to be too inflexible to exhaustively describe the structure of real texts. This misconception was dispelled by the theoretical development of formal grammars and the emergence of linguistically-oriented treebanks.[1] In particlar, Combinatory Categorial Grammar (CCG) (Steedman, 1996, 2000) and CCGbank (Hockenmaier and Steedman, 2005) gave rise to the subsequent developments of CCG parsers such as C&C parser (Clark and Curran, 2007) and EasyCCG parser (Lewis and Steedman, 2014), and proved that wide-coverage CCG parsers could be generated from treebanks in a similar process to probablistic CFG parsers.

This trend has also impacted research on Japanese syntax and parsers. Bekki (2010) revealed that CCG, as a syntactic theory, enables us to provide a wide-coverage syntactic description of the Japanese language. It motivated the development of the Japanese CCGBank (Uematsu et al., 2013), followed by Japanese CCG parsers such as Jigg (Noji and Miyao, 2016) and depccg (Yoshikawa et al., 2017).

The difficulty in developing the Japanese CCGBank lay in the absence of CFG treebanks for the Japanese language at that time.[2] While CCGbank was generated from the Penn Treebank, which is a CFG treebank, the only large-scale treebank available for Japanese was the Kyoto Corpus[3], which is a dependency tree corpus, from which Uematsu et al. (2013) attempted to construct a Japanese CCGBank by automatic conversion.

The syntactic structures of CCG have more elaborated information than those of CFG, such as argument structures and syntactic features. Thus, it is inevitable that a dependency tree, which has even less information than that of CFG, must be supplemented with a great deal of linguistic information. Uematsu et al. (2013) had to guess them systematically, which is not an obvious process, and ad-hoc rules had to be stipulated in many places to accomplish it, including the "passive/causative suffixes as $S\backslash S$ analysis," which we will discuss in Section 3.

Since CCGBank serves as both training and evaluation data for CCG parsers, syntactic descriptions

[1] To mention a few, the LinGO Redwoods treebank (Oepen et al., 2002) contains English sentences annotated with Head-driven Phrase Structure Grammar (HPSG) parse trees. The INESS treebank repository (Rosén et al., 2012) offer Lexical Functional Grammar (LFG) treebanks such as The ParGram Parallel Treebank (ParGramBank) (Sulger et al., 2013), which provides ten typologically different languages.

[2] Recently, a large-scale CFG treebank for the Japanese language is available as a part of NINJAL parsed corpus of modern Japanese `https://npcmj.ninjal.ac.jp/`, and there is also an attempt to generate a treebank of better quality by using it (Kubota et al., 2020). However, the questions of what is empirically problematic about the Japanese CCGBank and, more importantly, why it is, remain undiscussed. The importance of answering these questions as we do in this paper is increasing, given that attempts to generate a CCGBank from a dependency corpus such as Universal Dependency are still ongoing (cf. Tran and Miyao (2022)).

[3] `https://github.com/ku-nlp/KyotoCorpus`

Proceedings of the 21st International Workshop on Treebanks and Linguistic Theories (TLT, GURT/SyntaxFest 2023), pages 32 - 36
March 9-12, 2023 ©2023 Association for Computational Linguistics

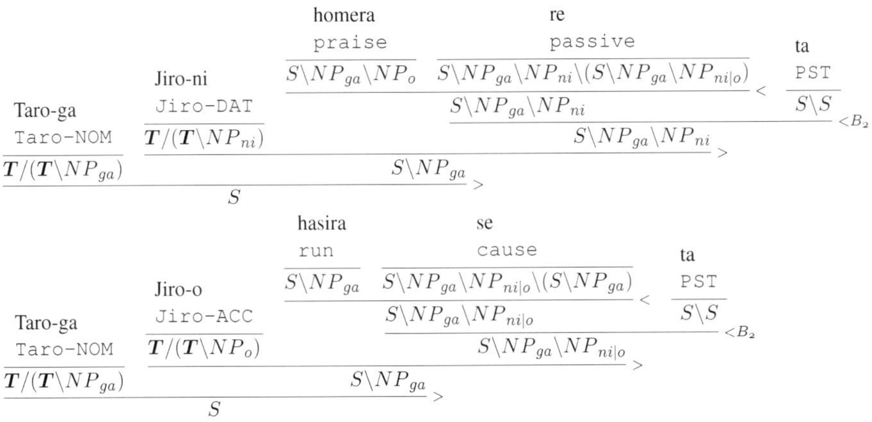

Figure 1: Syntactic structures of (1) and (2) in Bekki (2010)

in CCGBank set an upper bound on CCG parser performance, which inherit any empirical fallacies in CCGBank: thus the validity of the syntactic structures in CCGBank is important. However, little research from the perspective of formal syntax has been conducted regarding the adequacy of syntactic structures contained in treebanks.

This paper aims to assess the syntactic structures exhibited by the Japanese CCGbank from the viewpoint of theoretical linguistics. Specifically, we focus on the syntax and semantics of case alternation in passive and causative constructions in Japanese, a linguistic phenomenon analyzed differently in the standard Japanese CCG and CCGBank, and show that the syntactic analysis of the Japanese CCGBank contains empirical fallacies.

2 Passive and Causative Constructions in Japanese

We first present some empirical facts about Japanese passives and causatives and how they are described in the standard Japanese CCG (Bekki, 2010). *Ga*-marked noun phrases (henceforth NP_{ga}) in passive sentences correspond to *ni*-marked noun phrases (henceforth NP_{ni}) or *o*-marked noun phrases (henceforth NP_o) in the corresponding active sentences, which is expressed as (1) in the form of inferences.

(1) Taro-ga Jiro-ni homera-re-ta
Taro-NOM Jiro-DAT praise-passive-PST
$\Longrightarrow$ Jiro-ga Taro-o home-ta
Jiro-NOM Taro-ACC praise-PST
(trans.) 'Taro is praised by Jiro.' $\Longrightarrow$ 'Jiro praised Taro.'

Next, NP_{ni} or NP_o in causative sentences correspond to NP_{ga} in the corresponding active sentences, which is also expressed in the form of inference as in (2).

(2) Taro-ga Jiro-{ni|o}
Taro-NOM Jiro-{DAT|ACC}
hasira-se-ta $\Longrightarrow$ Jiro-ga hasit-ta
run-causative-PST Jiro-NOM run-PST
(trans.) 'Taro made Jiro run.' $\Longrightarrow$ 'Jiro run.'

According to Bekki (2010), the syntactic structure of the left-side sentences of (1) and (2) are as shown in Figure 1.

For simplicity (omitting analysis of tense, etc.), let us assume that the semantic representations of *Taro-ga*, *Jiro-{ni|o}*, *homera*, *hasira*, and *ta* are respectively defined as $\lambda P.P(\mathbf{t})$,$\lambda P.P(\mathbf{j})$, $\lambda y.\lambda x.\lambda k.(e:ev) \times \mathbf{praise}(e,x,y) \times ke$, $\lambda x.\lambda k.(e:ev) \times \mathbf{run}(e,x) \times ke$, id by using event semantics (Davidson, 1967) with continuations (Chierchia, 1995) in terms of DTS (dependent type semantics) (Bekki and Mineshima, 2017), where id is the identity function and ev is the type for events.

Then the core of the analysis of case alternation is to define semantic representations of the passive suffix *re* and the causative suffix *se*, homomorphically to their syntactic categories, as

(3) Passive suffix *re*: $\lambda P.\lambda y.\lambda x.Pxy$

(4) Causative suffix *se*:
$\lambda P.\lambda y.\lambda x.\lambda k.Py(\lambda e.\mathbf{cause}(e,x) \times ke)$

In words, both suffixes *know* the argument structure of its first argument, namely, the verb. In

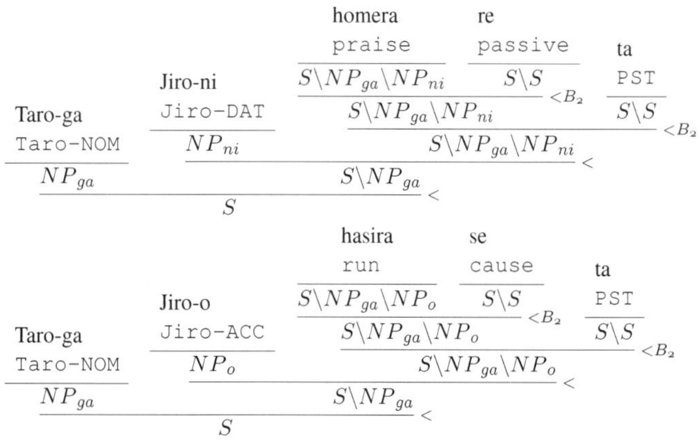

Figure 2: Syntactic structures of (1) and (2) in CCGBank

passive constructions, NP_{ga} corresponds to the NP_o or NP_{ni}, and NP_{ni} corresponds to NP_{ga}, in their active counterparts. In causative constructions, $NP_{ni|o}$ corresponds to NP_{ga} in their active counterparts. Assuming the event continuation k is replaced by the term $\lambda e.\top$ at the end of the semantic composition (where $\top$ is an enumeration type with only one proof term and plays the role of "true"), the semantic composition ends up in the following representations for the left-side sentences of (1) and (2), respectively.

(5) $(e : ev) \times \mathbf{praise}(e, \mathbf{j}, \mathbf{t}) \times \top$

(6) $(e : ev) \times \mathbf{run}(e, \mathbf{j}) \times \mathbf{cause}(e, \mathbf{t}) \times \top$

These respectively entail the right-side sentences of (1) and (2), the semantic representations of which are (7) and (8) respectively, so the inferences (1) and (2) are correctly predicted.

(7) $(e : ev) \times \mathbf{praise}(e, \mathbf{j}, \mathbf{t}) \times \top$

(8) $(e : ev) \times \mathbf{run}(e, \mathbf{j}) \times \top$

The validity of this analysis can be verified by inference data on various constructions including passives and causatives. In particular, causatives can be nested in passives in Japanese, as in (9).

(9) Jiro-ga Taro-ni
Jiro-NOM Taro-DAT
hasira-sera-re-ta $\Longrightarrow$ Taro-ga
run-causative-passive-PST Taro-NOM
Jiro-o hasira-se-ta
Jiro-ACC run-causative-PST
(lit.) 'Jiro was made run by Taro.' $\Longrightarrow$ 'Taro made Jiro run.'

The constituent *hasira-sera-re* is the passivization of *hasira-sera*, the matrix predicate of the left-side sentence of (2) that is equivalent to the right-side sentence of (9), and thus also entails the right-side sentence of (2). The semantic representation of *hasira-sera-re* is obtained by a functional application of (4) to the semantic representation of *hasira*, followed by a functional application of (3), as follows.

(10) $\lambda y.\lambda x.\lambda k.$
$(e : ev) \times \mathbf{run}(e, x) \times \mathbf{cause}(e, y) \times ke$

Therefore, the semantic representation of the left-side of (9) is $(e : ev) \times \mathbf{run}(e, \mathbf{j}) \times \mathbf{cause}(e, \mathbf{t}) \times \top$, which is equal to (6), so it is correctly predicted to entail the left and right-sides of (2). Thus, the passive/causal analysis in Bekki (2010) robustly predicts and explains the process from syntactic structures to semantic representations, and inferences.

3 ccg2lambda and the $S\backslash S$ analysis

Analysis using a compositional semantic system ccg2lambda (Martínez-Gómez et al., 2016) relies on the syntactic structures output by the Japanese CCG parsers Jigg or depccg. As mentioned in Section 1, the output of these CCG parsers depends on Japanese CCGBank. In Japanese CCGBank, the lexical assignments for the left-side sentences of (1) and (2) are as shown in Figure 2, in which both the passive suffix *re* and the causative suffix *se* have the syntactic category $S\backslash S$.

Let us glance over how non-passive sentences in CCGBank are semantically analyzed. The semantic representation of the two-place predicate *homera* is given as follows (slightly simplified).

(11) $\lambda Q_2 Q_1 C_1 C_2 K.$

$$Q_1(\lambda x_1.Q_2(\lambda x_2.\exists e(K(\textbf{praise}, e)$$
$$\& C_1(x_1, e, \textbf{Ag}) \& C_2(x_2, e, \textbf{Th}))))$$

This appears to be considerably more complex than that of *homera* in the previous section. This is because in ccg2lambda, the relations between **Ag** (=Agent) and x_1, e and between **Th** (=Theme) and x_2, e are relativized by the higher-order variables C_1, C_2. After taking an NP_{ni} for Q_2 and an NP_{ga} for Q_1 to become the constituent of syntactic category S, ccg2lambda applies to it the function $\lambda S.S(\lambda xeT.(T(e) = x), \lambda xeT.(T(e) = x), id)$. This causes $\lambda xeT.(T(e) = x)$ to be assigned to C_1 and C_2 to specify $\textbf{Ag}(e) = x_1$ and $\textbf{Th}(e) = x_2$, and id to be assigned to K. Assuming $\lambda P.P(\textbf{t})$ and $\lambda P.P(\textbf{j})$ for the semantic representations of *Taro-ga* and *Jiro-ni*, the semantic representation of the right-side of (1) is obtained as (12), which is a standard neo-Davidsonian semantic representation (Parsons, 1990) for *Jiro praised Taro*.

(12) $\exists e(\textbf{praise}(e) \,\&\, \textbf{Ag}(e) = \textbf{j} \,\&\, \textbf{Th}(e) = \textbf{t})$

By contrast, in ccg2lambda the semantic representation of *re* is overwritten by the *semantic template* as

(13) $\lambda Q_2 Q_1 C_1 C_2 K.V(Q_2, Q_1,$
$\lambda x_1 eT.C_1(x_1, e, \textbf{Th}), \lambda x_2 eT.C_2(x_2, e, \textbf{Ag}), K)$

V is instantiated by the semantic representation of the adjacent transitive verb (=*homera* in this case). The semantic representation of *homera-re* thus becomes

(14) $\lambda Q_2 Q_1 C_1 C_2 K.Q_1(\lambda x_1.Q_2(\lambda x_2.\exists e($
$K(\textbf{praise}, e) \,\&\, C_1(x_1, e, \textbf{Th}) \,\&\, C_2(x_2, e, \textbf{Ag}))))$

That is, the semantic roles received by C_1, C_2 in (11) are discarded, and instead C_1 is given **Th** and C_2 is given **Ag**. By applying $\lambda P.P(\textbf{t})$, $\lambda P.P(\textbf{j})$, and $\lambda S.S(\lambda xeT.(T(e) = x), \lambda xeT.(T(e) = x), id)$ sequentially, the left-side of (1) becomes

(15) $\exists e(\textbf{praise}(e) \,\&\, \textbf{Ag}(e) = \textbf{j} \,\&\, \textbf{Th}(e) = \textbf{t})$

Because this is the same as (12), the inference (1) is correctly predicted. Similarly, for causative suffixes, given a semantic template

(16) $\lambda Q_2 Q_1 C_1 C_2 K.V(Q_2, Q_1,$
$\lambda x_1 eT.C_1(x_1, e, \textbf{Cause}), \lambda x_2 eT.C_2(x_2, e, \textbf{Ag}), K)$

the semantic representation of *hasira-se* is obtained as follows.

(17) $\lambda Q_2 Q_1 C_1 C_2 K.Q_1(\lambda x_1.Q_2(\lambda x_2.\exists e($
$K(\textbf{run}, e) \,\&\, C_1(x_1, e, \textbf{Cause}) \,\&\, C_2(x_2, e, \textbf{Ag}))))$

Thus, the left-side of the (2) will be

(18) $\exists e(\textbf{run}(e) \,\&\, \textbf{Cause}(e) = \textbf{t} \,\&\, \textbf{Ag}(e) = \textbf{j})$

which entails $\exists e(\textbf{run}(e) \& \textbf{Ag}(e) = \textbf{j})$, the right-side of (2), so the inference (2) is also correctly predicted.

However, this analysis produces incorrect predictions for nesting: the semantic representation of *hasira-sera-re* is obtained by applying (13) to (17), which ends up in (19).

(19) $\lambda Q_2 Q_1 C_1 C_2 K.Q_1(\lambda x_1.Q_2(\lambda x_2.\exists e($
$K(\textbf{run}, e) \,\&\, C_1(x_1, e, \textbf{Th}) \,\&\, C_2(x_2, e, \textbf{Ag}))))$

Notice that (19) is identical to the one obtained by applying passive suffix *re* directly to *hasira* (i.e., *hasira-re*). From here, neither the right-side of (9) = (2) nor the left-side of (2) is implied.

This error occurs because the passive suffix globally assumes that the first argument is given **Th** and the second argument is given **Ag**. On the contrary, the nesting example shows that the passive suffix connects the first and the second arguments in matrix with the second and the first argument of the verb, respectively. Capturing this behaviour of the passive suffix requires the verb's first and second arguments to be accessible from the syntax and the semantics of the passive suffix, which means the syntactic category of the passive suffix should be exactly $S\backslash NP_{ga}\backslash NP_{ni}\backslash(S\backslash NP_{ga}\backslash NP_{ni|o})$.

4 Conclusion

In this paper, we showed that the syntactic analysis of Japanese CCGBank together with the semantic analysis of ccg2lambda produces false predictions for passive and causative nesting, which means that the current syntactic analysis of passive/causative constructions in Japanese CCGBank does not have a semantic support that correctly predicts the inferences such as (1), (2), and (9). In other words, the claim that *re* and *se* have the syntactic category $S\backslash S$ cannot be maintained. Since the standard analysis described in Section 2 correctly explains all of those inferences, the burden of proof is clearly on the CCGBank side.

An important implication of this paper is that there is a need for outreach to the linguistic community, where not all linguists regard a treebank as an output of a linguistic analysis. We suggest that we should treat treebanks as outputs of some linguistic analyses and try to provide counterexamples in this way in order to keep treebanks and also the subsequent development of syntactic parsers sound from the linguistic perspective.

Acknowledgements

We thank the anonymous reviewers for their comments and suggestions. This work was partially supported by JST CREST Grant Number JPMJCR20D2, Japan, and JSPS KAKENHI Grant Number JP20K19868, Japan.

References

Daisuke Bekki. 2010. *Nihongo-Bunpoo-no Keisiki-Riron - Katuyootaikei, Toogohantyuu, Imigoosei - (trans. 'Formal Japanese Grammar: the conjugation system, categorial syntax, and compositional semantics')*. Kuroshio Publisher, Tokyo.

Daisuke Bekki and Koji Mineshima. 2017. Context-passing and underspecification in dependent type semantics. In *Modern Perspectives in Type Theoretical Semantics*, Studies of Linguistics and Philosophy, pages 11–41. Springer.

Gennaro Chierchia. 1995. *Dynamics of Meaning*. Chicago Press.

Stephen Clark and James. R. Curran. 2007. Widecoverage efficient statistical parsing with CCG and log-linear models. *Computational Linguistics*, 33(4):493–552.

Donald Davidson. 1967. The logical form of action sentences. In N. Rescher, editor, *The Logic of Decision and Action*. University of Pittsburgh Press, Pittsburgh.

Julia Hockenmaier and Mark J. Steedman. 2005. CCG-bank LDC2005T13. Linguistic Data Consortium.

Yusuke Kubota, Koji Mineshima, Noritsugu Hayashi, and Shinya Okano. 2020. Development of a general-purpose categorial grammar treebank. In *the 12th Language Resources and Evaluation Conference*, pages 5195–5201. European Language Resources Association.

Mike Lewis and Mark Steedman. 2014. A* CCG parsing with a supertag-factored model. In *the 2014 Conference on Empirical Methods in Natural Language Processing (EMNLP)*, pages 990–1000. Association of Computational Linguistics.

Pascual Martínez-Gómez, Koji Mineshima, Yusuke Miyao, and Daisuke Bekki. 2016. ccg2lambda: A computational semantics system. In *the Association of Computational Linguistics (ACL2016)*, pages 85–90.

Hiroshi Noji and Yusuke Miyao. 2016. Jigg: A framework for an easy natural language processing pipeline. In *the 54th Association of Computational Linguistics*, pages 103–108.

Stephan Oepen, Kristina Toutanova, Stuart Shieber, Christopher D. Manning, Dan Flickinger, and Thorsten Brants. 2002. The LinGO redwoods treebank: Motivation and preliminary applications. In *COLING 2002: The 17th International Conference on Computational Linguistics: Project Notes*.

Terence Parsons. 1990. *Events in the Semantics of English: A Study in Subatomic Semantics*. The MIT Press, Cambridge MA.

Victoria Rosén, Koenraad De Smedt, Paul Meurer, and Helge Dyvik. 2012. An open infrastructure for advanced treebanking. In *META-RESEARCH Workshop on Advanced Treebanking at LREC2012*, pages 22–29. Istanbul, Turkey.

Mark J. Steedman. 1996. *Surface Structure and Interpretation*. The MIT Press, Cambridge.

Mark J. Steedman. 2000. *The Syntactic Process (Language, Speech, and Communication)*. The MIT Press, Cambridge.

Sebastian Sulger, Miriam Butt, Tracy Holloway King, Paul Meurer, Tibor Laczkó, György Rákosi, Cheikh Bamba Dione, Helge Dyvik, Victoria Rosén, Koenraad De Smedt, Agnieszka Patejuk, Özlem Çetinoğlu, I Wayan Arka, and Meladel Mistica. 2013. ParGramBank: The Pargram Parallel Treebank. In *the 51st Annual Meeting of the Association for Computational Linguistics (ACL2013)*, pages 550–560.

Tu-Anh Tran and Yusuke Miyao. 2022. Development of multilingual CCG treebank via universal dependencies conversion. In *the 13th Conference on Language Resource and Evaluation (LREC2022)*, pages 5220–5233.

Sumire Uematsu, Takuya Matsuzaki, Hiroki Hanaoka, Yusuke Miyao, and Hideki Mima. 2013. Integrating multiple dependency corpora for inducing wide-coverage japanese CCG resources. In *the 51st Annual Meeting of the Association for Computational Linguistics*, volume 1, pages 1042–1051. Association for Computational Linguistics.

Masashi Yoshikawa, Hiroshi Noji, and Yuji Matsumoto. 2017. A* CCG parsing with a supertag and dependency factored model. In *the 55th Annual Meeting of the Association for Computational Linguistics (ACL2017)*, pages 277–287.

ICON: Building a Large-Scale Benchmark Constituency Treebank for the Indonesian Language

Ee Suan Lim[1*], Wei Qi Leong[1*], Ngan Thanh Nguyen[1], Dea Adhista[2], Wei Ming Kng[1], William Chandra Tjhi[1], Ayu Purwarianti[2,3]

[1]AI Singapore, Singapore [2]Prosa.ai, Indonesia [3]Institut Teknologi Bandung, Indonesia

eesuanlim@gmail.com {weiqi, ngan, wtjhi}@aisingapore.org

dea.adhista@prosa.ai weiming.kng@gmail.com

ayu@itb.ac.id

Abstract

Constituency parsing is an important task of informing how words are combined to form sentences. While constituency parsing in English has seen significant progress in the last few years, tools for constituency parsing in Indonesian remain few and far between. In this work, we publish ICON (Indonesian CONstituency treebank), the hitherto largest publicly-available manually-annotated benchmark constituency treebank for the Indonesian language with a size of 10,000 sentences and approximately 124,000 constituents and 182,000 tokens, which can support the training of state-of-the-art transformer-based models. We establish strong baselines on the ICON dataset using the Berkeley Neural Parser with transformer-based pre-trained embeddings, with the best performance of 88.85% F1 score coming from our own version of SpanBERT (IndoSpanBERT). We further analyze the predictions made by our best-performing model to reveal certain idiosyncrasies in the Indonesian language that pose challenges for constituency parsing.

1 Introduction

Constituency parsing is an important task of informing how words are combined to form sentences. It uses Context-Free Grammars (CFG) to assign a structure, usually in the form of a hierarchical syntactic parse tree, to a sentence. Parse trees can be used directly in applications such as grammar checking (Ng et al., 2013; Li et al., 2022) while linguistic features engineered through parsing can be used to boost the performance of downstream models for higher-level tasks such as semantic role labeling (Fei et al., 2021; Li et al., 2021), machine translation (Yang et al., 2020), natural language inference (Chen et al., 2017), opinion mining (Xia et al., 2021), text summarization (Xu and Durrett, 2019) and relation extraction (Jiang and Diesner, 2019).

There is another important family of grammar formalism called dependency grammar. While dependency parsing has become increasingly prevalent, this does not obviate the need for constituency parsing since the two can be used for different purposes. For span-labeling tasks such as coreference resolution, it has been argued that the explicit encoding of the boundaries of non-terminal phrases in constituency trees makes them more beneficial to the task than dependency trees (Jiang and Cohn, 2022).

The Indonesian language is the national and primary language of Indonesia, the world's fourth largest country by population at the time of writing with almost 275 million people (Aji et al., 2022). There has been mounting interest in the development of Indonesian natural language processing (NLP) although tools for constituency parsing remain few and far between. The progress in constituency parsing for the Indonesian language has been hampered by the absence of a large-scale benchmark dataset that can support the training of the current state-of-the-art (SOTA) transformer-based models, which have been pushing the envelope of English constituency parsing. In light of this, we introduce ICON (Indonesian CONstituency treebank), a 10,000-tree benchmark constituency parsing dataset for the Indonesian language. It is the hitherto largest publicly-available dataset for Indonesian constituency parsing. We also establish strong baselines on this treebank using the Berkeley Neural Parser (Kitaev and Klein, 2018) and a suite of pre-trained embeddings.

[*] Equal contribution

Proceedings of the 21st International Workshop on Treebanks and Linguistic Theories (TLT, GURT/SyntaxFest 2023), pages 37 - 53

The rest of the paper is organized as follows: Section 2 reviews related work. Section 3 looks at the ICON treebank in more detail. Section 4 explains the experiments we ran on the treebank and Section 5 puts forward findings from our analyses and sheds light on the challenges in Indonesian constituency parsing. Lastly, in Section 6, we present our conclusions and lay out suggestions for future works.

2 Related work

2.1 Constituency parsing treebanks

The Penn Treebank (PTB) corpus (Marcus et al., 1993) is one of the most widely-used datasets in constituency parsing for English. It consists of over 40,000 sentences from Wall Street Journal articles and uses five clause-level, 21 phrase-level and 36 part-of-speech (POS) tags. Following the successes of the PTB in enabling the training of much more accurate English parsers than previously known ones, similar projects were initiated for other languages as well. Notably, a multilingual constituency treebank was prepared for the SPMRL 2013 Shared Task for syntactic parsing (Seddah et al., 2013), with treebanks in nine typologically-diverse languages, namely Swedish, German, French, Polish, Korean, Arabic, Hebrew, Hungarian and Basque.

While treebanks in some other languages are relatively large and cover a wide range of genres, publicly-available constituency treebanks for the Indonesian language are relatively small and domain specific (see Table 1). They are therefore not ideal for the training of end-to-end deep neural networks which most of the current SOTA models are based on.

	Sentences	Tokens	Sources	Availability
INACL Treebank	15,813	Not available	English-translated sentences	Not available
IDN Treebank	1,030	30,953	Translated news from the PTB	https://github.com/famrashel/idn-treebank
Kethu Treebank	Same as IDN Treebank	Same as IDN Treebank	Same as IDN Treebank	https://github.com/ialfina/kethu/tree/master/kethu-2.0
Cendana Treebank	552	5,850	Online chat data at Traveloka	https://github.com/davidmoeljadi/INDRA/tree/master/tsdb/gold/Cendana
JATI Treebank	543	7,129	Dictionary relevant to food and beverages	Not available

Table 1: A comparison of size and sources of existing Indonesian constituency treebanks.

2.2 Constituency parsing models

Constituency parsing takes on two main approaches: chart-based and transition-based. There has only been a handful of papers on constituency parsing in Indonesian, and many of them took the transition-based approach. The first Indonesian constituency parser is a shift-reduce parser that utilizes an automatically-generated CFG from the treebank corpus, and it achieved an F1 score of 74.91% on the IDN treebank (Filino and Purwarianti, 2016). In a subsequent paper (Herlim and Purwarianti, 2018), another shift-reduce parser that uses beam search and structured learning was applied on the newer and larger INACL treebank but gave a lower F1 score of 50.3%. To enable a fair comparison with the first parser by Filino and Purwarianti (2016), this second shift-reduce parser was trained on the IDN treebank to give an F1 score of 74.0%. A more recent work (Arwidarasti et al., 2020) introduced an improved treebank called Kethu. The Kethu treebank resolved the compound-word problem in the IDN treebank and further adjusted the treebank to the PTB format. The Stanford CoreNLP transition-based parser (Manning et al., 2014), which employs beam search and global perceptron training, was trained on the Kethu treebank to give an F1 score of 69.97%.

We only know of one existing Indonesian constituency parser that uses the neural approach (Filino and Purwarianti, 2016). The first of two possible reasons for such a small number is that Indonesian transformer-based embeddings were previously not available. However, this has changed with the recent release of IndoBERTs (Koto et al., 2020; Wilie et al., 2020) and multilingual pre-trained language models like XLM-RoBERTa (Conneau et al., 2020) and mT5 (Xue et al., 2021). The latter have been shown to generalize well across natural language processing tasks (Devlin et al., 2019; Wu and Dredze, 2019; Conneau et al., 2020). A second possible reason is that neural end-to-end models require a large amount of training data which existing Indonesian constituency treebanks were not able to supply. To overcome this, we built a new 10,000-tree constituency dataset which allowed us to achieve SOTA performance using neural architectures.

3 ICON Dataset

3.1 Data sources and annotation

ICON[1] is hitherto the largest publicly-available manually-annotated corpus for the task of constituency parsing in Indonesian. It contains 3,000 sentences from Indonesian Wikipedia and 7,000 sentences from news articles of various genres obtained from Tempo, an Indonesian news agency, spanning the period from 1971 to 2016. An example of a tree in the ICON dataset can be found in Figure 1.

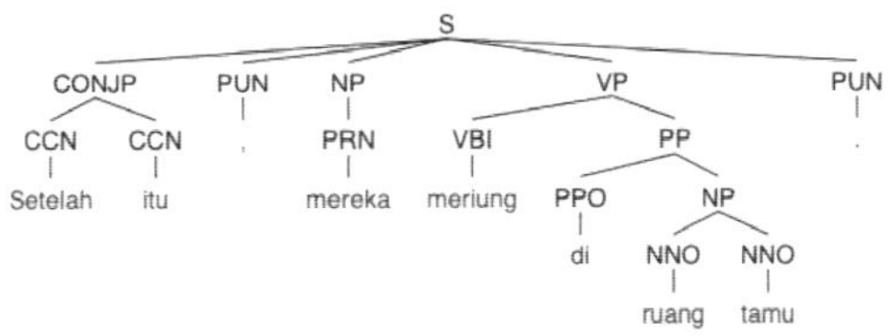

Figure 1: An example of a tree in the ICON dataset. The English equivalent of the parsed tree without POS tags would be: (S (CONJP After that) , (NP they) (VP gathered (PP in (NP the living room))) .)

The data was annotated by seven native Indonesian speakers, consisting of five annotators and two quality controllers. The annotators involved are undergraduates majoring in linguistics who have taken courses in syntax and semantics, while the quality controllers involved are linguistics graduates who have had more than two years of experience working in the field of NLP data annotation.

The annotation guidelines were formulated by the quality controllers using the PTB POS tagging (Santorini, 1990) and bracketing guidelines (Bies et al., 1995) for English as a reference with additional adaptations to account for the characteristics of the Indonesian language data. Thorough knowledge transfer sessions were then conducted by the quality controllers. Thereafter, annotators had to complete an assessment to evaluate their understanding of the guidelines. This feedback session allowed annotators to have a common understanding and deconflict any inter-annotator disagreements.

Clause-level tag	Definition	Count
S	Main clause and complete clause with final intonation	11,904
SINV	Inverted clause	1,288
CP	All types of complementizer phrases and clauses	4,057
RPN	Relative clause	3,977
SBARQ	Complete interrogative clause	64
SQ	Yes-or-no question	3

Table 2: Definition and count of clause-level tags.

Phrase-level tag	Definition	Count
ADJP	Adjectival phrase	3,035
WHADJP	Adjectival phrase consisting of wh-premodifier and head is an adjective	6
ADVP	Adverbial phrase	928
WHADVP	Wh-adverbial phrase	140
CONJP	Conjunction spanning more than a single word	243
FRAG	Fragmented sentence	77
INTJ	Interjection	103
NP	Noun phrase	55,736
WHNP	Wh-noun phrase	104
PP	Prepositional phrase	14,698
WHPP	Wh-prepositional phrase	8
PNT	Parenthetical	93
QP	Quantifier phrase	727
UCP	Unlike coordinated phrase	224
VP	Verb phrase	26,713

Table 3: Definition and count of phrase-level tags.

POS tag	Definition	Count
NNO	Noun	44,006
NNP	Proper noun	28,540
PPO	Preposition	14,233
CSN	Subordinating conjunction	3,123
PRR	Relative pronoun	3,979
PRI	Interrogative pronoun	143
PRK	Clitic pronoun	1,697
PRN	Pronoun	2,452
VBI	Intransitive verb	8,858
VBT	Transitive verb	6,292
VBP	Passive verb	4,954
VBL	Linking verb (copula)	966
TAME	Tense, Aspect, Modality, Evidentiality marker	2,859
CCN	Coordinating conjunction	5,082
INT	Interjection	103
ADJ	Adjective	6,588
ADV	Adverb	6,882
NEG	Negation	1,548
NUM	Numeric value	5,103
KUA	Quantifier	1,690
ART	Article	4,563
PAR	Particle	353
SYM	Symbol	374
PUN	Punctuation	27,727

Table 4: Definition and count of POS tags.

[1] https://github.com/aisingapore/seacorenlp-data/tree/main/id/constituency

	Train		Development		Test		Total
	Count	%	Count	%	Count	%	Count
Sentences	8,000	80.00%	1,000	10.00%	1,000	10.00%	10,000
Tokens	145,794	80.06%	18,291	10.04%	18,030	9.90%	182,115
Clause-level tags	17,084	80.23%	2,149	10.09%	2,060	9.67%	21,293
Phrase-level tags	82,357	80.09%	10,349	10.06%	10,129	9.85%	102,835
Word-level (POS) tags	145,794	80.06%	18,291	10.04%	18,030	9.90%	182,115
	Avg (tokens)		Avg (tokens)		Avg (tokens)		Avg (tokens)
Sentence length		15.61		15.71		15.40	15.43
Tree depth		8.47		8.44		8.38	8.46

Table 5: Statistics of the ICON dataset.

3.2 Deviations from PTB guidelines

Although the annotation guidelines for ICON were based mainly on the PTB guidelines, there were several changes that were made in order to adapt them to the Indonesian language. These include changes to the POS and constituent tagsets as well as the handling of null elements and functional tags.

3.3 Dataset statistics and characteristics

The ICON dataset consists of six clause-level, 15 phrase-level and 24 POS tags (see Tables 2, 3 and 4) and is split into train, development and test sets using a 8:1:1 ratio (see Table 5 for the statistics for each split). The train, development and test sets were well stratified across the number of tokens, sentence length, tree depth, POS tag count and constituent label count. Distribution of the labels, tree depth and sentence length can be found in Appendix A.

3.4 Comparison with the Kethu treebank

The most recent Indonesian constituency parser (Arwidarasti et al., 2020) uses a treebank called Kethu. It is derived from the IDN treebank and is a publicly-available treebank which is not domain specific. There are differences between ICON and Kethu. First, their constituent and POS tagsets differ. The ICON treebank splits the SBAR label into CP and RPN while Kethu uses SBAR as per the PTB guidelines. ICON also uses CONJP whereas Kethu does not. Second, the Kethu treebank uses null elements and functional tags but the ICON treebank does not. Third, between the two, ICON, which is 9.7 times larger than Kethu, can better support the training of SOTA transformer-based models, which requires large amounts of data.

4 Training models with ICON

To establish a baseline on the ICON treebank, which could be used as a benchmark for future works on Indonesian constituency parsing, we trained the Berkeley Neural Parser (Kitaev and Klein, 2018) on the treebank with a suite of Indonesian and multilingual pre-trained language embeddings.

4.1 Model architecture

We chose the Berkeley Neural Parser (Kitaev and Klein, 2018) because it performed well for English constituency parsing on the PTB and achieved an F1 score of 95.1%. Also, the model architecture includes a POS tagger and does not require additional data like dependency treebanks to train model parameters.

Employing the chart-based method to constituency parsing, the encoder in the Berkeley Neural Parser (Kitaev and Klein, 2018) first takes in words in a sentence, embeds them by passing them through a pre-trained language model like BERT (Devlin et al., 2019) and transforms these representations using self-attention. The span vector is then constructed by subtracting the representation associated with the start of the span from the representation associated with the end of the span. The decoder part of the neural model consists of a span classifier that is used to give a score to the label in each span. To get the score for an entire parse tree, the scores of the constituent spans are summed up. Finally, a modified version of the Cocke–Younger–Kasami (CKY) algorithm (Kasami, 1965; Younger, 1967) searches over all possible trees to identify the highest-scoring tree for a given sentence.

4.2 Pre-trained language embeddings

Indonesian embeddings. In order to adapt the Berkeley Neural Parser to the Indonesian language, we replaced the English embeddings with IndoBERT embeddings, which are Indonesian transformer-based embeddings found in the IndoLEM paper (Koto et al., 2020) and the IndoNLU paper (Wilie et al., 2020) (see Appendix B for more details).

Since the Berkeley Neural Parser looks at spans of text and it has been shown that SpanBERT (Joshi et al., 2020) produces superior results for span-based NLP tasks, we developed and added our very own version of Indonesian SpanBERT, called IndoSpanBERT, to the list of pre-trained embeddings to be used in our experiments. As the name suggests, SpanBERT focuses on spans–the Masked Language Modeling (MLM) objective of BERT is modified to mask random spans instead of random tokens. The model is then trained using span-boundary representations to predict the contents of the masked spans. We used the IndoLEM dataset (Koto et al., 2020) for pretraining and it was tokenized by IndoLEM's IndoBERT's WordPiece tokenizer. 16 A100 40GB GPUs were used for training with a maximum of 512 tokens. The base model was trained with a batch size of 8,192 and took 600,000 training steps (75 hours) to converge whereas the large model was trained with a batch size of 4,096 and took 280,000 steps (72 hours) to converge.

Multilingual embeddings. Multilingual masked language models have improved the state of many cross-lingual understanding tasks as well as natural language understanding tasks for each language (Devlin et al., 2019; Wu and Dredze, 2019; Conneau et al., 2020). This is done by pre-training large Transformer models (Vaswani et al., 2017) on a single, multilingual corpus. Sub-word tokenizers like SentencePiece (Kudo and Richardson, 2018) enabled this process by facilitating the sharing of vocabulary learnt across various languages. The larger corpora used for training such models as compared to those used to train monolingual models have also contributed to the success of multilingual embeddings (Conneau et al., 2020). To see their effects on constituency parsing, we included XLM-RoBERTa (Conneau et al., 2020), BERT-Base Multilingual Uncased (Devlin et al., 2019), mT5 (Xue et al., 2021) and XGLM-1.7B (Lin et al., 2021) embeddings in our experiments (see Appendix C).

English Embeddings. We included English BERT embeddings (Devlin et al., 2019) in our experiments. The F1 score that can be achieved using English embeddings could be used as a baseline to compare against the F1 scores of models using Indonesian and multilingual embeddings.

4.3 Experiment results

We established strong baselines on the ICON treebank using the Berkeley Neural Parser (Kitaev and Klein, 2018) and a suite of pre-trained embeddings (see Table 6).

Embedding	Language	Precision	Recall	F1
Base embeddings				
BERT	English	83.67	83.79	83.73
IndoLEM	Indonesian	88.32	**89.30**	88.81
IndoNLU	Indonesian	86.97	87.90	87.43
IndoSpanBERT	Indonesian	**88.52**	89.19	**88.85**
BERT-Base, Multilingual	Multilingual	86.80	87.23	87.01
mT5	Multilingual	86.81	88.64	87.71
XGLM-1.7B	Multilingual	84.81	85.04	84.92
XLM-RoBERTa	Multilingual	87.30	88.60	87.94
Large embeddings				
BERT	English	83.81	84.22	84.01
IndoNLU	Indonesian	88.11	**88.97**	**88.54**
IndoSpanBERT	Indonesian	88.03	**88.97**	88.49
mT5	Multilingual	88.18	88.77	88.47
XLM-RoBERTa	Multilingual	**88.29**	88.68	88.48

Table 6: Summary of experiment results.

IndoSpanBERT and IndoLEM gave comparable F1 scores on the test set of 88.85% and 88.81% respectively.

We used grid search to derive the optimum set of hyperparameters for the Berkeley Neural Parser using IndoSpanBERT and they are as follows: batch_size 32, learning_rate 0.00005, subbatch_max_tokens 1500, num_layers 8 and num_heads 8.

Comparing against other Indonesian parsers. For reference, prior works reported the following F1 scores when testing their parsers on their respective test sets: 74.91% (Filino and Purwarianti, 2016), 74.0% (Herlim and Purwarianti, 2018) and 69.97% (Arwidarasti et al., 2020). Since the test sets are different across the various parsers, it might not be very meaningful to compare F1 scores. We intend to perform a fairer comparison by comparing the performance of the parsers when used in a downstream task like machine translation (Meng et al., 2013; Ma et al., 2018; Yang et al., 2020), natural language inference (Chen et al., 2017) or question answering (Zhu et al., 2022).

Comparing across various embeddings. Comparing the F1 scores across the various pre-trained language embeddings for the experiments we have conducted, we made the following observations, some of which merit further research and are beyond the scope of this paper.

Firstly, having IndoSpanBERT scoring the highest F1 score is in line with the English SpanBERT experiment findings (Joshi et al., 2020). This suggests that IndoSpanBERT could be used to improve the results of other Indonesian span-based tasks such as question answering, relation extraction and coreference resolution.

Secondly, the base and large versions of English BERT did not perform too badly despite being applied to Indonesian, which is from a different language family. The best Indonesian model (using IndoSpanBERT-base) achieved an F1 score of 88.85% whereas the English model (using English BERT-base) achieved an F1 score of 83.73%. This is certainly an interesting finding which could be explored further in future works.

Thirdly, when comparing across the base pre-trained embeddings, the monolingual Indonesian ones performed better than the multilingual ones. The larger Indonesian corpus used in multilingual pre-training as well as the transfer learning from other languages did not seem to benefit Indonesian constituency parsing. For example, multilingual mT5, which has the largest known number of Indonesian tokens (69 billion tokens) amongst all the pre-trained embeddings used in this paper, gave an F1 score of 87.71% whereas the model that used IndoLEM embeddings, which were pre-trained with just 220 million words, gave an F1 score of 88.81%.

5 Analysis

A breakdown of the performance of the best model (IndoSpanBERT-base) by constituent labeling and POS tagging can be found in Appendices D and E.

An in-depth error analysis of the predictions made by our trained parser revealed certain idiosyncrasies in the Indonesian language that pose challenges for constituency parsing. Word order is relatively flexible in Indonesian (Stack, 2005; Irmawati et al., 2017) despite the lack of morphological case markings. Furthermore, the fact that predicates in Indonesian are not only verbal, like in English, but can also be nominal, adjectival and prepositional (Sneddon et al., 2010), means that the CFG production rules are going to be much more diverse and difficult to predict for parsers. In addition, the presence of mechanisms such as topicalization as well as object voice (Arka and Manning, 1998; Sneddon et al., 2010; Djenar, 2018; Jeoung, 2020) allows verb-initial and verb-final word orders, even if the neutral word order of Indonesian is SVO (Donohue, 2007; Chung, 2008; Sneddon et al., 2010; Dryer, 2013). Other than these issues, we explore three additional problems in detail in the following sections–the ambiguity in POS in Indonesian, structural ambiguity in NPs with demonstratives as well as difficulties in parsing coordinated structures.

5.1 Ambiguity in POS

Categorial ambiguity is rife in Indonesian (Teeuw, 1962; Tjia, 2015), especially between adjectives and adverbs, verbs and adjectives, and prepositions and conjunctions. Depending on context, words such as *mau* and *suka* could be interpreted as auxiliaries or verbs or even both (Jeoung, 2020). We find that the parser, despite its excellent performance on POS tagging (with a F1 score of 95% and above for most categories), still falters on ADJ (86.36%), ADV (92.37%) and VBI (90.88%). This is further reflected in the low bracketing F1 scores for the ADJP (68.18%) and ADVP (71.06%) constituents. This is likely due to the fact that the parser cannot rely on morphology to distinguish reliably between categories. Certain adjectives can be used as adverbs without morphological changes (Sasangka et al., 2000; Sneddon et al., 2010), unlike in English where the suffix *-ly* can be used to distinguish ADV from ADJ. Furthermore, a single affix in Indonesian can be associated with different word classes (Sneddon et al., 2010; Mahdi, 2012; Denistia and Baayen, 2022) (see Examples 1, 2 and 3 (Sasangka et al., 2000; Sneddon et al., 2010) for the functions of *ke-/-an* circumfixation).

(1) Verb + ke-/-an → Verb/Noun

a. Joni **kejatuhan** mangga.
Joni **was fallen on** by a mango.
(Passive voice/Perfective aspect)

b. **Kejatuhan** Majapahit terjadi di awal abad ke 16.

The **fall** of Majapahit occurred in the early 16th century. (Noun formation)

(2) Adjective + ke-/-an → Adjective/Noun

a. **Ketinggian** air mencapai satu meter.
The water **level (height)** is up to one meter. (Abstract noun formation)

b. Nadanya **ketinggian**. Aku tidak bisa menyanyikannya.
The note is **too high**. I cannot sing it. (Excessive degree)

(3) Noun + ke-/-an → Noun/Adjective

a. Jika memakai kebaya, Darni tampak sangat **keibuan**.
When she wears a kebaya, Darni looks very **motherly**. (Adjective formation)

b. Raja Mulawarman memerintah **Kerajaan** Hindu tertua di Indonesia.
King Mulawarman ruled the oldest Hindu **kingdom** in Indonesia. (Noun formation)

Furthermore, there is also ambiguity between the categories of adjectives and verbs in Indonesian (Teeuw, 1962; Sasangka, 2000; Mahdi, 2012; Tjia, 2015). While literature on the subject has not gone as far as to argue for the absence of adjectives in Indonesian, as has been done for the Korean language (Kim, 2002), it has explored the notion that adjectives might be better viewed as stative verbs (Sneddon et al., 2010), a perspective that has been adopted by many a linguist for languages of Mainland Southeast Asia (MSEA), such as for the Kra-Dai languages (Pittayaporn, 2021) and Vietic languages (Alves, 2021). This ambiguity is in part due to the fact that both verbs and adjectives can be predicative in Indonesian, as well as the fact that certain affixes are common to both categories. For example, the prefixes *ter-* in terhormat, *me-* in menarik and *ber-* in berbahaya are commonly used to form both adjectives and verbs (Sasangka, 2000; Musgrave, 2013). In any case, for the initial version of the ICON dataset, we adopted the approach of distinguishing between the two categories by gradability (Keraf, 1984; Kridalaksana, 1986; Effendi, 1995). If a word is gradable, it is considered to be an adjective and not a verb.

5.2 Structural ambiguity in NPs with demonstratives

In Indonesian, demonstratives in a NP are preceded by all other constituents nested within the NP (Sneddon et al., 2010). This can cause structural ambiguity when there is more than one noun preceding the demonstrative or when a relative clause ending with a noun precedes the demonstrative (Sneddon et al., 2010). The demonstrative could be a modifier of the noun immediately preceding it or of the head of the entire NP (see Figure 2).

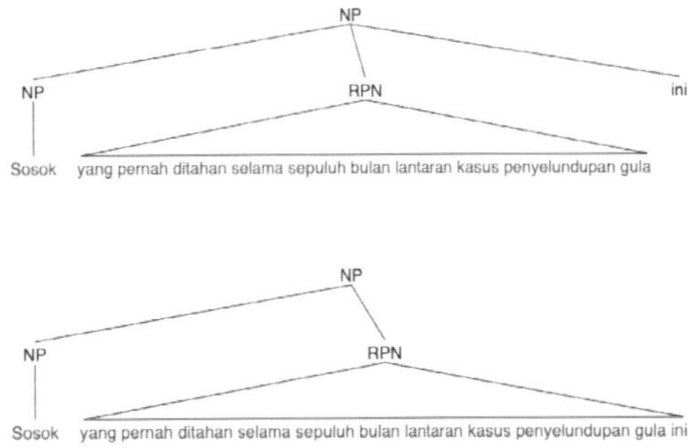

Figure 2: A case of demonstrative attachment ambiguity in which *ini* (this) can modify the head of the entire noun phrase (*Sosok*) or the NP immediately preceding it (*kasus penyelundupan gula*). POS tags and the internal structure of the relative clause have been hidden due to space constraints.

This ambiguity can usually be resolved with more discourse context (Hirst, 1984), but this is unfortunately not available in the ICON dataset (or in the Kethu dataset for that matter) since the text data comprises individual sentences that do not belong together in the same discourse. This makes it difficult even for a human annotator to decide on the most germane interpretation. A possible improvement to the dataset could therefore be to explore using entire documents for the text data, like in OntoNotes (Weischedel et al., 2013), instead of using unrelated sentences.

5.3 Challenges in parsing coordinated structures

Coordination has been mentioned in the literature as a major challenge in constituency parsing (Hogan, 2007; Maier et al., 2012), especially when unlike syntactic categories are involved (Prolo, 2006). We find that this is true for our model's performance on the ICON dataset as well, with a bracketing F1 score of 41.02% for UCP when evaluated on the validation dataset.

It is perhaps more complicated in Indonesian to determine the level of coordination between constituents, or indeed to determine whether there is even coordination in the first place, due to the tendency for coordinating conjunctions and even coordinating punctuations to be missing in coordinated structures. The fact that there are so many cross-categorial ambiguities (as explained in the preceding sections) and that predicates in Indonesian can be nominal, verbal, adjectival or even prepositional probably do not make this task any easier. In fact, we found that many of the UCP constituents were incorrectly annotated by the annotators due to the difficulty involved. These errors will be fixed in subsequent revisions of the treebank.

An interesting finding was that in cases where the model picked up on the coordination of unlike syntactic categories but failed to parse it as a UCP constituent, the label VP was predicted instead. While an investigation of the possible reasons behind this error, such as through an analysis of attention weights, is beyond the scope of this paper, we could venture a plausible preliminary hypothesis. As Prolo (2006) asserted, UCP coordination is not random, and coordination can only occur when two constituents fulfill the same grammatical function. It is therefore perhaps the case that when coordinating two unlike constituents which are predicative in nature (see Example 4), the model implicitly associates the coordinated structure with predication which is in turn associated with VPs given the central role of verbs in predication. This is in fact in line with suggestions in the literature to mix syntactic categories and grammatical function when dealing with UCPs (Prolo, 2006).

(4) (S (NP Tedi) (UCP (PP juga (PP di sana)) tapi (VP lolos)))
Tedi was there too but got away.

6 Conclusion

In conclusion, we have published ICON, the largest publicly-available manually-annotated benchmark constituency treebank for the Indonesian language with a size of 10,000 sentences and approximately 124,000 constituents and 182,000 tokens. As part of the process of building the treebank, we also re-evaluated and revamped the constituent tagset and POS tagset in use in existing treebanks to ensure that the labels are relevant and suitable for the grammatical features of the Indonesian language. In addition, we have established strong baselines on the ICON dataset using the Berkeley Neural Parser with transformer-based pre-trained embeddings, with our own IndoSpanBERT and the existing IndoLEM giving F1 scores of 88.85% and 88.81% respectively.

Moving forward, there are still certain parts of the treebank that can be improved or are worth a second look. Some possible aspects to be worked on are as follows:

1. The ambiguity between ADJ and VBI should probably be scrutinized more to arrive at a linguistically accurate rule for differentiating between the two classes.

2. SBARQ and SQ constituents are relatively lacking in the dataset (67 out of 21293 clause-level tags). In order to improve and allow for better evaluation of parsers' ability to parse questions, having more questions in the dataset might be beneficial.

Beyond improvements to the dataset, there are other research questions that could be explored as well:

1. How much do downstream tasks benefit from constituency parse trees in Indonesian? In what ways can we incorporate these syntactic features into models?

2. How much further could we push the performance of constituency parsers for the Indonesian language with other model architectures, such as using the label attention layer and head-driven phrase structure grammar (Mrini et al., 2020)?

We hope that this work will be an important catalyst for the development of better Indonesian constituency parsers and that it will enable research in linguistic phenomena and syntax-enhanced models for NLP in Indonesian.

Acknowledgements

This work is supported by the National Research Foundation, Singapore under its AI Singapore Programme. First and foremost, the authors would like to thank the annotation and quality control team at Prosa.ai, including Dea Adhista, Hanung Wahyuning Linuwih, Rayditya Brillian Prima, and Menik Lestari, for their professionalism and dedication in ensuring that the data is of good quality. Second, the authors would like to thank Lih Yan Wong for her contributions to the initial exploration stage of the experiments, Alvin Tan Pengshi for helping to preprocess the raw treebank data into the bracketed notation, and Haniah Wafa for helping to explore the possibility of comparing different parsers using a downstream machine translation task. Last but not least, the authors would also like to thank Datasaur.ai for providing the data annotation platform for the project.

References

Alham Fikri Aji, Genta Indra Winata, Fajri Koto, Samuel Cahyawijaya, Ade Romadhony, Rahmad Mahendra, Kemal Kurniawan, David Moeljadi, Radityo Eko Prasojo, Timothy Baldwin, Jey Han Lau, and Sebastian Ruder. 2022. One Country, 700+ Languages: NLP Challenges for Underrepresented Languages and Dialects in Indonesia. In *Proceedings of the 60th Annual Meeting of the Association for Computational Linguistics (Volume 1: Long Papers)*. Association for Computational Linguistics, 7226–7249. https://doi.org/10.18653/v1/2022.acl-long.500.

Mark J. Alves. 2021. Typological profile of Vietic. In *The Languages and Linguistics of Mainland Southeast Asia: A comprehensive guide*. De Gruyter Mouton, Berlin, Boston, 469–498. https://doi.org/10.1515/9783110558142-022.

I Wayan Arka and Christopher D. Manning. 1998. Voice and grammatical relations in Indonesian: A new perspective. In *Proceedings of the LFG98 Conference*. CSLI Publications.

Jessica Arwidarasti, Ika Alfina, and Adila Krisnadhi. 2020. Adjusting Indonesian Multiword Expression Annotation to the Penn Treebank Format. In *2020 International Conference of Asian Language Processing (IALP)*. https://doi.org/10.1109/IALP51396.2020.9310479.

Ann Bies, Mark Ferguson, Karen Katz, and Robert MacIntyre. 1995. Bracketing Guidelines for Treebank II Style Penn Treebank Project. *Technical Report*. University of Pennsylvania, Philadelphia, Pennsylvania.

Qian Chen, Xiaodan Zhu, Zhen-Hua Ling, Si Wei, Hui Jiang, and Diana Inkpen. 2017. Enhanced LSTM for Natural Language Inference. In *Proceedings of the 55th Annual Meeting of the Association for Computational Linguistics (Volume 1: Long Papers)*. Association for Computational Linguistics, 1657–1668. https://doi.org/10.18653/v1/P17-1152.

Sandra Chung. 2008. Indonesian clause structure from an Austronesian perspective. *Lingua*, 118, 10 (2008), 1554–1582. https://doi.org/10.1016/j.lingua.2007.08.002.

Alexis Conneau, Kartikay Khandelwal, Naman Goyal, Vishrav Chaudhary, Guillaume Wenzek, Francisco Guzmán, Edouard Grave, Myle Ott, Luke Zettlemoyer, and Veselin Stoyanov. 2020. Unsupervised Cross-lingual Representation Learning at Scale. In *Proceedings of the 58th Annual Meeting of the Association for Computational Linguistics*. Association for Computational Linguistics, 8440–8451. https://doi.org/10.18653/v1/2020.acl-main.747.

Karlina Denistia and R. Harald Baayen. 2022. The morphology of Indonesian: Data and quantitative modeling. In *The Routledge Handbook of Asian Linguistics, 1st edition*. Routledge, London, United Kingdom, 605–634. https://doi.org/10.4324/9781003090205.

Jacob Devlin, Ming-Wei Chang, Kenton Lee, and Kristina Toutanova. 2019. BERT: Pre-training of Deep Bidirectional Transformers for Language Understanding. In *Proceedings of the 2019 Conference of the North American Chapter of the Association for Computational Linguistics: Human Language Technologies, (Volume 1: Long and Short Papers)*. Association for Computational Linguistics, 4171–4186. https://doi.org/10.18653/v1/N19-1423.

Dwi Noverini Djenar. 2018. Constituent order and information structure in Indonesian discourse. In *Perspectives on information structure in Austronesian languages*. Language Science Press, Berlin, Germany, 177–205. https://doi.org/10.5281/zenodo.1402545.

Mark Donohue. 2007. Word order in Austronesian from north to south and west to east. *Linguistic Typology*, 11 (2007), 349–391. https://doi.org/10.1515/lingty.2007.026.

Matthew S. Dryer. 2013. Order of Subject, Object and Verb. In *Dryer, Matthew S. & Haspelmath, Martin (Eds.), The World Atlas of Language Structures Online*. Max Planck Institute for Evolutionary Anthropology. https://wals.info/chapter/81.

S. Effendi. 1995. Kata Sifat dan Kata Keterangan dalam Bahasa Indonesia. *Bahasa dan Sastra*, 12, 2 (1995), 1–53.

Hao Fei, Shengqiong Wu, Yafeng Ren, Fei Li, and Donghong Ji. 2021. Better Combine Them Together! Integrating Syntactic Constituency and Dependency Representations for Semantic Role Labeling. In *Findings of the Association for Computational Linguistics: ACL-IJCNLP 2021*. Association for Computational Linguistics, 549–559. https://doi.org/10.18653/v1/2021.findings-acl.49.

Mario Filino and Ayu Purwarianti. 2016. Indonesian shift-reduce constituent parser. In *2016 International Conference on Data and Software Engineering (ICoDSE)*. 1-6. https://doi.org/10.1109/ICODSE.2016.7936118.

Robert Herlim and Ayu Purwarianti. 2018. Indonesian Shift-Reduce Constituency Parser Using Feature Templates & Beam Search Strategy. In *5th International Conference on Advanced Informatics: Concept Theory and Applications (ICAICTA)*. 54–59. https://doi.org/10.1109/ICAICTA.2018.8541292.

Graeme Hirst. 1984. A Semantic Process for Syntactic Disambiguation. In *Proceedings of the Fourth AAAI Conference on Artificial Intelligence (AAAI'84)*. AAAI, 148–152.

Deirdre Hogan. 2007. Coordinate Noun Phrase Disambiguation in a Generative Parsing Model. In *Proceedings of the 45th Annual Meeting of the Association of Computational Linguistics*. Association for Computational Linguistics, 680–687. https://aclanthology.org/P07-1086.

Budi Irmawati, Hiroyuki Shindo, and Yuji Matsumoto. 2017. A Dependency Annotation Scheme to Extract Syntactic Features in Indonesian Sentences. *International Journal of Technology*, 8, 5 (2017), 957–967. https://doi.org/10.14716/ijtech.v8i5.878.

Helen Jeoung. 2020. Categorial ambiguity in mau, suka, and other Indonesian predicates. *Language*, 96, 3 (2020), 157–172. https://doi.org/10.1353/lan.2020.0053.

Fan Jiang and Trevor Cohn. 2022. Incorporating Constituent Syntax for Coreference Resolution. *arXiv*. https://doi.org/10.48550/arXiv.2202.10710.

Ming Jiang and Jana Diesner. 2019. A Constituency Parsing Tree based Method for Relation Extraction from Abstracts of Scholarly Publications. In *Proceedings of the Thirteenth Workshop on Graph-Based Methods for Natural Language Processing (TextGraphs-13)*. Association for Computational Linguistics, 186–191. https://doi.org/10.18653/v1/D19-5323.

Mandar Joshi, Danqi Chen, Yinhan Liu, Daniel S. Weld, Luke Zettlemoyer, and Omer Levy. 2020. SpanBERT: Improving Pre-training by Representing and Predicting Spans. *Transactions of the Association for Computational Linguistics*, 8 (2020), 64–77. https://doi.org/10.1162/tacl_a_00300.

Tadao Kasami. 1965. An efficient recognition and syntax-analysis algorithm for context-free languages. *Technical Report AFCLR-65-758*. Air Force Cambridge Research Laboratory, Bedford, MA.

Gorys Keraf. 1984. *Tatabahasa Indonesia*. Nusa Indah.

Min-joo Kim. 2002. Does Korean have adjectives? *MIT Working Papers in Linguistics*, 43, (2002), 71–89.

Nikita Kitaev and Dan Klein. 2018. Constituency Parsing with a Self-Attentive Encoder. In *Proceedings of the 56th Annual Meeting of the Association for Computational Linguistics (Volume 1: Long Papers)*. Association for Computational Linguistics, 2676–2686. https://doi.org/10.48550/arXiv.1805.01052.

Fajri Koto, Afshin Rahimi, Jey Han Lau, and Timothy Baldwin. 2020. IndoLEM and IndoBERT: A Benchmark Dataset and Pre-trained Language Model for Indonesian NLP. In *Proceedings of the 28th International Conference on Computational Linguistics*. International Committee on Computational Linguistics, 757–770. https://doi.org/10.18653/v1/2020.coling-main.66.

Harimurti Kridalaksana. 1986. *Kelas Kata dalam Bahasa Indonesia*. Gramedia.

Taku Kudo and John Richardson. 2018. SentencePiece: A simple and language independent subword tokenizer and detokenizer for Neural Text Processing. In *Proceedings of the 2018 Conference on Empirical Methods in Natural Language Processing: System Demonstrations*. Association for Computational Linguistics, 66–71. https://doi.org/10.18653/v1/D18-2012.

Zuchao Li, Kevin Parnow, and Hai Zhao. 2022. Incorporating rich syntax information in Grammatical Error Correction. *Information Processing and Management*, 59, 3 (2022). https://doi.org/10.1016/j.ipm.2022.102891

Zuchao Li, Hai Zhao, Shexia He, and Jiaxun Cai. 2021. Syntax Role for Neural Semantic Role Labeling. *Computational Linguistics*, 47, 3 (2021), 529–574. https://doi.org/10.1162/coli_a_00408.

Xi Victoria Lin, Todor Mihaylov, Mikel Artetxe, Tianlu Wang, Shuohui Chen, Daniel Simig, Myle Ott, Naman Goyal, Shruti Bhosale, Jingfei Du,

Ramakanth Pasunuru, Sam Shleifer, Punit Singh Koura, Vishrav Chaudhary, Brian O'Horo, Jeff Wang, Luke Zettlemoyer, Zornitsa Kozareva, Mona Diab, Veselin Stoyanov, and Xian Li. 2021. Few-shot Learning with Multilingual Language Models. *arXiv*. https://doi.org/10.48550/arXiv.2112.10668.

Chunpeng Ma, Akihiro Tamura, Masao Utiyama, Tiejun Zhao, and Eiichiro Sumita. 2018. Forest-Based Neural Machine Translation. In *Proceedings of the 56th Annual Meeting of the Association for Computational Linguistics (Volume 1: Long Papers)*. Association for Computational Linguistics, 1253–1263. https://doi.org/10.18653/v1/P18-1116.

Waruno Mahdi. 2012. Distinguishing Cognate Homonyms in Indonesian. *Oceanic Linguistics*, 51, 2 (2012), 402–449.

Wolfgang Maier, Sandra Kübler, Erhard Hinrichs, and Julia Krivanek. 2012. Annotating Coordination in the Penn Treebank. In *Proceedings of the Sixth Linguistic Annotation Workshop*. Association for Computational Linguistics, 166–174. https://aclanthology.org/W12-3624.

Christopher Manning, Mihai Surdeanu, John Bauer, Jenny Finkel, Steven Bethard, and David McClosky. 2014. The Stanford CoreNLP Natural Language Processing Toolkit. In *Proceedings of 52nd Annual Meeting of the Association for Computational Linguistics: System Demonstrations*. Association for Computational Linguistics, 55–60. https://doi.org/10.3115/v1/P14-5010.

Mitchell P. Marcus, Beatrice Santorini, and Mary Ann Marcinkiewicz. 1993. Building a Large Annotated Corpus of English: The Penn Treebank. *Computational Linguistics*, 19, 2 (1993), 313–330. https://aclanthology.org/J93-2004.

Fandong Meng, Jun Xie, Linfeng Song, Yajuan Lü, and Qun Liu. 2013. Translation with Source Constituency and Dependency Trees. In *Proceedings of the 2013 Conference on Empirical Methods in Natural Language Processing*. Association for Computational Linguistics, 1066–1076. https://aclanthology.org/D13-1108.

Khalil Mrini, Franck Dernoncourt, Quan Hung Tran, Trung Bui, Walter Chang, and Ndapa Nakashole. 2020. Rethinking Self-Attention: Towards Interpretability in Neural Parsing. In *Findings of the Association for Computational Linguistics: EMNLP 2020*. Association for Computational Linguistics, 731–742. https://doi.org/10.18653/v1/2020.findings-emnlp.65.

Simon Musgrave. 2013. Functional categories in the syntax and semantics of Malay. In *Tense, aspect, mood, and evidentiality in languages of Indonesia*. PKBB Universitas Katolik Indonesia Atma Jaya, Jakarta, 135–152.

Hwee Tou Ng, Siew Mei Wu, Yuanbin Wu, Christian Hadiwinoto, and Joel Tetreault. 2013. The CoNLL-2013 Shared Task on Grammatical Error Correction. In *Proceedings of the Seventeenth Conference on Computational Natural Language Learning: Shared Task*. Association for Computational Linguistics, 1–12. https://aclanthology.org/W13-3601.

Pittayawat Pittayaporn. 2021. Typological profile of Kra-Dai languages. In *The Languages and Linguistics of Mainland Southeast Asia: A comprehensive guide*. De Gruyter Mouton, Berlin, Boston, 433–468. https://doi.org/10.1515/9783110558142-021.

Carlos A. Prolo. 2006. Handling Unlike Coordinated Phrases in TAG by Mixing Syntactic Category and Grammatical Function. In *Proceedings of the 8th International Workshop on Tree Adjoining Grammar and Related Formalisms*. Association for Computational Linguistics, 137–140. https://aclanthology.org/W06-1520.

Beatrice Santorini. 1990. Part-of-speech Tagging Guidelines for the Penn Treebank Project. *Technical Report*. University of Pennsylvania, Philadelphia, Pennsylvania.

Sry Satriya Tjatur Wisnu Sasangka, Titik Indiyatini, and Nantje Harijati Widjaja. 2000. *Adjektiva dan Adverbia dalam Bahasa Indonesia*. Pusat Bahasa Departemen Pendidikan Nasional Jakarta.

Djamé Seddah, Reut Tsarfaty, Sandra Kübler, Marie Candito, Jinho D. Choi, Richárd Farkas, Jennifer Foster, Iakes Goenaga, Koldo Gojenola, Yoav Goldberg, Spence Green, Nizar Habash, Marco Kuhlmann, Wolfgang Maier, Joakim Nivre, Adam Przepiórkowski, Ryan Roth, Wolfgang Seeker, Yannick Versley, Veronika Vincze, Marcin Woliński, Alina Wróblewska, and Eric Villemonte de la Clérgerie. 2013. Overview of the SPMRL 2013 Shared Task: A Cross-Framework Evaluation of Parsing Morphologically Rich Languages. In *Proceedings of the Fourth Workshop on Statistical Parsing of Morphologically Rich Languages*. Association for Computational Linguistics, 146–182. https://aclanthology.org/W13-4917.

James Neil Sneddon, Alexander Adelaar, Dwi Noverini Djenar, and Michael C. Ewing. 2010. *Indonesian Reference Grammar, 2nd edition*. Allen & Unwin.

Maggie Stack. 2005. Word Order and Intonation in Indonesian. In *Lexical Semantic Ontology Working*

Papers in Linguistics 5: Proceedings of Workshop in General Linguistics. Linguistics Student Organization, 168–182.

Alex Teeuw. 1962. Some problems in the study of word-classes in Bahasa Indonesia. *Lingua*, 11 (1962), 409–421. https://doi.org/10.1016/0024-3841(62)90050-5.

Johnny Tjia. 2015. Grammatical relations and grammatical categories in Malay; The Indonesian prefix meN- revisited. *Wacana*, 16, 1 (2015), 105–132.

Ashish Vaswani, Noam Shazeer, Niki Parmar, Jakob Uszkoreit, Llion Jones, Aidan N. Gomez, Lukasz Kaiser, Illia Polosukhin. 2017. Attention Is All You Need. In *31st Conference on Neural Information Processing Systems (NIPS 2017)*. https://doi.org/10.48550/arXiv.1706.03762.

Ralph Weischedel, Martha Palmer, Mitchell Marcus, Eduard Hovy, Sameer Pradhan, Lance Ramshaw, Nianwen Xue, Ann Taylor, Jeff Kaufman, Michelle Franchini, Mohammed El-Bachouti, Robert Belvin, and Ann Houston. 2013. OntoNotes Release 5.0. *Linguistic Data Consortium*. Retrieved from https://catalog.ldc.upenn.edu/LDC2013T19.

Bryan Wilie, Karissa Vincentio, Genta Indra Winata, Samuel Cahyawijaya, Xiaohong Li, Zhi Yuan Lim, Sidik Soleman, Rahmad Mahendra, Pascale Fung, Syafri Bahar, and Ayu Purwarianti. 2020. IndoNLU: Benchmark and Resources for Evaluating Indonesian Natural Language Understanding. In *Proceedings of the 1st Conference of the Asia-Pacific Chapter of the Association for Computational Linguistics and the 10th International Joint Conference on Natural Language Processing*. Association for Computational Linguistics, 843–857. https://aclanthology.org/2020.aacl-main.85.

Shijie Wu and Mark Dredze. 2019. Beto, Bentz, Becas: The Surprising Cross-Lingual Effectiveness of BERT. In *Proceedings of the 2019 Conference on Empirical Methods in Natural Language Processing and the 9th International Joint Conference on Natural Language Processing (EMNLP-IJCNLP)*. Association for Computational Linguistics, 833–844. https://doi.org/10.18653/v1/D19-1077.

Qingrong Xia, Bo Zhang, Rui Wang, Zhenghua Li, Yue Zhang, Fei Huang, Luo Si, and Min Zhang. 2021. A Unified Span-Based Approach for Opinion Mining with Syntactic Constituents. In *Proceedings of the 2021 Conference of the North American Chapter of the Association for Computational Linguistics: Human Language Technologies*. Association for Computational Linguistics, 1795–1804. https://doi.org/10.18653/v1/2021.naacl-main.144.

Jiacheng Xu and Greg Durrett. 2019. Neural Extractive Text Summarization with Syntactic Compression. In *Proceedings of the 2019 Conference on Empirical Methods in Natural Language Processing and the 9th International Joint Conference on Natural Language Processing (EMNLP-IJCNLP)*. Association for Computational Linguistics, 3292–3303. https://doi.org/10.18653/v1/D19-1324.

Linting Xue, Noah Constant, Adam Roberts, Mihir Kale, Rami Al-Rfou, Aditya Siddhant, Aditya Barua, and Colin Raffel. 2021. mT5: A Massively Multilingual Pre-trained Text-to-Text Transformer. In *Proceedings of the 2021 Conference of the North American Chapter of the Association for Computational Linguistics: Human Language Technologies*. Association for Computational Linguistics, 483–498. https://doi.org/10.18653/v1/2021.naacl-main.41.

Jian Yang, Shuming Ma, Dongdong Zhang, Zhoujun Li, and Ming Zhou. 2020. Improving Neural Machine Translation with Soft Template Prediction. In *Proceedings of the 58th Annual Meeting of the Association for Computational Linguistics*. Association for Computational Linguistics, 5979–5989. https://doi.org/10.18653/v1/2020.acl-main.531.

Daniel H. Younger. 1967. Recognition and parsing of context-free languages in time n^3. Information and Control, 10, 2 (1967), 189–208. https://doi.org/10.1016/S0019-9958(67)80007-X.

Fangyi Zhu, Lok You Tan, See-Kiong Ng, and Stéphane Bressan. 2022. Syntax-Informed Question Answering with Heterogeneous Graph Transformer. In *Database and Expert Systems Applications: 33rd International Conference, DEXA 2022, Vienna, Austria, August 22–24, 2022, Proceedings, Part I*. Springer-Verlag, Berlin, Heidelberg, 17–31. https://doi.org/10.1007/978-3-031-12423-5_2.

Appendices

A Distribution of labels, tree depth and sentence length across splits

		Train		Development		Test		Total
		Count	%	Count	%	Count	%	Count
S	Main clause and complete clause with final intonation	9,557	80.28%	1,183	9.94%	1,164	9.78%	11,904
SINV	Inverted clause	1,042	80.90%	126	9.78%	120	9.32%	1,288
CP	All types of complementizer phrases and clauses	3,238	79.81%	427	10.53%	392	9.66%	4,057
RPN	Relative clause	3,193	80.29%	407	10.23%	377	9.48%	3,977
SBARQ	Complete interrogative clause	51	79.69%	6	9.38%	7	10.94%	64
SQ	Yes-or-no question	3	100.00%	0	0.00%	0	0.00%	3

Table 7: Statistics of clause-level tags.

		Train		Development		Test		Total
		Count	%	Count	%	Count	%	Count
ADJP	Adjectival phrase	2,429	80.03%	284	9.36%	322	10.61%	3,035
WHADJP	Adjectival phrase consisting of wh-premodifier and head is an adjective	3	50.00%	2	33.33%	1	16.67%	6
ADVP	Adverbial phrase	751	80.93%	81	8.73%	96	10.34%	928
WHADV P	Wh-adverbial phrase	116	82.86%	10	7.14%	14	10.00%	140
CONJP	Conjunction spanning more than a single word	192	79.01%	19	7.82%	32	13.17%	243
FRAG	Fragmented sentence	63	81.82%	6	7.79%	8	10.39%	77
INTJ	Interjection	85	82.52%	10	9.71%	8	7.77%	103
NP	Noun phrase	4,4678	80.16%	5,652	10.14%	5,406	9.70%	55,736
WHNP	Wh-noun phrase	80	76.92%	9	8.65%	15	14.42%	104
PP	Prepositional phrase	1,1746	79.92%	1,518	10.33%	1,434	9.76%	14,698
WHPP	Wh-prepositional phrase	2	25.00%	1	12.50%	5	62.50%	8
PNT	Parenthetical	70	75.27%	11	11.83%	12	12.90%	93
QP	Quantifier phrase	584	80.33%	69	9.49%	74	10.18%	727
UCP	Unlike coordinated phrase	179	79.91%	23	10.27%	22	9.82%	224
VP	Verb phrase	21,379	80.03%	2,654	9.94%	2,680	10.03%	26,713

Table 8: Statistics of phrase-level tags.

		Train		Development		Test		Total
		Count	**%**	**Count**	**%**	**Count**	**%**	**Count**
NNO	Noun	35,182	79.95%	4,494	10.21%	4,330	9.84%	44,006
NNP	Proper noun	22,940	80.38%	2,860	10.02%	2,740	9.60%	28,540
PPO	Preposition	11,369	79.88%	1,469	10.32%	1,395	9.80%	14,233
CSN	Subordinating conjunction	2,500	80.05%	324	10.37%	299	9.57%	3,123
PRR	Relative pronoun	3,187	80.10%	416	10.45%	376	9.45%	3,979
PRI	Interrogative pronoun	108	75.52%	14	9.79%	21	14.69%	143
PRK	Clitic pronoun	1,378	81.20%	151	8.90%	168	9.90%	1,697
PRN	Pronoun	1,987	81.04%	254	10.36%	211	8.61%	2,452
VBI	Intransitive verb	7,088	80.02%	888	10.02%	882	9.96%	8,858
VBT	Transitive verb	5,033	79.99%	624	9.92%	635	10.09%	6,292
VBP	Passive verb	3,969	80.12%	510	10.29%	475	9.59%	4,954
VBL	Linking verb (copula)	777	80.43%	109	11.28%	80	8.28%	966
TAME	Tense, Aspect, Modality, Evidentiality marker	2,267	79.29%	284	9.93%	308	10.77%	2,859
CCN	Coordinating conjunction	4,038	79.46%	509	10.02%	535	10.53%	5,082
INT	Interjection	86	83.50%	9	8.74%	8	7.77%	103
ADJ	Adjective	5,296	80.39%	640	9.71%	652	9.90%	6,588
ADV	Adverb	5,520	80.21%	652	9.47%	710	10.32%	6,882
NEG	Negation	1,242	80.23%	153	9.88%	153	9.88%	1,548
NUM	Numeric value	4,079	79.93%	480	9.41%	544	10.66%	5,103
KUA	Quantifier	1,347	79.70%	186	11.01%	157	9.29%	1,690
ART	Article	3,624	79.42%	449	9.84%	490	10.74%	4,563
PAR	Particle	292	82.72%	33	9.35%	28	7.93%	353
SYM	Symbol	291	77.81%	36	9.63%	47	12.57%	374
PUN	Punctuation	22,194	80.04%	2,747	9.91%	2,786	10.05%	27,727

Table 9: Statistics of POS tags.

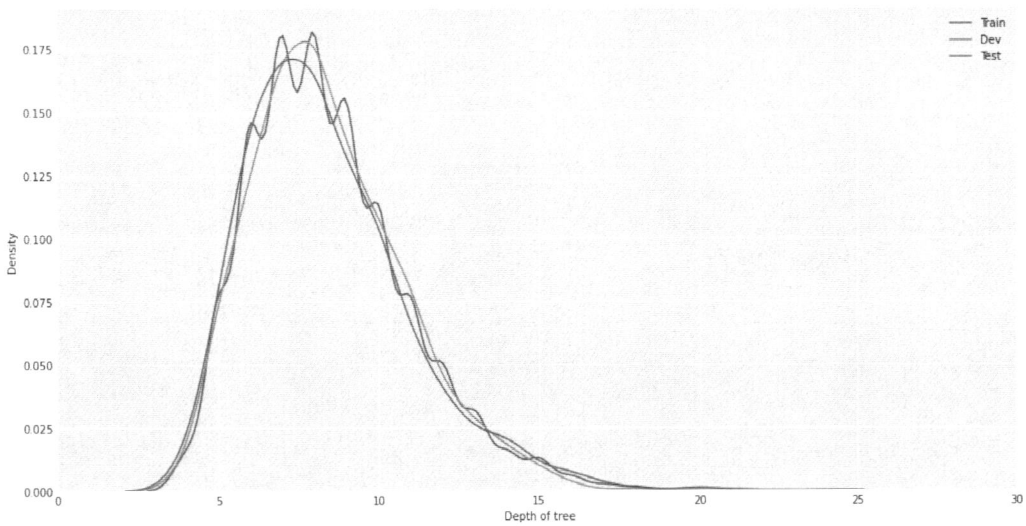

Figure 3: Distribution of tree depth in train, development and test sets.

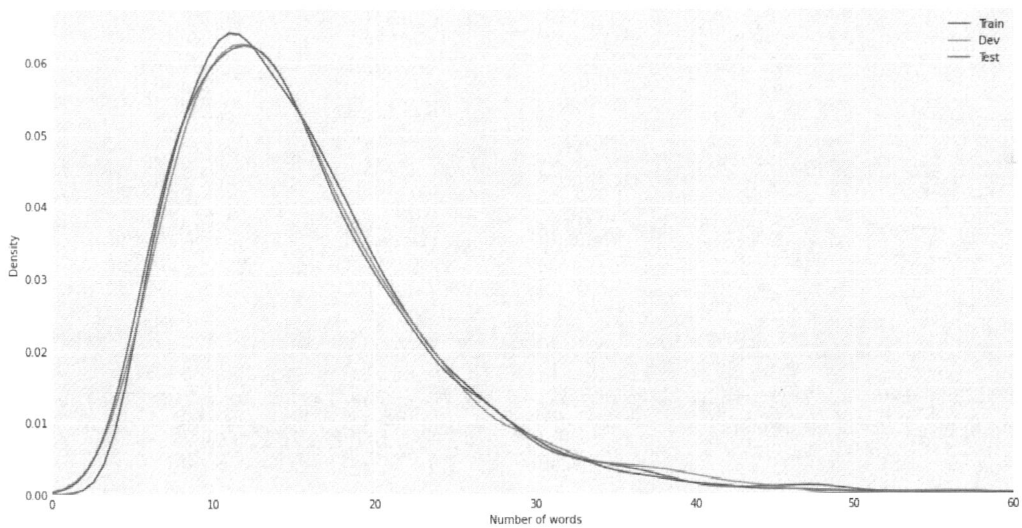

Figure 4: Distribution of sentence length in train, development and test sets.

B A comparison of Indonesian embeddings

	IndoNLU IndoBERT (Wilie et al., 2020)	**IndoLEM IndoBERT (Koto et al., 2020)**	**IndoSpanBERT (ours)**
Data sources	News, web corpus, Wikipedia, Twitter, etc.	News, web corpus, Wikipedia	Same as IndoLEM IndoBERT
Data size	3.6B words (23GB)	220M words (3.9GB)	
Tokenization algorithm	SentencePiece	WordPiece	
Vocabulary size	30,522	31,923	
Number of parameters	Base: 125M Large: 335M	Base: 110M	Base: 108M Large: 334M

Table 10: Table comparing Indonesian pre-trained language embeddings used in our experiments. M stands for million, B stands for billion and GB stands for gigabytes.

C A comparison of multilingual embeddings

	XLM-RoBERTa (Conneau et al., 2020)	**BERT-Base, Multilingual Uncased (Devlin et al., 2019)**	**mT5 (Xue et al., 2021)**	**XGLM (Lin et al., 2021)**
Data sources	CC-100, a filtered version of CommonCrawl, covering 100 languages	Wikipedia, covering 102 languages	mC4, a version of CommonCrawl, covering 101 languages	A subset of CC100-XL, covering 68 CommonCrawl snapshots and 134 languages
Overall data size	Number of tokens not available (2.5TB)	Data size not available	6.3T tokens (size not available)	1.9T tokens (8.4TB)
Indonesian data size	22.7B tokens (148.3GB)	Data size not available	69B tokens (size not available)	15B tokens (67.51GB)
Tokenization algorithm	SentencePiece	WordPiece	SentencePiece	SentencePiece
Vocabulary size	250,000	110,000	250,000	250,000
Number of parameters	Base: 270M Large: 550M	Base: 120M	Base: 580M Large: 1.2B	XGLM-1.7B: 1.7B

Table 11: Table comparing multilingual pre-trained language embeddings used in our experiments. M stands for millions, B stands for billions, T stands for trillions, GB stands for gigabytes and TB stands for terabytes.

D Model performance by constituent labeling

Constituent	Count	Recall	Precision	F1 score
ADJP	284	68.66	67.71	68.18
ADVP	81	66.67	76.06	71.06
CONJP	19	84.21	88.89	86.49
CP	427	89.23	85.62	87.39
FRAG	6	66.67	66.67	66.67
INTJ	10	80.00	72.73	76.19
NP	5,652	90.06	89.46	89.76
PP	1,518	92.09	90.66	91.37
PRN	11	72.73	100.00	84.21
QP	69	76.81	67.95	72.11
RPN	407	93.61	89.44	91.48
S	1,183	93.15	94.19	93.67
SBARQ	6	66.67	100.00	80.00
SINV	126	87.30	84.62	85.94
UCP	23	34.78	50.00	41.02
VP	2,654	90.99	89.44	90.21
WHNP	9	44.44	80.00	57.14

Table 12: Model performance by constituent labeling.

E Model performance by POS tagging

POS tag	Count	Recall	Precision	F1 score
ADJ	640	86.56	86.16	86.36
ADV	652	92.79	91.95	92.37
ART	449	91.76	94.06	92.90
CCN	509	97.25	97.25	97.25
CSN	324	95.99	91.20	93.53
INT	9	88.89	72.73	80.00
KUA	186	94.62	93.62	94.12
NEG	153	99.35	98.06	98.70
NNO	4,494	95.68	96.22	95.95
NNP	2,860	96.43	95.43	95.93
NUM	480	96.67	97.27	96.97
PAR	33	96.97	91.43	94.12
PPO	1,469	98.16	98.97	98.56
PRI	14	92.86	100.00	96.30
PRK	151	90.07	83.95	86.90
PRN	254	96.06	95.69	95.87
PRR	416	98.56	99.03	98.79
PUN	2,747	99.93	99.89	99.91
SYM	36	88.89	88.89	88.89
TAME	284	98.94	98.94	98.94
VBI	888	89.19	92.63	90.88
VBL	109	100.00	100.00	100.00
VBP	510	98.24	97.08	97.66
VBT	624	94.87	94.27	94.57

Table 13: Model performance by POS tagging.

Parsing Early New High German: Benefits and limitations of cross-dialectal training

Christopher Sapp
Department of Germanic Studies
Indiana University
csapp@iu.edu

Daniel Dakota
Department of Linguistics
Indiana University
ddakota@iu.edu

Elliott Evans
Department of Germanic Studies
Indiana University
evansell@iu.edu

Abstract

Historical treebanking within the generative framework has gained in popularity. However, there are still many languages and historical periods yet to be represented. For German, a constituency treebank exists for historical Low German, but not Early New High German. We begin to fill this gap by presenting our initial work on the Parsed Corpus of Early New High German (PCENHG). We present the methodological considerations and workflow for the treebank's annotations and development. Given the limited amount of currently available PCENHG treebank data, we treat it as a low-resource language and leverage a larger, closely related variety—Middle Low German—to build a parser to help facilitate faster post-annotation correction. We present an analysis on annotation speeds and conclude with a small pilot use-case, highlighting potential for future linguistic analyses. In doing so we highlight the value of the treebank's development for historical linguistic analysis and demonstrate the benefits and challenges of developing a parser using two closely related historical Germanic varieties.

1 Introduction

The most common system for historical treebanks in the generative framework is the Penn family of parsed historical corpora. These are valuable resources for analyzing syntactic change and have resulted in an explosion of research in this area, including the annual Diachronic Generative Syntax Conference and *Journal of Historical Syntax*. The Germanic family is well-represented (see section 3.1), with the exception of High German (HG). Our broader research agenda seeks to fill this gap by creating a parsed corpus of Early New High German (ENHG; 1350-1650).

Although there is no Penn-style treebank for any stage of HG on which to train a parser[1], there does exist the Corpus of Historical Low German (CHLG; Booth et al., 2020), which we can use as a starting point. The Low German (LG) language subsumes northern dialects that preserve proto-Germanic **p, *t,* and **k*, while HG varieties partially or fully reflect the HG consonant shift (*p>pf, t>ts, k>x,* etc.) and include all central and southern dialects and Modern Standard German. Despite these phonological differences and the characterization of LG and HG as separate languages, they are highly similar in lexis and syntax (Salveit, 1970; Rösler, 1997), although this syntactic similarity is questioned by Booth et al. (2020).

We introduce the first stages of the Parsed Corpus of Early New High German, along with the current workflow for developing the treebank and the supporting rationale for our chosen annotation and methodology. We explore a strategy of training a parser on historical texts from the CHLG treebank to help facilitate and aid in creating an ENHG treebank. In addition to initial parsing experiments to provide basic insights into the effectiveness of a cross-variety parser, we perform a small pilot case study to highlight potential linguistic challenges and use-cases for the treebank.

2 Related Work

2.1 Historical Treebanking

The Penn system for historical corpora is refined and expanded from the Penn Treebank (Marcus et al., 1993). This constituency-based annotation captures both linear and hierarchical relations between words and allows a variety of complex syntactic configurations to be queried. There exist Penn-style historical corpora for several Germanic languages: three large corpora for historical English (Kroch, 2020; Taylor et al., 2003b, 2006), Icelandic Parsed Historical Corpus (Wallenberg et al., 2011), Penn Parsed Corpus of Historical Yiddish (Santorini, 2021), and CHLG, but not yet for any

[1] Neither Tiger (Brants et al., 2004) nor TüBa-DZ (Telljohann et al., 2015) are annotated with a PTB style framework.

Proceedings of the 21st International Workshop on Treebanks and Linguistic Theories (TLT, GURT/SyntaxFest 2023), pages 54 - 66
March 9-12, 2023

stage of High German.

Penn-style historical corpora are produced by an iterative process of automatic annotation and manual correction (Taylor et al., 2003a). If texts are already POS tagged, a typical parsing workflow is outlined by Booth et al. (2020): 1) basic/shallow rule-based parsing, 2) manual correction, embedding clauses and inserting empty categories, 3) rule-based validation and flagging of errors, and 4) manual correction of flagged errors. Manual correction is especially vital because medieval texts are not standardized, and researchers in diachronic syntax expect to query sentences that are accurately parsed.

2.2 Annotation Development

Each historical corpus in the Penn family slightly adapts the tagset of the Penn Parsed Corpora of Historical English (Kroch, 2020), either for language-specific reasons or to resolve inconsistencies in the tagsets of prior corpora. CHLG departs significantly from this (Booth et al., 2020): although it uses Penn-type tags for higher syntactic nodes, the POS tags are a variant of the the Stuttgart-Tübingen Tagset (STTS; Schiller et al., 1995, 1999). In CHLG, each terminal node is split into meta information and the wordform:

(1) *grotem*

```
(ADJA (META (CASE dat) (GEND neut)
            (LEMMA grōt) (NUM sg))
      (ORTHO grotem))
```

Our syntactic labels are largely as in CHLG, but for the heads, we were faced with the choice to adapt one of the Penn tagsets to historical German (making our corpus easily searchable by the diachronic generative syntax community) or keep the tagset of our source texts (making the corpus most similar to CHLG). We have chosen to use a modified form of the Penn tagset, because a) the STTS encodes some basic syntactic information, resulting in redundancy with higher constituents (Booth et al., 2020), b) researchers most likely to use our corpus are more familiar with Penn-type annotations, and c) most Penn corpora and many others (e.g. the SPMRL shared task (Seddah et al., 2013, 2014)) attach morphological information to the POS tag. Following HeliPaD (Walkden, 2016), we attach morphology and lemma to the POS tag and terminal, respectively:

(2) *grossem*

```
(ADJ^D^SG grossem=groß)
```

2.3 Historical Parsing

Some work exists on automatic syntactic analysis of German historical texts. Koleva et al. (2017) perform experiments with both a memory-based learning approach and a CRF model for POS tagging Middle Low German; a single mixed cross-genre, cross-city model yields the best results.

Ortmann (2020) shows that topological field identification models derived form modern German do not show good performance when applied to Early New High German, as the often extremely long sentences in ENHG are problematic. Follow up work in chunking (Ortmann, 2021b) and automatic phrase recognition (Ortmann, 2021a) yield similar findings, with increased sentence length causing additional errors, but including historical data in the training helps performance.

Full constituency parsing of Modern British English is performed by Kulick et al. (2014), obtaining results similar to that of the Penn Treebank. Kulick et al. (2022) develop the first parser for Early Modern English (1700-1914), noting that experiments using in-domain embeddings outperform those trained on Modern English.

Perhaps the most directly related work to ours is that of Arnardóttir and Ingason (2020), who build a single neural parsing pipeline for the Icelandic Parsed Historical Corpus. While achieving good performance when using a mix of data in the train, development, and test sets, they noted that performance drops when parsers were trained and tested on different time periods, with modern data showing more performance loss on older data than vice versa. One notable decision was the conversion of all historical texts to modern Icelandic spelling. We do not perform any such normalization and expect a large amount of dialectal and diachronic variation, but note that parsers have shown to be surprisingly adaptable to errors and inconsistencies in historical texts (Kulick et al., 2022).

3 Methodology

3.1 Treebanks

Historical treebanks are used to investigate changes that would be difficult to detect in a corpus that is only morphologically tagged. Treebanks in the Penn family can be analyzed using CorpusSearch 2 (CS2; Randall et al., 2004), a program whose query language is intuitive to generative syntacticians (e.g. `CP-SUB* dominates NP-OB1` returns direct objects in subordinate clauses).

Corpus of Historical Low German The CHLG treebank contains 20 Middle Low German (MLG) texts from 1279-1580, resulting in over 170,000 words. Phrase/clause labels are adapted from Kroch (2020). The tagset for terminal nodes is the Historisches Niederdeutsch-Tagset (HiNTS; Barteld et al., 2018), a variant of the Stuttgart-Tübingen Tagset (STTS; Schiller et al., 1995, 1999) adapted for historical Low German, see (1).

Parsed Corpus of Early New High German (PCENHG): currently consists of 5 texts with approx. 39,000 words.[2] Ultimately, this will be a structured corpus, aiming for one text from each of 10-12 regions for each 50-year time period between 1350 and 1650 (64 texts, approx. 600,000 words). Texts are adapted from the Referenzkorpus Frühneuhochdeutsch (ReF; Wegera et al., 2021); the texts come divided into sentences and POS-tagged using the Historisches Tagset (HiTS; Dipper et al., 2013), similar to the tagset of CHLG.

We selected three texts to be the first parsed and manually corrected texts for the PCENHG:

- *Neues Buch Köln*: chronicle of the city of Cologne from about 1360; Ripuarian dialect; 189 sentences = 10,027 words

- *Fierrabras*: fiction from 1533; Moselle Franconian; 401 sentences = 10,274 words

- *Wahrhaftig Historia*: Hans Staden's 1557 travel narrative; Rhine Franconian; currently 269 sentences = 4,251 words

These were chosen because they fall within the timespan of the CHLG and are from the north-west of the ENHG area, thus assumed to be lexically and grammatically closer than more southerly texts to the texts of CHLG. The three texts are Middle German, a dialect group of HG that retains some consonants of LG to varying degrees on a roughly north-south continuum. The dialect of Cologne (*Neues Buch*) shares the most features with LG, with fewer LG features in the Moselle Franconian *Fierrabras* and the fewest LG features in Rhine Franconian *Wahrhaftig Historia*. The locations of the texts vis-a-vis LG are illustrated in Figure 1.[3]

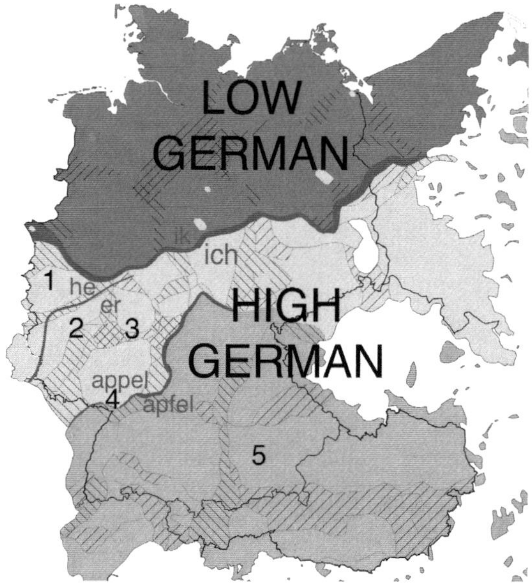

Figure 1: LG and HG. Texts in this study: 1=*Neues Buch*, 2=*Fierrabras*, 3=*Historia*, 4=*Karrenritter*, 5=*Geistliche Mai*

Trebank	Train	Dev	Test	Total
CHLG	9 997	999	833	11 829
Neues Buch	100	50	39	189
Fierrabras	200	101	100	401
Historia	140	68	60	268

Table 1: Treebank statistics for currently available gold annotated sentences with the train, development, and test splits.

3.2 Parsers

One unknown is whether a particular parser may be optimal for our workflow of post-correction, as different parsing strategies may produce different results given textual characteristics. We choose to perform preliminary experiments with two parsers that have yielded state-of-the-art results, the Berkeley Neural Parser (Kitaev et al., 2019) and the SuPar Neural CRF Parser (Zhang et al., 2020).

Berkeley Neural Parser decouples predicting the optimal representation of a span (i.e. input sequence) from predicting the optimal label, requiring only that the resultant output form a valid tree. This not only removes the underlying grammars found in traditional PCFG parsers, but also direct correlations between a constituent and a label (Fried et al., 2019). A CKY (Kasami, 1965; Younger, 1967; Cocke and Schwartz, 1970) style inference algorithm is used at test time. The parser

[2]The corpus can be found at `https://ipchg.iu.edu`

[3]Map adapted from Wiesinger et al.; labels are our own.

uses a self-encoder and can use BERT embeddings for word representations while additionally allowing POS tag prediction to be used as an auxiliary loss task.

SuPar Neural CRF Parser is a two-stage parser, that, similarly to the Berkeley parser, produces a constituent and then a label, and uses a BiLSTM encoder to compute context-aware representations by employing two different MLP layers indicating both left and right word boundaries. Each candidate is scored over the two representations using a biaffine operation (Dozat and Manning, 2017), and the CKY algorithm is used when parsing to obtain the best tree.

Experimental Setup Treebanks have both traces and empty categories removed before training—standard preprocessing for PTB-style treebanks. Features experimented with include: word+char, word+dbmdz BERT embeddings (Devlin et al., 2019)[4], and word+char+dbmdz embeddings. Results are reported including grammatical functions (GFs) using the SPMRL shared task scorer (Seddah et al., 2013, 2014), unless otherwise noted.

3.3 Workflow

As shown in Figure 2, our production of a text involves an iterative process of machine parsing and hand correcting, illustrated here with a relative clause from *Fierrabras*, sentence 36. We first download a .negra file of the text from the ReF:

(3)
```
der PRELS - SB 508
mit APPR - AC 502
golt NA - NK 502
koestlich ADJV - MO 506
belegt VVPPD - HD 506
was VAFIN - HD 508
```

The text is then parsed with a neural parser. However, because texts in the ReF have gold POS tags, we replace the POS tags from the output of the parser with the original POS tags:

(4)
```
(WNP(PRELS der))(IP-SUB(PP(APPR
mit)(NP(NA golt)))(ADVP(ADJV
koestlich))(VVPPD belegt)(VAFIN
was)
```

[4] https://github.com/dbmdz/berts; We also experimented with deepset AI embeddings, but found they consistently yielded worse performance than dbmdz embeddings, most likely due to WordPiece differences (see Reimann and Dakota (2021) for discussion).

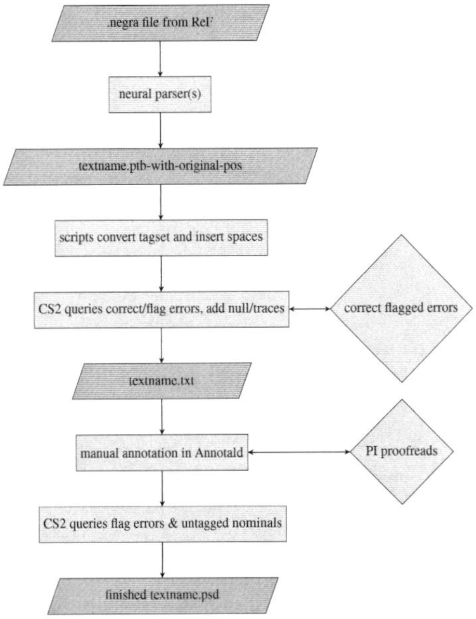

Figure 2: Parsing and correcting workflow

This serves a) to ensure POS tags that are more accurate than the parser output and b) as a check on the syntactic parsing in case of a mismatch between the (gold) POS tag and (machine-parsed) higher constituents.

We then execute several scripts on the parsed texts. An R script converts the STTS-style tags to an intermediate version of our tagset. The intermediate tags are Penn-style tags but maintain some of the fine-grained distinctions of the STTS that aid manual annotation, e.g. distinguishing relative pronouns from determiners:

(5)
```
(WNP(D-relative der))(IP-SUB(PP(P
mit)(NP(N golt)))(ADVP(ADV
koestlich))(VBN-adj-pred-adv
belegt)(AUX-finite was)
```

Sed scripts insert spaces between nodes, making the sentences readable by CS2. CS2 corpus revision queries correct and/or flag errors and insert (when possible) null subjects and traces:

(6)
```
(WNP (D-relative der)) (IP-SUB
(NP-SBJ *pro*-CHECK) (PP (P
mit) (NP (N golt))) (ADVP (ADV
koestlich)) (VBN-adverbial?
belegt) (BEDI^3^SG was)
```

Some flagged errors are manually corrected between queries. The result is passed to an annotator, who using Annotald (Ingason et al., 2018) corrects the parse, assembles higher-level constituents if

Test	Features	SuPar			Berkeley		
		R	P	F	R	P	F
Neues Buch	word+char	39.15	38.71	38.93	28.75	44.53	34.94
	word+dbmdz	40.46	38.43	39.42	39.65	44.45	41.91
	word+dbmdz+char	43.47	41.34	42.38	40.29	46.39	**43.12**
Fierrabras	word+char	31.31	29.91	30.59	22.22	36.75	27.69
	word+dbmdz	36.11	33.39	34.70	42.51	45.78	44.08
	word+dbmdz+char	37.60	34.82	36.15	43.59	47.13	**45.29**

Table 2: Results for SuPar and Berkeley parsers using CHLG trained model and testing on 100 sentences of two different texts from ENHG

necessary, and ensures that GFs are correct. For example, because (6) was not automatically parsed as a relative clause, the CS2 query inserted a null subject instead of a trace; the annotator must embed the clause in CP-REL with null C, add a trace coindexed with the relative pronoun, and delete the extraneous null subject. All sentences are proofread by an expert annotator and returned to the annotator for further correction. Finally, more CS2 queries flag remaining errors and spread case/number tags to any untagged nominals; any flagged errors are again manually corrected. Final gold parse:

(7)
```
(CP-REL (WNP-SBJ-2 (D^N^SG der))
(C 0) (IP-SUB (NP-SBJ *T*-2) (PP
(P mit) (NP (N^D^SG golt))) (ADVP
(ADV koestlich)) (VBN belegt)
(BEDI^3^SG was)))
```

4 Parsing Experiments

4.1 CHLG on ENHG

It is unclear how many sentences we need to build an ENHG-only parsing model, and given that developing a large-scale treebank is a costly and timely process, we treat our current ENHG treebank as a low-resource language and aim to determine how we can facilitate faster annotations. One approach is to leverage the closely related CHLG, given its linguistic relatedness and much larger size. We are not aware of any standard train/development/test splits for the CHLG treebank, and with the limited number of sentences for ENHG, all experiments should be viewed as exploratory and with caution, as different chosen splits may yield noticeably different performance metrics (Dakota and Kübler, 2017), particularly as treebanks may scale in size in the future.

We first trained a parser only with the CHLG treebank using the numbers specified in Table 1 and parsed *Neues Buch* and *Fierrabras*. We then hand-corrected the first 100 sentences from each of the texts and used these sentences as an initial test set to determine to what extent we can use the CHLG treebank to parse the ENHG texts, results of which are presented in Table 2.

Results show, unsurprisingly, that a combination of word+char+dmbdz embeddings yields the best performance for both parsers. However, we see different trends between the parsers. One is that SuPar seems to favor recall over precision, while Berkeley is favoring precision over recall, which is particularly noticeable in the word+char experiments. The large discrepancy is diminished greatly for Berkeley once dmbdz embeddings are utilized, but still precision is favored. We also see that while both parsers achieve simlar performance on *Neues Buch*, Berkeley is significantly better than SuPar once dbmdz embeddings are utilized for *Fierrabras*. Additionally, *Fierrabras* seems to benefit more from the addition of the dmbdz embeddings than *Neues Buch*. One reason may be that dmdbz's embeddings are based on Modern Standard German, and *Fierrabras* is closer to Modern Standard German both temporally (by almost 200 years) and dialectally (i.e., it exhibits fewer Low German characteristics, see section 5 for additional analyses).

4.2 CHLG and ENHG

Based on Table 2, we choose the Berkeley parser for all additional experiments, as it slightly outperforms SuPar. Another rationale is the auxiliary task that predicts POS tags. In our experimental setup, SuPar uses only lexical information (i.e., different word representations), meaning it is more sensitive to lexical variation. The auxiliary task employed by Berkeley may help with such variation more effectively due to including POS information via the auxiliary task. Given that the data is

Train	Dev	Test	R	P	F	POS
CHLG	CHLG	50ENHG	40.89	45.66	43.15	00.00
100ENHG	50ENHG	50ENHG	38.62	63.67	48.07	73.37
CHLG+100ENHG	50ENHG	50ENHG	57.29	67.03	61.77	86.90
CHLG	CHLG	197ENHG	41.68	46.16	44.25	00.03
450ENHG	211ENHG	197ENHG	53.60	68.66	60.20	87.31
CHLG+450ENHG	211ENHG	197ENHG	61.24	70.60	65.69	90.88

Table 3: Results of ENHG and concatenated CHLG+ENHG parsers compared to a base CHLG parser. The number of ENHG sentences is prefixed in each column (e.g., 450ENHG is 450 ENHG sentences).

non-standardized and shows both lexical and syntactic changes, a parser that is potentially more robust to such changes is advantageous. Additionally, while currently annotated texts have gold POS accessible, this will not always be the case going forward. Having the parser still predict POS tags is then optimally beneficial, since many state-of-the-art parsers may choose not to use them or predict them, and it eliminates the need to train a separate POS tagger for future non-POS tagged texts.[5]

Due to a limited number of initial sentences, we perform a set of experiments in which we randomly divide the 200 sentences five times, selecting 100 training sentences, 50 development sentences, and 50 test sentences respectively in each case. We perform two experiments, one in which we only use the 100 sentences for training and another in which we concatenate the 100 sentences with the full CHLG treebank, while in both we use the 50 development and test sentences respectively. Such concatenation setups have proven beneficial in various dependency parsing experiments between dialects and related languages (Velldal et al., 2017; Mompelat et al., 2022). We compare the results against using the initially trained CHLG-only model from Table 2 and report averages over the five runs.

Results show that even 100 trained and 50 development sentences can outperform the CHLG-only model. However, we also see that concatenating the CHLG sentences with the 100 ENHG train sentences results in a substantial boost in performance, in particular to recall and POS accuracy. This is somewhat surprising given that CHLG has a different tagset, but it may be that the parser is able to recognize different lexical items as belonging to a specific language variety, and both treebanks use a similar phrase level annotation scheme, which helps identify higher-level projections.

After parsing and correcting an additional 659 sentences from *Neues Buch*, *Fierrabras*, and *Historia*, we perform a repeat of the same three experiments we did on our initial 200 gold annotated sentences, only now with 450 train sentences, and development and test sets of 211 and 197 respectively. We find that the performance of the CHLG-only model shows no significant change compared to when it is tested on the original 50 sentences, suggesting it can parse the available texts with a high degree of stability due to its linguistic relatedness and likely large number of higher-level projections relevant to ENHG, albeit still yielding suboptimal parses.

While the concatenation of the CHLG and 450 ENHG sentences still yields the best performance, the gap between the concatenation model and the ENHG model is substantially reduced both in terms of F-score and POS accuracy, and is still driven mostly by an increase in recall. This suggests we are approaching a threshold of ENHG sentences needed to build ENHG-only models that can yield results similar to that of models concatenated with the CHLG treebank and will no longer benefit substantially from the CHLG.

4.3 Post-Correction Annotation

One desired advantage of training a parser is to facilitate faster human annotations via post-correction. In order to examine if we can improve the rate of manual annotation, we collect statistics from a single expert annotator from two additional texts, initially parsed using different approaches.

For the shallow parse, we begin not with the output of a neural parser but simply with the terminals and POS tags from ReF. From there, the process

[5] We note that SuPar can utilize tag embeddings as features; however, they are not internally predicted, rather the POS tags must be provided at both train and test time. Thus we would still need to train an external POS tagger for any future data without gold POS tags when using this feature as input.

Text	Model	Words/Hr
Karrenritter	shallow	392
Karrenritter	GFs	340
Geistliche	shallow	273
Geistliche	GFs	352
Geistliche	noGFs	361

Table 4: Words annotated per hour on additional texts using different models: shallow (CorpusSearch queries), noGFs (model without grammatical functions), GFs (model with grammatical functions).

is much like that outlined in 3.3: convert the POS tags, insert spaces, and run CS2 corpus revision queries. These rule based-queries (e.g. build NP out of any adjacent D, ADJ, and/or N; build PP out of adjacent P and NP; build subordinate clause after subordinator, relative clause after a relative pronoun, etc.) function together as a basic parser.

For a parsing model, we have two variations, one with grammatical functions (GFs) and one without (noGFs), both of which are trained using the full CHLG treebank and adding all 859 gold annotated sentences from the first three ENHG texts, while still optimizing on CHLG.

The two additional texts are:

- *Karrenritter*: fiction; ca. 1430; South Rhine Franconian; 540 sentences = 10,041 words
- *Geistliche Mai*: medidation on the crucifix; 1529; Bavarian; currently 100 sentences = 3,045 words

The results in Table 4 suggest that, when the text is syntactically simple like *Karrenritter* (mean sentence length of 18.6 words), correcting from the output of the neural parser is no faster than correcting from a minimally parsed text. However, in a syntactically more complex text such as *Geistliche Mai* (mean length 30.5 words), manual correction is much faster when the text was parsed by a neural parser, either with or without GFs. Example sentences from each text (see Appendix A, Fig 3 and 4) illustrate that sentences from *Karrenritter* are not only shorter but also structurally less complex than those from *Geistliche*.

5 Dialectal differences: case study of *he/er*

There are several exploratory uses for historical treebanking, predominantly the ability to identify and analyze diachronic changes in syntactic structures. A more computational use is to examine how effectively we can develop parsers that cover a range of historical changes, as well as dialectal variation, in a language.

To demonstrate use-cases for both on the PCENHG, we train a parser on a single text and parse the other texts to 1) explore the difficulty in cross-textual parsing given diachronic, dialect, domain, and genre differences and 2) analyze parser outputs of a single, high-frequency function word which has two distinct forms but a single syntactic representation across the different dialects.

5.1 Cross-Text Parsing Results

Table 5 presents results for training and testing on the various texts. Perhaps most striking is the fact that the CHLG-only model produces better parsers on *Fierrabras* and *Historia* than on *Neues Buch*, although the latter is linguistically closest to LG. However, both *Fierrabras* and *Historia* have noticeably shorter sentences (mean sentence length 25.6 and 15.8 words, resp.) than *Neues Buch* (mean length 53 words), thus the parser may just be able to create more efficient trees on the shorter sentences, which are often syntactically simpler. Not only does *Neues Buch* have a noticeable issue in recall, while the other two texts show a better balance, it also has low scores in every experimental setup, except training on itself, with substantially lower scores when training on the other ENHG texts, which also have noticeably shorter sentences. This suggests that the characterization of dialects as similar on traditional (phonological) criteria does not guarantee ease of parsing, due to idiosyncratic properties of particular texts. We also face the challenges of both genre and domain differences in combination with diachronic changes, making efficient cross-textual parsing difficult, let alone building a single unified parsing model.

5.2 *he/er* Analysis

To further illustrate these capabilities, we perform a pilot investigation involving the pronouns *he* and *er* (both of which are Eng. 'he', the masculine nominative singular personal pronoun). The pronoun *he* is found in LG and in Cologne (*Neues Buch*) while *er* is used in the rest of HG (see Fig 1). The dialect of Cologne is transitional between LG and HG for this feature (and several others).

When training on CHLG, we see that the parser is effectively able to correctly project the lexeme *he* in *Neues Buch* to a NP-SBJ, but struggles noticeably with *er* found in *Fierrabras*. Instead, *er* is

Train & Dev	Test	R	P	F	POS
CHLG	Neues Buch	31.76	40.11	35.45	00.06
	Fierrabras	47.63	49.32	48.46	00.00
	Historia	58.55	59.89	59.21	00.00
Neues Buch	Neues Buch	38.83	56.32	45.97	76.53
	Fierrabras	35.29	60.16	44.49	66.01
	Historia	40.92	71.82	52.13	70.54
Fierrabras	Neues Buch	18.80	42.50	26.07	63.08
	Fierrabras	57.00	76.21	65.22	88.06
	Historia	45.66	64.10	53.47	81.65
Historia	Neues Buch	15.66	17.01	16.31	61.48
	Fierrabras	40.45	53.57	46.10	76.99
	Historia	52.76	67.51	59.23	84.29

Table 5: Results for training and testing on different texts.

Train & Dev	Test	Correct	Error
CHLG	Neues Buch	30	2
	Fierrabras	6	40
	Historia	1	2
Neues Buch	Neues Buch	31	1
	Fierrabras	43	3
	Historia	2	1
Fierrabras	Neues Buch	13	19
	Fierrabras	46	0
	Historia	3	0
Historia	Neues Buch	15	17
	Fierrabras	44	2
	Historia	3	0

Table 6: Phrase projection error counts for lexemes *he* or *er* when training on one text and testing on another.

often projected to a NP-OB2 (i.e. indirect object). This is probably due to the fact that *er* is never masc.nom.sg. 'he' in CHLG but rather fem.dat.sg. 'her' or even possessive 'her/their'. Such findings are in line with previous research, showing that increasing differences in lexicon and syntactic structure limit the effectiveness of cross-dialect parsing (see Chiang et al. (2006) for difficulties in Arabic dialect parsing within a PTB framework).

However, training on *Neues Buch*, from the transitional dialect of Cologne, does not show performance degradation seen from CHLG. On *Fierrabras*, it is able to correctly project most *er*, despite being trained where *he* is the realized form. This may be because Cologne and Middle German are HG dialects with similar pronoun systems, with the sole exception of *he/er*, and the parser is able to overcome this difference via POS and syntactic inferences. This is partially supported by the fact that more than half the time *er* is tagged as a determiner in *Fierrabras*, but this does not result in error propagation, since such instances still successfully project to a NP-SBJ. On the other hand, we see that models trained on *Historia* and *Fierrabras* are able to successfully parse *er* in *Fierrabras* and *Historia*, respectively, but show mixed results on *he* in *Neues Buch*.

While parsing on closely related languages or dialects can be successful, important factors, such as irreconcilable differences in function words, can limit the effectiveness. When differences between varieties are more superficial, however, a parser can more adequately overcome minor lexical and syntactic variation.

6 Conclusion

We have introduced the Parsed Corpus of Early New High German. Its introduction and continued development presents an additional resource for research both on diachronic syntax and on parsing.

We have begun construction of the treebank by successfully utilizing a treebank from a closely related language to develop a base parsing system that helps speed up the annotation process. We use a cyclical process in which outputs are sent through a workflow that automates various post-correction requirements, before finally being hand-corrected by an expert annotator, with the new gold sentences able to be used to train a new parser.

As our gold treebank for ENHG continues to grow, we should be able to reduce our dependence on the CHLG treebank. However, we have also shown that while there are lexical and some syntactic differences between the texts, higher-level projections still benefit from the mixing since many of the rules are applicable in both varieties, even in the presence of lexical and lower-level syntactic differences, as indicated by the case study of *he/er* variation.

Once the Parsed Corpus of Early New High German is complete, we expect to use it to train a model that can parse both Middle High German (1050-1350) and Modern German (1650-present). This will allow the completion of a parsed corpus of the whole history of HG (as well as providing a source of possible additional data for developing additional PTB-style treebanks of Modern Standard German). Such a timespan and the variation in texts will also allow us to contribute simultaneously to both cross-domain and diachronic parsing research, in particular using a single unified model.

References

Þórunn Arnardóttir and Anton Karl Ingason. 2020. A Neural Parsing Pipeline for Icelandic Using the Berkeley Neural Parser. In Costanza Navarretta and Maria Eskevich, editors, *Proceedings of CLARIN 2020*, pages 48–51.

Fabian Barteld, Sarah Ihden, Katharina Dreessen, and Ingrid Schröder. 2018. HiNTS: A Tagset for Middle Low German. In *Proceedings of the Eleventh International Conference on Language Resources and Evaluation (LREC 2018)*, pages 3940–3945, Miyazaki, Japan. European Language Resources Association (ELRA).

Hannah Booth, Anne Breitbarth, Aaron Ecay, and Melissa Farasyn. 2020. A Penn-Style Treebank of Middle Low German. In *Proceedings of the 12th Conference on Language Resources and Evaluation (LREC 2020)*, pages 766–775.

Sabine Brants, Stefanie Dipper, Peter Eisenberg, Silvia Hansen, Esther König, Wolfgang Lezius, Christian Rohrer, George Smith, and Hans Uszkoreit. 2004. TIGER: Linguistic Interpretation of a German Corpus. *Journal of Language and Computation.*

David Chiang, Mona Diab, Nizar Habash, Owen Rambow, and Safiullah Shareef. 2006. Parsing Arabic Dialects. In *11th Conference of the European Chapter of the Association for Computational Linguistics*, pages 369–376, Trento, Italy.

John Cocke and Jacob Schwartz. 1970. Programming Languages and Their Compilers. Technical report, Courant Institute of Mathematical Sciences, New York.

Daniel Dakota and Sandra Kübler. 2017. Towards Replicability in Parsing. In *Proceedings of the International Conference on Recent Advances in Natural Language Processing, RANLP 2017*, pages 185–194, Varna, Bulgaria.

Jacob Devlin, Ming-Wei Chang, Kenton Lee, and Kristina Toutanova. 2019. BERT: Pre-training of deep bidirectional transformers for language understanding. In *Proceedings of the 2019 Conference of the North American Chapter of the Association for Computational Linguistics: Human Language Technologies (NAACL-HLT)*, pages 4171–4186, Minneapolis, MN.

Stefanie Dipper, Karin Donhauser, Thomas Klein, Sonja Linde, Stefan Muller, and Klaus-Peter Wegera. 2013. HiTS: ein Tagset fur historische Sprachstufen des Deutschen. *Journal for Language Technology and Computational Linguistics, Special Issue*, (28):85–137.

Timothy Dozat and Christopher Manning. 2017. Deep biaffine attention for neural dependency parsing. In *5h International Conference on Learning Representations (ICLR 2017)*, Toulon, France.

Daniel Fried, Nikita Kitaev, and Dan Klein. 2019. Cross-Domain Generalization of Neural Constituency Parsers. In *Proceedings of the 57th Annual Meeting of the Association for Computational Linguistics*, pages 323–330, Florence, Italy.

Anton Ingason, Jana Beck, and Aaron Ecay. Annotald, v1.13.10 [online]. 2018.

Tadao Kasami. 1965. An Efficient Recognition and Syntax-Analysis Algorithm for Context-Free Languages. Technical report, AFCRL-65-75, Air Force Cambridge Research Laboratory.

Nikita Kitaev, Steven Cao, and Dan Klein. 2019. Multilingual Constituency Parsing with Self-Attention and Pre-Training. In *Proceedings of the 57th Annual Meeting of the Association for Computational Linguistics*, pages 3499–3505, Florence, Italy.

Mariya Koleva, Melissa Farasyn, Bart Desmet, Anne Breitbarth, and Veronique Hoste. 2017. An automatic part-of-speech tagger for Middle Low German. *International Journal of Corpus Linguistics*, 22:107–140.

Anthony Kroch. Penn Parsed Corpora of Historical English [online]. 2020.

Seth Kulick, Anthony Kroch, and Beatrice Santorini. 2014. The Penn Parsed Corpus of Modern British English: First Parsing Results and Analysis. In *Proceedings of the 52nd Annual Meeting of the Association for Computational Linguistics (Volume 2: Short Papers)*, pages 662–667, Baltimore, Maryland.

Seth Kulick, Neville Ryant, and Beatrice Santorini. 2022. Penn-Helsinki Parsed Corpus of Early Modern English: First Parsing Results and Analysis. In *Findings of the Association for Computational Linguistics: NAACL 2022*, pages 578–593, Seattle, United States.

Mitchell P. Marcus, Mary Ann Marcinkiewicz, and Beatrice Santorini. 1993. Building a Large Annotated Corpus of English: The Penn Treebank. *Computational Linguistics*, 19(2):313–330.

Ludovic Mompelat, Daniel Dakota, and Sandra Kübler. 2022. How to Parse a Creole: When Martinican Creole Meets French. In *Proceedings of the The 28th International Conference on Computational Linguistics (COLING 2022)*, pages 4397–4406.

Katrin Ortmann. 2020. Automatic Topological Field Identification in (Historical) German Texts. In *Proceedings of the The 4th Joint SIGHUM Workshop on Computational Linguistics for Cultural Heritage, Social Sciences, Humanities and Literature*, pages 10–18, Online.

Katrin Ortmann. 2021a. Automatic Phrase Recognition in Historical German. In *Proceedings of the 17th Conference on Natural Language Processing (KONVENS 2021)*, pages 127–136, Düsseldorf, Germany.

Katrin Ortmann. 2021b. Chunking Historical German. In *Proceedings of the 23rd Nordic Conference on Computational Linguistics (NoDaLiDa)*, pages 190–199, Reykjavik, Iceland (Online).

Beth Randall, Anthony Kroch, and Beatrice Santorini. CorpusSearch 2 [online]. 2004.

Sebastian Reimann and Daniel Dakota. 2021. Examining the Effects of Preprocessing on the Detection of Offensive Language in German Tweets. In *Proceedings of the 17th Conference on Natural Language Processing (KONVENS 2021)*, pages 159–169, Online.

Irmtraud Rösler. 1997. *Satz, Text, Sprachhandeln: Syntaktische Normen der mittelniederdeutschen Sprache und ihre soziofunktionalen Determinanten*. Heidelberg: Winter.

Laurits Salveit. 1970. Befehlsausdrücke in mittelniederdeutschen Bibelubersetzungen. In Dietrich Hoffmann, editor, *Gedenkschrift für William Foerst*, pages 278–89. Böhlau.

Beatrice Santorini. Penn Parsed Corpus of Historical Yiddish, v1.0 [online]. 2021.

Anne Schiller, Simone Teufel, Christine Stöcker, and Christine Thielen. 1995. Guidelines für das Tagging deutscher Textkorpora mit STTS. Technical report, Universität Stuttgart and Universität Tübingen.

Anne Schiller, Simone Teufel, Christine Stöckert, and Christine Thielen. 1999. Guidelines für das Tagging deutscher Textkorpora mit STTS (Kleines und großes Tagset). Technical report, Universität Stuttgart and Universität Tübingen.

Djamé Seddah, Sandra Kübler, and Reut Tsarfaty. 2014. Introducing the SPMRL 2014 Shared Task on Parsing Morphologically-rich Languages. In *Proceedings of the First Joint Workshop on Statistical Parsing of Morphologically Rich Languages and Syntactic Analysis of Non-Canonical Languages*, pages 103–109, Dublin, Ireland.

Djamé Seddah, Reut Tsarfaty, Sandra Kübler, Marie Candito, Jinho D. Choi, Richárd Farkas, Jennifer Foster, Iakes Goenaga, Koldo Gojenola Galletebeitia, Yoav Goldberg, Spence Green, Nizar Habash, Marco Kuhlmann, Wolfgang Maier, Joakim Nivre, Adam Przepiórkowski, Ryan Roth, Wolfgang Seeker, Yannick Versley, Veronika Vincze, Marcin Woliński, Alina Wróblewska, and Eric Villemonte de la Clergerie. 2013. Overview of the SPMRL 2013 Shared Task: A Cross-Framework Evaluation of Parsing Morphologically Rich Languages. In *Proceedings of the Fourth Workshop on Statistical Parsing of Morphologically-Rich Languages*, pages 146–182, Seattle, Washington, USA.

Ann Taylor, Mitchell Marcus, and Beatrice Santorini. 2003a. The Penn treebank: An overview. In *Treebanks: Building and Using Parsed Corpora, ed. by Anne Abeillé*, pages 5–22. Kluwer: Dordrecht, Netherlands.

Ann Taylor, Arja Nurmi, Anthony Warner, Susan Pintzuk, and Terttu Nevalainen. Parsed Corpus of Early English Correspondence [online]. 2006.

Ann Taylor, Anthony Warner, Susan Pintzuk, and Frans Beths. York-Toronto-Helsinki Parsed Corpus of Old English Prose [online]. 2003b.

Heike Telljohann, Erhard Hinrichs, Sandra Kübler, Heike Zinsmeister, and Kathrin Beck. 2015. Stylebook for the Tübingen Treebank of Written German (TüBa-D/Z). Seminar für Sprachwissenschaft, Universität Tübingen, Germany.

Erik Velldal, Lilja Øvrelid, and Petter Hohle. 2017. Joint UD Parsing of Norwegian Bokmål and Nynorsk. In *Proceedings of the 21st Nordic Conference on Computational Linguistics*, pages 1–10, Gothenburg, Sweden.

George Walkden. 2016. The HeliPaD: a parsed corpus of Old Saxon. *International Journal of Corpus Linguistics*, 21(4):559–571.

Joel C. Wallenberg, Anton Karl Ingason Ingason, Einar Freyr Sigurðsson, and Eiríkur Rögnvaldsson. Icelandic Parsed Historical Corpus (IcePaHC) Version 0.9 [online]. 2011.

Klaus-Peter Wegera, Hans-Joachim Solms, Ulrike Demske, and Stefanie Dipper. Referenzkorpus Frühneuhochdeutsch (1350–1650) Version 1.0 [online]. 2021.

Peter Wiesinger, Klass Heeroma, and Werner König. German dialect continuum in 1900. `https://commons.wikimedia.org/wiki/File:German_dialect_continuum_in_1900_(according_to_Wiesinger,_Heeroma_%26_K%C3%B6nig).png`. Accessed: 2022-11-05.

Daniel Younger. 1967. Recognition and parsing of context-free languages in n^3. *Information and Control*, 10(2):189–208.

Yu Zhang, Houquan Zhou, and Zhenghua Li. 2020. Fast and Accurate Neural CRF Constituency Parsing. In *Proceedings of the Twenty-Ninth International Joint Conference on Artificial Intelligence, IJCAI-20*, pages 4046–4053.

A Appendix

The following examples from our corpus illustrate the finished product of the annotation workflow outlined in section 3.3. They also exemplify that the shorter sentences from *Karrenritter* (mean sentence length 18.6 words; the illustrated sentence is 19 words) are generally less complex than relatively longer sentences from *Geistliche Mai* (mean length 30.5 words; the illustrated sentence is 33 words). Note that the example from *Geistliche Mai* not only has more embedded clauses (here: a relative clause inside an adverbial clause) but also more complex NPs, with many NPs containing possessives (NP-POS) and/or appositives (NP-PRN).

```
( (IP-MAT (QP-1 (Q^A^SG alles))
          (HVDS^3^SG het)
          (NP-SBJ (PRO^N^SG er))
          (NP-OB1 (PRO^A^SG s)
                  (QP *ICH*-1)
                  (CP-ADV *ICH*-2))
          (NP-OB2 (PRO^D^SG ir))
          (NEG nit)
          (VBN gesagt)
          (PP (P vmb)
              (NP (Q^A^SG alle) (D^A^SG diß) (N^A^SG welt)))
          (CODE <,>)
          (CP-ADV-2 (WADVP-3 (WADV wie))
                    (C 0)
                    (IP-SUB (ADVP *T*-3)
                            (NP-SBJ (PRO^N^SG es))
                            (PP (P zwuschen)
                                (NP (NP (PRO^D^SG im))
                                    (CONJP (CONJ vnd)
                                           (NP (PRO$^D^SG siner)
                                               (N^D^SG frauwen)))))
                            (VBDI^3^SG stund)))
         (CODE <.>))
  (ID 1430.NN.Karrenritter.SRhFrk.,13))
```

Figure 3: Example of 19-word sentence from *Karrenritter*

```
( (IP-MAT (PP (P in)
              (NP (D^D^SG dem)
                  (ADJ^D^SG xij)
                  (N^D^SG spiegelein)
                  (NP-PRN (N^D^SG m))))
          (VBI^2^SG schau)
          (CODE <,>)
          (CP-ADV (WADVP-1 (WADV wye))
                  (C 0)
                  (IP-SUB (ADVP *T*-1)
                          (NP-SBJ (D^N^SG dys)
                                  (ADJ^N^SG hochwyrdig)
                                  (N^N^SG creucz))
                          (BEPI^3^SG ist)
                          (NP-PRD (D^N^SG dye)
                                  (ADJP (NP-POS (Q^G^PL aller) (N^G^PL halltum))
                                        (ADJS^N^SG reychest))
                                  (N^N^SG manstrancz)
                                  (CODE <,>)
                                  (CP-REL (WPP-2 (P in) (WNP (D^A^SG dye)))
                                          (C 0)
                                          (IP-SUB (PP *T*-2)
                                                  (VBN gefast)
                                                  (BEPI^3^SG ist)
                                                  (BEN gewossen)
                                                  (NP-SBJ (D^N^SG der)
                                                          (ADJ^N^SG heyllig)
                                                          (NP-POS (Q^G^PL aller)
                                                                  (ADJ^G^PL heyllligen))
                                                          (CODE <,>)
                                                          (NP-PRN (D^N^SG der)
                                                                  (VBN^N^SG vergot)
                                                                  (N^N^SG mensch))
                                                          (NP-PRN (NPR^N^SG xpsen)))
                                                  (PP (P mit)
                                                      (NP (PRO$^D^SG seiner)
                                                          (ADJ^D^SG salligen)
                                                          (N^D^SG sell))))))))
              (CODE <.>))
     (ID 1529.Fridolin.GeistlicheMai.Bavaria.,98))
```

Figure 4: Example of 33-word sentence from *Geistliche Mai*

Semgrex and Ssurgeon, Searching and Manipulating Dependency Graphs

John Bauer
HAI
Stanford University
horatio@cs.stanford.edu

Chloé Kiddon
Dept of Computer Science
Stanford University
chloe.kiddon@gmail.com *

Eric Yeh
SRI International
eric.yeh@sri.com

Alex Shan
Dept of Computer Science
Stanford University
azshan@stanford.edu

Christopher D. Manning
Linguistics & Computer Science
Stanford University
manning@stanford.edu

Abstract

Searching dependency graphs and manipulating them can be a time consuming and challenging task to get right. We document *Semgrex*, a system for searching dependency graphs, and introduce *Ssurgeon*, a system for manipulating the output of *Semgrex*. The compact language used by these systems allows for easy command line or API processing of dependencies. Additionally, integration with publicly released toolkits in Java and Python allows for searching text relations and attributes over natural text.

1 Introduction

With the rapid growth in languages supported by Universal Dependencies (Nivre et al., 2020), being able to easily and quickly search over dependency graphs greatly simplifies processing of UD datasets. Tools which allow for searching of specific relation structures greatly simplify the work of linguists interested in specific syntactic constructions and researchers extracting relations as features for downstream tasks. Furthermore, converting existing dependency treebanks from non-UD sources to match the UD format is valuable for adding additional data to Universal Dependencies, and doing this conversion automatically greatly reduces the time needed to add more datasets to UD. Accordingly, several tools have been developed for searching, displaying, and converting existing datasets.

In this paper, we describe *Semgrex*, a tool which searches for regex-like patterns in dependency graphs, and *Ssurgeon*, a tool to rewrite dependency graphs using the output of *Semgrex*. Both systems are written in Java, with Java API and command line tools available. In addition, there is a Python interface, including using displaCy (Honnibal et al., 2020) as a library to visualize the results of searches and transformation operations. The tools can be used programmatically to enable further processing of the results or used via the included command line tools. Furthermore, a web interface[1] shows the results of applying patterns to raw text.

Semgrex was released as part of CoreNLP (Manning et al., 2014). As such, it has been used in several projects (section 4). Several existing uses of *Semgrex* make use of it via the API, one of the strengths of the system, such as the OpenIE relation extraction of (Angeli et al., 2015).

More recently, we have added new pattern matching capabilities such as exact edge matching, a new python interface, and performance improvements. The previously unpublished *Ssurgeon* adds useful new capabilities for transforming dependency graphs.

Many of the features described here are similar to those in Grew-Match (Guillaume, 2021) and Semgrex-Plus (Tamburini, 2017). Similar to *Ssurgeon*, Semgrex-Plus uses *Semgrex* to find matches for editing, but *Ssurgeon* supports a wider range of operations. Compared with Grew-Match, *Semgrex* and *Ssurgeon* have the ability to start with raw text and search for dependency relations directly.

2 Semgrex

Semgrex and *Ssurgeon* are publicly released as part of the CoreNLP software package (Manning et al.,

*Chloé Kiddon is now at Google Research.

[1] https://corenlp.run/

Proceedings of the 21st International Workshop on Treebanks and Linguistic Theories (TLT, GURT/SyntaxFest 2023), pages 67 - 73
March 9-12, 2023

Attribute		
word	pos	lemma
ner	idx	upos

Table 1: Commonly used attributes of words

2014)[2]. *Semgrex* reads dependency trees from CoNLL-U files or parses dependencies from raw text using the associated CoreNLP parser.

Search patterns are composed of two pieces: node descriptions and relations between nodes. A search is executed by iterating over nodes, comparing each word to the node search pattern and checking its relationships with its neighbors using the relation search patterns.

2.1 Node Patterns

Dependency graphs of words and their dependency relations are represented internally using a directed graph, with nodes representing the words and labeled edges representing the dependencies.

When searching over nodes, the most generic node description is empty curly brackets. This search matches every node in the graph:

```
{}
```

Within the brackets, any attributes of the words available to *Semgrex* can be queried. For example, to query a person's name:

```
{word:Beckett}
```

It is possible to use standard string regular expressions, using the match semantics, within the attributes:

```
{word:/Jen.*/}
```

A node description can be negated. For example, this will match any word, as long as it does not start with Jen, Jenny, Jennifer, etc.

```
!{word:/Jen.*/}
```

Node descriptions can also be combined:

```
{word:/Jen.*/;tag:NNP}
```

See Table 1 for a list of commonly used word attributes. Note that `ner` may require a tool which provides NER annotations, such as (Manning et al., 2014) (Java) or (Qi et al., 2020) (Python), as those are typically not part of UD treebanks.

Relation	Meaning
A < B	A is the dependent of B
A > B	A is the governor of B
A << B	A is part of a chain of deps to B
A >> B	A is part of a chain of govs to B
A . B	idx(A) == idx(B) − 1
A .. B	idx(A) < idx(B)
A - B	idx(A) == idx(B) + 1
A -- B	idx(A) > idx(B)
A $+ B	C, A < C, B < C, idx(A) == idx(B) − 1
A $- B	C, A < C, B < C, idx(A) == idx(B) + 1
A $++ B	C, A < C, B < C, idx(A) < idx(B)
A $-- B	C, A < C, B < C, idx(A) > idx(B)
A >++ B	A gov B, idx(A) < idx(B)
A >-- B	A gov B, idx(A) > idx(B)
A <++ B	A dep B, idx(A) < idx(B)
A <-- B	A dep B, idx(A) > idx(B)

Table 2: Relations between words

2.2 Relation Patterns

Adding relations between nodes allows for searching over graph structures, making *Semgrex* a powerful search tool over dependency graphs. The relations used can be from any dependency formalism, although CoreNLP and Stanza both use Universal Dependencies by default.

The simplest relations are parent and child:

```
{word:Dep} < {word:Gov}
{word:Gov} > {word:Dep}
```

Many relations consider word order as well, such as the sister relations: + indicates the word on the left of the relation comes first, and − indicates the word on the right comes first:

```
{word:A} $+ {word:B}
{word:A} $- {word:B}
```

See Table 2 for a list of supported relations.

Relations can have labels, in which case the types on the edge between nodes must match:

```
{} <nsubj {}
```

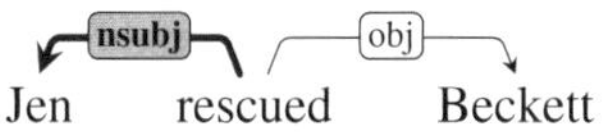

A special token matches exactly at root, such as in this example from the UD conversion of EWT (Silveira et al., 2014):

```
{$} > {}
```

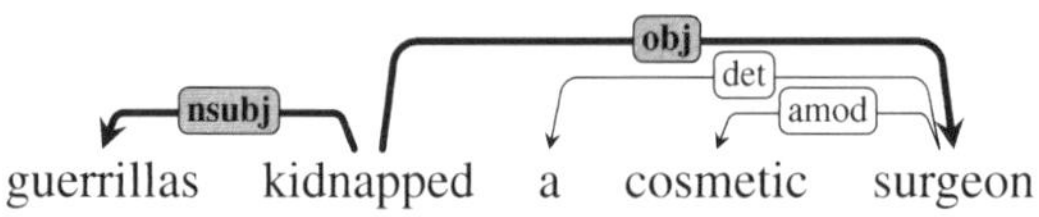

[2] `https://stanfordnlp.github.io/CoreNLP/`

Relations can be chained. Without parentheses, subsequent relations all apply to the same node; brackets denote that the later relations apply between the nodes in brackets as opposed to the head of the expression.

```
{} >nsubj {} >obj {}
```

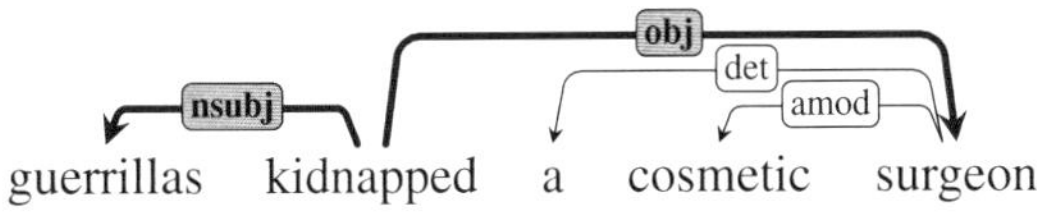


```
{} >obj ({} >amod {})
```

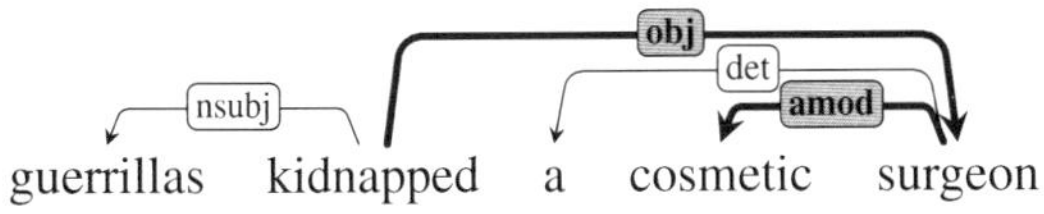

More advanced conjunction and disjunction operations are also possible. The JavaDoc[3] reference describes the complete syntax.

2.3 Named Nodes and Relations

It is possible to name one or more nodes as part of a *Semgrex* pattern. This allows for relations between three or more nodes using backreferences. When a node is named in a backreference, it must be the exact same node as the first instance for the pattern to match.

```
{word:running}
  >nsubj ({} >conj {}=C)
  >nsubj {}=C
```

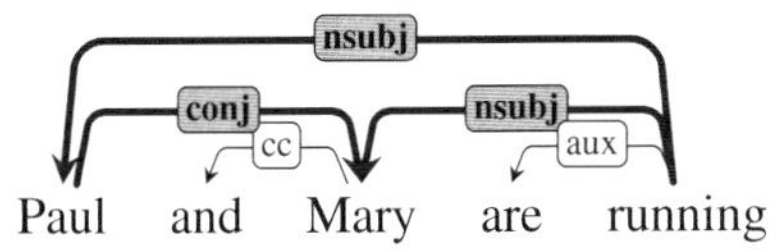

It is also possible to name the edges. This is useful when combined with *Ssurgeon*, which can manipulate an edge based on its name.

```
{word:running}
  >nsubj ({} >conj=conj {}=C)
  >nsubj {}=C
```

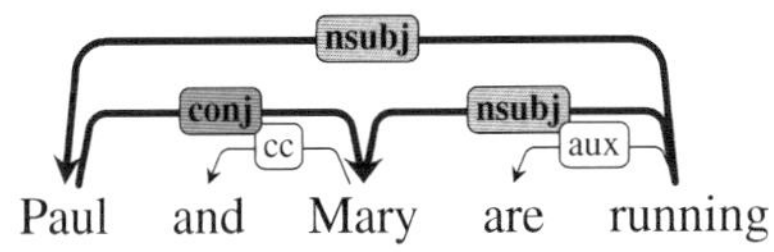

[3] https://nlp.stanford.edu/nlp/javadoc/javanlp/edu/stanford/nlp/semgraph/semgrex/SemgrexPattern.html

2.4 Concrete Example

Here are a couple examples from a slot filling task using *Semgrex*. Both examples search for "son" or "daughter" in relation to possible family members. (Angeli et al., 2014)

This matches "John's daughter, Logan, ..."

```
{lemma:/son|daughter|child/}
 >/nmod:poss/ {ner:PERSON}=ent
 >appos {ner:PERSON}=slot
```

This matches "Tommy, son of John, ..."

```
{ner:PERSON}=slot
 >appos
   ({lemma:/son|daughter|child/}
    >/nmod:of/ {ner:PERSON}=ent)
```

2.5 Implementation Notes

Under the hood, the tool is built using JavaCC[4] to process input patterns.

The graphs are implemented as a collection of edges as relations, with nodes storing indices and the text information such as word, lemma, and POS. To represent edges to hidden copy nodes, nodes can be pointers to the same underlying data with a copy index on them. An example where this happens is *I went over the river and through the woods*, where the unstated *went* before *through the woods* is represented as a copy node.

Nodes are searched in topographical order if possible, and in index order if not, with the intention of making a canonical ordering on the search results.

3 Ssurgeon

Ssurgeon is an extension of *Semgrex* which includes rules to rewrite dependency graphs.

A pattern in *Ssurgeon* is a pattern for *Semgrex* with required named nodes and/or edges, depending on the edit type, along with a edit definition.

3.1 Edge Editing

To add a new edge, the edit pattern must specify the governor, the dependent, and the edge type. The *Ssurgeon* pattern will add an edge to each match of the *Semgrex* pattern.

For example, in the previous "Paul and Mary are running" graph, the following would add the second $nsubj$ if it did not already exist. This would be useful for making enhanced dependencies, as basic UD has $conj(Paul, Mary)$ but not

[4] https://javacc.github.io/javacc/documentation/grammar.html

$nsubj(running, Mary)$.) If the edge already exists, this rule does not add a duplicate edge.

```
{word:running}=A
  >nsubj
  ({}=B >conj {}=C)

addEdge -gov A -dep C
        -reln nsubj
```

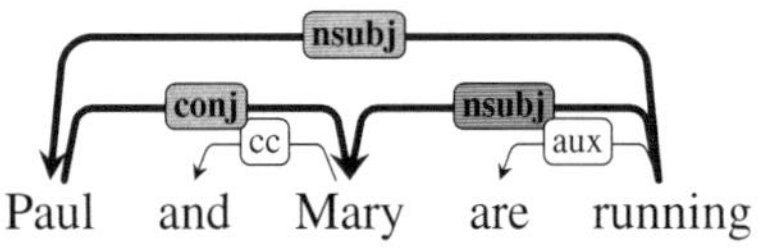

There are two mechanisms for deleting an edge. The first deletes an edge between two named nodes, and the second deletes a named edge. All edges which match the *Semgrex* pattern will be deleted.

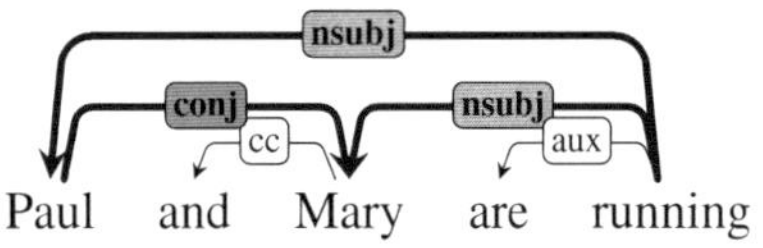


```
{word:running}
  >nsubj {}=B
  >nsubj ({}=C !== {}=B)

removeEdge -gov B -dep C
           -reln conj
```

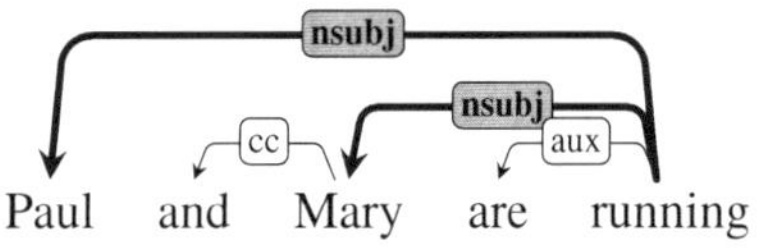

Alternatively, $removeNamedEdge$ removes a labeled edge:

```
{word:running}
  >nsubj {}=B
  >nsubj ({}=C >conj=conj {}=B)

removeNamedEdge -edge conj
```

There is also a mechanism for relabeling an edge, such as might be handy when mapping dependency graphs from one formalism to another:

```
{word:running}
  >nsubj {}=B
  >nsubj ({}=C >conj=conj {}=B)

relabelNamedEdge
  -edge conj -reln dep
```

3.2 Node Editing

There are mechanisms to add a node, remove a subgraph starting from a node, and alter the content of a node.

To add a node, specify a position, a node to attach it to, and a relation. The position can be at the start or end of a sentence or relative to an existing node. For this modification, it is necessary to add a guard to the *Semgrex* expression, or it will enter an infinite loop of adding unlimited new nodes to the graph.

Note that in the following example, searching for a word with no *det* and adding a *det* to the node is already sufficient to prevent runaway nodes.

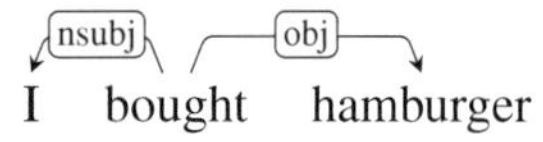


```
{word:bought}
  >dobj ({}=A !>det {})

addNode
  -word=a -reln det
  -gov A -position +A
```

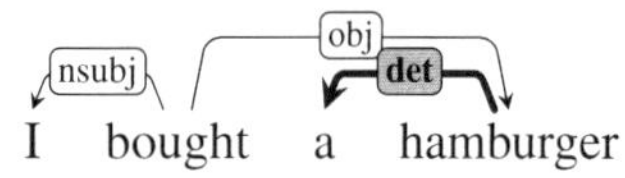

4 Usage

Semgrex has been used for task-specific processing of academic work (Shah et al., 2018), news summarization (Li et al., 2016), text-to-scene generations (Chang et al., 2014), relation extraction (Chaganty et al., 2017), and processing medical documents (Profitlich and Sonntag, 2021).

Ssurgeon was used internally to simplify sentences using their dependencies as an extension to the textual entailment system in (Chambers et al., 2007).

The Java API and command line interfaces are part of the Java package CoreNLP (Manning et al., 2014)[5]. The python client is available via Stanza (Qi et al., 2020)[6] The code is actively maintained as of 2023, and suggestions for additional *Semgrex* relations, *Ssurgeon* operations, or other improvements are welcome at our github repo[7].

[5]https://stanfordnlp.github.io/CoreNLP/

[6]https://stanfordnlp.github.io/stanza/

[7]https://github.com/stanfordnlp/CoreNLP

4.1 Python Integration

Both *Semgrex* and *Ssurgeon* have Python APIs. This allows for operations on the results of Stanza (Qi et al., 2020) on natural language or using the API in Stanza to read and process existing UD datasets.

Here is an example of using *Semgrex* on the results of parsing an article on disease transmission with Stanza to find out what insect vectors transmit a disease. The search patterns here are abridged for readability.

```
EXPR = """
{word:/transmitted/} >/obl|advcl/
 ({word:/^(?!bite|biting|bites).*$/}=vector
  >/case|mark/ {word:/by|from|through/})
"""

def process_text(parser, text):
   doc = parser(text)
   results = semgrex.process_doc(doc, EXPR)
   facts = OrderedDict()
   for sentence_results, sentence in zip(results.result,
                                          doc.sentences):
      if sentence.text in facts:
         # already seen this exact sentence!
         # results will be exactly the same
         continue
      facts[sentence.text] = []
      for pattern_result in results.result:
         if len(pattern_result.match) == 0:
            continue
         for match in pattern_result.match:
            for named_node in match.node:
               new_fact = "  {}: {}".format(named_node.name,
                   sentence.tokens[named_node.index-1].text)
               if new_fact not in facts[sentence.text]:
                  facts[sentence.text].append(new_fact)
   return facts
```

Also included is a mechanism to display graphs as search results, thanks to an API call to displaCy (Honnibal et al., 2020).

5 Related Work

The analysis of dependency treebanks, especially Universal Dependencies, has a long history of using dependency searching and rewriting tools.

Constituency treebanks such as the Penn Treebank (Marcus et al., 1993) predate Universal Dependencies. To analyze such constituency datasets, Tgrep (Pito, 1993) and its successor Tgrep2 (Rohde, 2003) set the initial standard for searching tree structured data. Tregex and Tsurgeon (Levy and Andrew, 2006) extended the language and added functionality to rewrite constituency trees.

Semgrex was one of the earliest tools to address the problem of searching in dependency graphs. It was previous briefly described in a paper on entailment that was the first to use *Semgrex*, (Chambers et al., 2007), although that paper did not include *Ssurgeon* or fully explain the usage of *Semgrex*. *Semgrex* has been used by other research several times in the following years.

The authors of the UD_Italian-VIT (Alfieri and Tamburini, 2016) dataset used an extension of *Semgrex*, Semgrex-Plus (Tamburini, 2017), to convert the dependency form of VIT to Universal Dependencies. Semgrex-Plus adds edge creation, edge deletion, and word relabeling to a *Semgrex* result.

Also connected with UniversalDependencies are multiple search engines which allow for easier viewing of the treebanks. Tündra (Martens, 2013) allows for searching of a variety of treebanks using the TIGERSearch format (Lezius et al., 2002).[8] Additional treebanks not part of UD are included (Martens and Passarotti, 2014), although recent UD updates have not been incorporated.

Grew-Match (Guillaume, 2021)[9] hosts a website which allows for searching of existing UD and other dependency datasets. The interface is frequently updated, hosting the latest 2.11 treebanks as of January 2023.

(Heinecke, 2019) provides a web interface to backend parsers such as (Straka et al., 2016) and provides search, visual editing, and automatic pattern matching and replacement. However, it does not include a command line tool.

Other tools include UDeasy (Brigada Villa, 2022), which provides a graphical interface which allows for searching of UD treebanks or any other dependency formalism. spaCy reimplemented *Semgrex* as part of the 3.0 release, adding the DependencyMatcher tool (Honnibal et al., 2020).[10] UDapi (Popel et al., 2017) provides mechanisms for searching dependency graphs, parsing text, visualizing the graphs, and manipulating the graphs themselves. Odin is a rule-based event extraction framework over dependency structures (Valenzuela-Escarcega et al., 2016).

6 Conclusion

We have introduced *Semgrex* and *Ssurgeon*, flexible, simple systems for dependency matching and dependency tree manipulation.

7 Acknowledgements

We would like to thank the reviewers for their helpful feedback on this work.

[8] https://www.ims.uni-stuttgart.de/documents/ressourcen/werkzeuge/tigersearch/doc/html/QueryLanguage.html

[9] http://universal.grew.fr/

[10] https://spacy.io/api/dependencymatcher

References

Linda Alfieri and Fabio Tamburini. 2016. (Almost) automatic conversion of the Venice Italian Treebank into the merged Italian dependency treebank format. In *CLiC-it/EVALITA*.

Gabor Angeli, Sonal Gupta, Melvin Johnson, Christopher D. Manning, Julie Tibshirani, Jean Wu, and Sen Wu. 2014. Stanford's distantly supervised slot filling systems for KBP 2014.

Gabor Angeli, Melvin Jose Johnson Premkumar, and Christopher D. Manning. 2015. Leveraging linguistic structure for open domain information extraction. In *Proceedings of the 53rd Annual Meeting of the Association for Computational Linguistics and the 7th International Joint Conference on Natural Language Processing (Volume 1: Long Papers)*, pages 344–354, Beijing, China. Association for Computational Linguistics.

Luca Brigada Villa. 2022. UDeasy: a tool for querying treebanks in conll-u format. In *Proceedings of the Workshop on Challenges in the Management of Large Corpora (CMLC-10)*, pages 16–19, Marseille, France. European Language Resources Association.

Arun Tejasvi Chaganty, Ashwin Paranjape, Jason Bolton, Matthew Lamm, Jinhao Lei, Abigail See, Kevin Clark, Yuhao Zhang, Peng Qi, and Christopher D. Manning. 2017. Stanford at TAC KBP 2017: Building a trilingual relational knowledge graph. In *Text Analysis Conference*.

Nathanael Chambers, Daniel Cer, Trond Grenager, David Hall, Chloe Kiddon, Bill MacCartney, Marie-Catherine de Marneffe, Daniel Ramage, Eric Yeh, and Christopher D. Manning. 2007. Learning alignments and leveraging natural logic. In *Proceedings of the ACL-PASCAL Workshop on Textual Entailment and Paraphrasing*, pages 165–170, Prague. Association for Computational Linguistics.

Angel X. Chang, Manolis Savva, and Christopher D. Manning. 2014. Learning spatial knowledge for text to 3D scene generation. In *EMNLP*.

Bruno Guillaume. 2021. Graph matching and graph rewriting: GREW tools for corpus exploration, maintenance and conversion. In *Proceedings of the 16th Conference of the European Chapter of the Association for Computational Linguistics: System Demonstrations*, pages 168–175, Online. Association for Computational Linguistics.

Johannes Heinecke. 2019. ConlluEditor: a fully graphical editor for universal dependencies treebank files. In *Proceedings of the Third Workshop on Universal Dependencies (UDW, SyntaxFest 2019)*, pages 87–93, Paris, France. Association for Computational Linguistics.

Matthew Honnibal, Ines Montani, Sofie Van Landeghem, and Adriane Boyd. 2020. spaCy: Industrial-strength Natural Language Processing in Python.

Roger Levy and Galen Andrew. 2006. Tregex and tsurgeon: tools for querying and manipulating tree data structures. In *Proceedings of the Fifth International Conference on Language Resources and Evaluation (LREC'06)*, Genoa, Italy. European Language Resources Association (ELRA).

Wolfgang Lezius, Hannes Biesinger, and Ciprian-Virgil Gerstenberger. 2002. Tigersearch manual.

Wei Li, Lei He, and Hai Zhuge. 2016. Abstractive news summarization based on event semantic link network. In *Proceedings of COLING 2016, the 26th International Conference on Computational Linguistics: Technical Papers*, pages 236–246, Osaka, Japan. The COLING 2016 Organizing Committee.

Christopher Manning, Mihai Surdeanu, John Bauer, Jenny Finkel, Steven Bethard, and David McClosky. 2014. The Stanford CoreNLP natural language processing toolkit. In *Proceedings of 52nd Annual Meeting of the Association for Computational Linguistics: System Demonstrations*, pages 55–60, Baltimore, Maryland. Association for Computational Linguistics.

Mitchell P. Marcus, Beatrice Santorini, and Mary Ann Marcinkiewicz. 1993. Building a large annotated corpus of English: The Penn Treebank. *Computational Linguistics*, 19(2):313–330.

Scott Martens. 2013. Tündra: A web application for treebank search and visualization. In *Proceedings of The Twelfth Workshop on Treebanks and Linguistic Theories (TLT12)*, pages 133–144, Sofia.

Scott Martens and Marco Passarotti. 2014. Thomas Aquinas in the TüNDRA: Integrating the index Thomisticus treebank into CLARIN-D. In *Proceedings of the Ninth International Conference on Language Resources and Evaluation (LREC'14)*, pages 767–774, Reykjavik, Iceland. European Language Resources Association (ELRA).

Joakim Nivre, Marie-Catherine de Marneffe, Filip Ginter, Jan Hajič, Christopher D. Manning, Sampo Pyysalo, Sebastian Schuster, Francis Tyers, and Daniel Zeman. 2020. Universal Dependencies v2: An evergrowing multilingual treebank collection. In *Proceedings of the Twelfth Language Resources and Evaluation Conference*, pages 4034–4043, Marseille, France. European Language Resources Association.

Richard Pito. 1993. Tgrep user manual.

Martin Popel, Z. Žabokrtský, and Martin Vojtek. 2017. UDapi: Universal api for universal dependencies. In *UDW@NoDaLiDa*.

Hans-Jürgen Profitlich and Daniel Sonntag. 2021. A case study on pros and cons of regular expression detection and dependency parsing for negation extraction from german medical documents. technical report. *ArXiv*, abs/2105.09702.

Peng Qi, Yuhao Zhang, Yuhui Zhang, Jason Bolton, and Christopher D. Manning. 2020. Stanza: A Python natural language processing toolkit for many human languages. In *Proceedings of the 58th Annual Meeting of the Association for Computational Linguistics: System Demonstrations*.

Douglas Rohde. 2003. Tgrep2 user manual.

Sapan Shah, Dhwani Vora, B. P. Gautham, and Sreedhar Reddy. 2018. A relation aware search engine for materials science. *Integrating Materials and Manufacturing Innovation*, 7:1–11.

Natalia Silveira, Timothy Dozat, Marie-Catherine de Marneffe, Samuel Bowman, Miriam Connor, John Bauer, and Chris Manning. 2014. A gold standard dependency corpus for English. In *Proceedings of the Ninth International Conference on Language Resources and Evaluation (LREC'14)*, pages 2897–2904, Reykjavik, Iceland. European Language Resources Association (ELRA).

Milan Straka, Jan Hajič, and Jana Straková. 2016. UDPipe: Trainable pipeline for processing CoNLL-U files performing tokenization, morphological analysis, POS tagging and parsing. In *Proceedings of the Tenth International Conference on Language Resources and Evaluation (LREC'16)*, pages 4290–4297, Portorož, Slovenia. European Language Resources Association (ELRA).

Fabio Tamburini. 2017. Semgrex-plus: a tool for automatic dependency-graph rewriting. In *Proceedings of the Fourth International Conference on Dependency Linguistics (Depling 2017)*, pages 248–254, Pisa,Italy. Linköping University Electronic Press.

Marco Antonio Valenzuela-Escarcega, Gus Hahn-Powell, and Mihai Surdeanu. 2016. Odin's runes: A rule language for information extraction. In *LREC*.

Mapping AMR to UMR: Resources for Adapting Existing Corpora for Cross-Lingual Compatibility

Julia Bonn[1], Skatje Myers[1], Jens E. L. Van Gysel[2], Lukas Denk[2], Meagan Vigus[2], Jin Zhao[3], Andrew Cowell[1], William Croft[2], Jan Hajič[4], James H. Martin[1], Alexis Palmer[1], Martha Palmer[1], James Pustejovsky[3], Zdenka Urešová[4], Rosa Vallejos[2], Nianwen Xue[3]

[1]University of Colorado, Boulder, [2]University of New Mexico
[3]Brandeis University, [4]Charles University, Prague

Corresponding author: julia.bonn@colorado.edu

Abstract

This paper presents detailed mappings between the structures used in Abstract Meaning Representation (AMR) and those used in Uniform Meaning Representation (UMR). These structures include general semantic roles, rolesets, and concepts that are largely shared between AMR and UMR, but with crucial differences. While UMR annotation of new low-resource languages is ongoing, AMR-annotated corpora already exist for many languages, and these AMR corpora are ripe for conversion to UMR format. Rather than focusing on semantic coverage that is new to UMR (which will likely need to be dealt with manually), this paper serves as a resource (with illustrated mappings) for users looking to understand the fine-grained adjustments that have been made to the representation techniques for semantic categories present in both AMR and UMR.

1 Introduction

Even with the overwhelming improvement in performance in Natural Language Processing (NLP) brought about by recent transformer architectures (Vaswani et al., 2017; Radford et al., 2018; Liu et al., 2021), there is an enduring interest in symbolic meaning representations in the community. In the decade since English Abstract Meaning Representations (AMRs) were launched, they have become increasingly popular and feature in several successful NLP applications (Bonial et al., 2020; Zhang and Ji, 2021; Fu et al., 2021). The 60K sentence dataset of English annotations available via LDC[1] has contributed significantly to this popularity. There is also growing interest in projecting English AMRs onto other languages to explore their suitability as a cross-lingual representation (Damonte and Cohen, 2017; Blloshmi et al., 2020; Uhrig et al., 2021; Oral et al., 2022; Cabezudo et al., 2022; Damonte and Cohen, 2022), with mixed success (Wein et al., 2022b; Wein and Schneider, 2022). In parallel with this exploration, a serious study has been made of the more English-centric aspects of AMRs, with the goal of moving AMRs in the direction of Uniform Meaning Representations (UMRs) as an annotation framework that can more readily be applied to all languages. As discussed in Van Gysel et al. (2021), UMR was developed with cross-linguistic scope in mind, paying careful attention to linguistic typology and typologically diverse languages. For researchers familiar with AMR, and especially for those who have already been annotating datasets in other languages with AMR-like annotations, it is important to understand exactly the ways in which AMR and UMR are similar and the crucial ways in which they differ, as discussed here. This should be of interest to anyone familiar with AMR who wants to adapt it to another language, or who already has an AMR dataset that can be retrofit to be more compatible with UMR.

In our previous UMR publications, we introduced the schema by explaining how it carves up conceptual space into categories that are applicable to typologically diverse languages (Vigus et al., 2020, 2019; Van Gysel et al., 2019). Special consideration has been given to the needs of field linguists who may be approaching semantic annotation for the first time as well as to the semantic coverage that is new for UMR, such as modal (Vigus et al., 2019), aspectual (Vigus et al., 2020) and scopal relations (Pustejovsky et al., 2019). In this paper we turn to more direct mappings from AMR-elements to UMR-elements.

We start by reviewing how AMR carves up conceptual space into graph elements (section 2), and then show how these elements overlay those of the UMR schema, focusing on retention, alteration and removal. Section 3 focuses on role-role mappings, section 4 on abstract roleset mappings, and section 5 on abstract concept mappings. We limit our discussion to sentence-level graphs. In the

[1]AMR 3.0: https://doi.org/10.35111/44cy-bp51

Proceedings of the 21st International Workshop on Treebanks and Linguistic Theories (TLT, GURT/SyntaxFest 2023), pages 74 - 95
March 9-12, 2023 ©2023 Association for Computational Linguistics

appendix, we illustrate these mappings with easily-digestible graphics.

As the developers of UMR, nothing would delight us more than a rush to convert existing AMR datasets to UMR. Indeed, AMR corpora already exist in a variety of languages: English[2], Chinese[3], Czech (Xue et al., 2014), Spanish (Migueles-Abraira et al., 2018; Wein et al., 2022a), Turkish (Oral et al., 2022; Azin and Eryiğit, 2019), Vietnamese (Linh and Nguyen, 2019), Portuguese (Anchiêta and Pardo, 2018; Sobrevilla Cabezudo and Pardo, 2019), Korean (Choe et al., 2019), Persian (Takhshid et al., 2022), and more. Some parallel corpora also exist (Damonte and Cohen, 2022; Li et al., 2017), which will be especially useful if converted to UMR. Much conversion of AMR corpora to UMR corpora should be able to be accomplished deterministically, with unique issues arising for each language.

The body of this paper pertains most directly to LDC's 3.0 English AMR release, which consists of 60,000 sentences, 7800 of which are annotated with Multisentence AMR (O'Gorman et al., 2018). English AMR has also been extended to special domain projects outside of the LDC release. [4] Sections 6.1 and 6.2 focus on existing Czech and Chinese data sets, considering issues that are expected to arise when converting existing AMR corpora to UMR format.

2 From AMR to UMR

UMR begins with sentence level graphs largely inherited from AMR. This paper describes the changes to AMR graph structures that will produce a first-pass UMR graph. In this section, we break AMR structures down into types, with subsequent sections describing how to map each type onto its UMR counterparts.

UMR improves on AMR in two major ways: first by adjusting the AMR schema to make it more cross-linguistically applicable, and second, by adding new semantic coverage to the schema in the form of sentence-level graph elements for tense, aspect, modality, and scope, as well as document-level dependency structures for temporal relations, modality, and coreference. See Vigus et al. (2019), Vigus et al. (2020), and Pustejovsky et al. (2019) for in depth instruction on these additions. The UMR-Writer (Zhao et al., 2021) also creates alignments between tokens in a surface level representation and elements in its graph.

AMR fails many non-English languages in two basic ways. First, the categories AMR uses to divide semantic space sometimes fail to cover necessary distinctions in a given language or fail to align with the language's category boundaries. Second, the style of morphosyntactic expression used by a language may be incompatible with conversion from surface forms to graph structures. AMR is based on predicate argument structures and assumes that a predicate and its arguments are distinct tokens that can each be plugged into its own node in the graph. This creates problems for polysynthetic and agglutinating languages in which an event, its modifiers, and its participants may all be morphologically bound together. Applying English-based AMR practices either disrupts surface lexical units or produces single node graphs so semantically specific that they are unlikely to come up twice in a corpus. Figure 3 (Appendix A.2) demonstrates the second point with a side-by-side comparison of AMR and UMR graphs for an Arapaho sentence and its English translation.

Language-specific Rolesets: AMR represents the semantics of a given sentence as a rooted, directed, acyclic graph consisting of nested predicate argument structures (Banarescu et al., 2013). Most of the predicate argument structures come in the form of lexical rolesets, taken from a valency lexicon associated with the language to be annotated. AMR was originally created with English in mind, and English AMR uses the English PropBank Roleset Lexicon (Palmer et al., 2005; Pradhan et al., 2022; Bonial et al., 2014; O'Gorman et al., 2018a,b). Chinese AMR relies on the Chinese PropBank, and Czech AMR uses the Czech PDT-Vallex valency lexicon (Hajič et al., 2003; Urešová et al., 2021).

In general, lexical rolesets are created for eventualities (events and states) and are ambiguous for the parts of speech used to express them. Rolesets consist of a predicate ID, for sense disambiguation, and a set of numbered roles with lexicalized descriptions that are considered semantically primary to the sense.

General Roles: In order to give structure to

[2] ISI's AMR main page: https://amr.isi.edu/

[3] Chinese AMR main page with release: https://www.cs.brandeis.edu/ clp/camr/camr.html

[4] These range in size from just over 1000 with DialAMR (Bonial et al., 2020) to 8000 with NIH THYME (Wright-Bettner et al., 2020) to over 10,000 for Minecraft SpatialAMR (Bonn et al., 2020), to mention only those we know well.

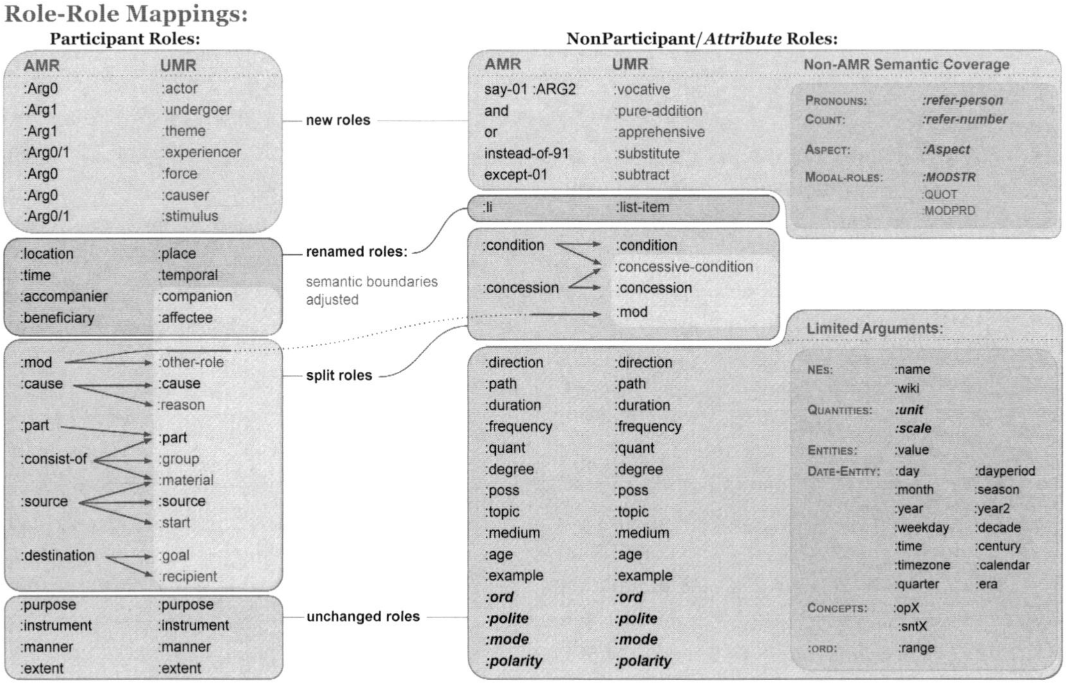

Figure 1: All AMR and UMR sentence-level roles, mapped. *Red text = new roles, blue text = role name changed, yellow highlight = semantic boundary shift.*

relations not covered by language-specific rolesets, AMR starts with general semantic roles (e.g., `:location`). These allow modification of entities and eventualities in a graph. Each role has a corresponding inverse role in the form `:<role>-of` (e.g., `:location-of`).

Abstract Rolesets: Sometimes, relations not covered by language-specific lexical rolesets need to be represented in a graph with a predicate (which has a variable), rather than a role (which does not). AMR uses Abstract Rolesets for this, broken down into several categories. First, most general roles have a corresponding reifying roleset (e.g., `:location`, `be-located-at-91`, with ARG1-theme and ARG2-location). Other Abstract Rolesets cover predication of implicitly understood relations such as entity-entity role relationships (`have-rel-role-91`) or inclusion (`include-91`).[5] In certain cases, AMR uses an existing language-specific roleset from English PropBank as an abstract roleset (e.g., `last-01` as a reification of `:duration`; `contrast-01` for contrast between clauses). There is no single comprehensive list of Abstract Rolesets readily available to AMR annotators either in the AMR editor[6] or the AMR guidelines.[7]

Abstract Concepts: AMR uses a limited set of Abstract Concepts in the graphs. These do not come with numbered arguments, but they may project one or more general roles as arguments (see the Limited Arguments in figure 1). Abstract Concepts include discourse relations such as `and`, `amr-unknown` (used for questions), quantity types (e.g., `temporal-quantity`, `volume-quantity`), entity types (e.g., `date-entity`), and concepts from the Named Entity Hierarchy. The NE concepts can be used to characterize implicit participants when needed.

3 Mapping Roles

In order to better serve a typologically diverse range of languages, UMR uses an updated set of general semantic roles. Many are taken directly from AMR, although some have been renamed, semantically expanded or contracted, or split. Others have been replaced with non-role strategies in UMR, and a small handful have been discontinued and not replaced. Changes are motivated by the cross-linguistic argument realization patterns in the ValPaL database (Vigus et al., 2020; Hartmann

[5]AMR frequently uses a `-91` suffix for these rolesets.

[6]`https://amr.isi.edu/editor.html`

[7]`https://github.com/amrisi/amr-guidelines/blob/master/amr.md`

et al., 2013). Each role in UMR still has an inverse and a roleset that reifies it. This section presents the ways in which roles have been adjusted to be more semantically comprehensive for UMR, as illustrated in Figure 1.

A major feature of UMR is the ability to use only general semantic roles for languages without roleset lexicons (see Stage 0 annotation in Van Gysel et al. (2021)). Due to this change, rather than having a single list of roles as in AMR, UMR groups its roles into Participant roles (primary arguments of eventualities), NonParticipant roles (other modifiers), and Attributes (roles that take only a fixed set of values). Most adjustments from AMR to UMR target Participant roles.

New roles: the concepts/roles in the top (pink) boxes in Figure 1 occur in AMR, but not as general roles. Of these, new participant roles (left) appear exclusively as numbered arguments (typically ARG0 or ARG1) of language-specific lexical rolesets, and new NonParticipant roles (right) as abstract concepts or abstract rolesets. The new NonParticipant roles are all discourse relation roles (see section 4) with the exception of `:vocative`, which AMR deals with by inferring an English-specific `say-01` roleset. A general role for vocatives is preferable for non-English corpora.

Renamed roles: the roles in the next boxes down in Figure 1 (purple) have been renamed so as to better describe the semantic categories they cover. `:companion` and `:affectee` both have shifted semantic boundaries compared to their AMR counterparts. `:companion` now applies to animate participants only ('I traveled *with Mary*') and is no longer to be used with entity modification (as in 'a pizza *with pineapple*'). Instances of the latter sort should be handled now with the appropriate topological (`:part`) or discourse relations (`and`) depending on the situation. `:affectee` now includes Maleficiaries as well as Beneficiaries, filling a sometimes uncomfortable gap in AMR. The other roles (`:place`, `:temporal`, and `:list-item`) are more cross-linguistically descriptive than their previous forms. `:place` and `:temporal` are better labels for participants that are abstract or metaphorically extended. Note that `:time` is still used for clock times under `date-entity`. `:list-item` replaces `:li`, which was considered too opaque a label.

Split roles: roles that are split into finer-grained categories to better support cross-linguistic semantic role diversity are next in Figure 1 (green). In most cases, the original role name has been retained but applied to a narrower category. The exceptions are AMR's `:consist-of` and `:destination`. `:consist-of` is dispreferred as a label because of its '`-of`' ending, which is ambiguous with inverse roles. `:destination` has been split across `:goal` and `:recipient` because of how `:destination`'s split contrasts with `:source`'s split. `:source` was split into three roles: `:source` (the Start-Point in motion events that involves separation of a Part from a Whole), `:start` (the Start-Point for other motion events), and `:material` (the Material in a creation event). `:destination` on the other hand was split along animacy lines, with `:recipient` being used for animate End-Points of sent-motion events, and `:goal` being used, in effect, for participants that contrast with any of the three `:source`-based roles. In other words, `:goal` captures End-points in motion events regardless of whether the entity in motion becomes part of the End-point, and also Products in creation events. `:goal` is considered to be more appropriately general than `:destination` across these types. `:consist-of` is also split across three narrower roles–`:part`, `:group`, and `:material`. These are largely topological distinctions.

In AMR, `:mod` is used as a catch-all role for modifiers with no clear home in one of the other roles. In UMR, we split this duty between `:mod` and `:other-role`. `:other-role` should be used as a catch-all Participant role, whereas `:mod` should be used as a catch-all NonParticipant role. In other words, `:mod` should still be used for demonstratives and the like. We note too that UMR is much more flexible about leaving surface concepts unannotated if they do not fit clearly into the schema, somewhat reducing the need for a catch-all role. (Exactly which concepts should be left unannotated for this reason is a question that needs to be resolved on a language-by-language basis, depending on how conceptual space is morphosyntactically distributed. Consider the option to omit 'just' and 'back-and-forth' as their own :mod nodes in the English UMR in Appendix A.2.) `:other-role` is more likely to be used by low-resource languages undergoing Stage 0 annotation.

Removed roles: UMR discontinues use of a number of roles (Appendix A.1). Some of these were simply shortcuts, while others do not fit into the current schema as roles. The most important removed role is `:domain`, which AMR used for identity relations in place of a copular roleset. `:domain` was used in places where property, object, or identity relations were expressed clausally. It was considered an inverse of `:mod`, so `:mod` has been given a new inverse, `:mod-of`. In UMR, these clausal expressions are now handled using the rolesets of nonprototypical predication (formerly 'nonverbal clauses'), discussed in section 4.

`:subset`, `:superset`, and `:subevent` have also been removed, although `:subset` is still used for entity coreference at the document level. `:subset` and `:superset` relations can still be represented in sentence-level graphs with `include-91` from AMR. Subevent relations can still be represented at the document level in UMR as part of the temporal dependency annotation (see UMR guidelines [8]). As for the shortcuts: these were not fully 'roles', they just triggered automatic creation of a related abstract roleset in the graph. The shortcuts are no longer used, but the rolesets they pointed to still are, in their UMR forms. The exception is `:cost`, which should now be treated with `:other-role`.

Inverse roles appear in the form `:<role>/:<role>-of` (as seen with `:mod/:Mod-of` above), with the inverse capitalized. As noted with `:consist-of`, UMR does not use base roles ending in `-of`, thus eliminating ambiguity.

4 Mapping Abstract Rolesets

4.1 Role-Reification Rolesets: Sometimes during annotation, relations typically handled with general roles need to be represented as a predicate in a graph. This need may arise for three different reasons. First, the relation might be expressed clausally (*'I'm in Chicago'*). Second, the relation may be split across sentences, as (*'What did you make?' 'Blankets.'*). This occurs especially frequently in casual dialogue corpora. Third, sometimes the relation itself needs a variable, either for coreference or modification.

AMR provides reified rolesets for most of its general roles, although there are a few holes, as with `:direction` and `:path`. Most of AMR's reifications are constructed fairly consistently. Those that were created for AMR had `-91` suffixes, but sometimes, English-specific rolesets were used. This turns out to be an uncomfortable set-up for annotation of non-English languages, since English-sourced roleset names may not be obviously identifiable as reifications (e.g., `last-01` for `:duration`, `concern-02` for `:topic`). Also problematically, the English-sourced rolesets don't always have exactly the same semantic coverage as the roles they reify. For example, `age-01` is aspectually-incompatible with `:age`, as it pertains to an aging event rather than a property. `age-01` also includes an `:ARG0` for the causer/agent of the aging event, which is not applicable to the `:age` role.

Because of these issues, the entire set of reified rolesets has been overhauled to bring them into alignment and make them more cross-linguistically appropriate. This involves new conventions for naming the rolesets and new conventions for naming and structuring their arguments. We believe these changes are a great improvement that will benefit all annotators moving forward.

Naming conventions: Reification rolesets are now named consistently, as follows: 1) each has a `-91` suffix. If multiple rolesets exist for the same concept, numbering continues with `-92` and so on; 2) each starts with a `have-` prefix, with the exception of `be-polite-91`, which we keep as a stylistic choice; 3) the content between '`have-`' and '`-91`' is the name of the role being reified. Appendix A.3 shows reification rolesets for all UMR roles.

Argument structuring conventions: Reification rolesets are also structured and numbered consistently now, as follows: 1) each roleset starts with `:ARG1`, as `:ARG0` is reserved for agentive/causal arguments; 2) `:ARG1` is used for the event or entity that would serve as the head of the unreified role in a graph, and `:ARG2` is for the value that would be annotated under the unreified role. Other arguments may be possible but are less conventionalized. See how the old reification for `:accompanier` was reconfigured as `have-companion-91` below:

```
accompany-01
    :ARG0 accompanier
    :ARG1 accompanied
    :ARG2 start point
    :ARG3 end point
have-companion-91
    :ARG1 event
    :ARG2 accompanier
```

Argument structure changes particularly affect mappings between prior English-sourced reification rolesets and their new UMR counterparts, since many of the English predicates (`cause-01`, `concern-02`) originated as rolesets for agentive verbs that started with `:ARG0`.

[8] UMR website: https://umr4nlp.github.io/web/

4.2 Rolesets for Nonprototypical Predication. Following Croft (2022) and Heine (1997), UMR has a set of `-91` rolesets for representing nonprototypical predication (previously referred to as nonverbal clause rolesets). Also following Croft, UMR has abandoned the 'nonverbal clause' terminology because annotators found it to be unclear. Although the term sounds like it excludes verbal expressions, it is in fact used to describe a set of semantic categories that can be expressed in many different ways cross-linguistically, including verbally.

Rolesets of nonprototypical predication cover five semantic categories first (possession, location, property predication, object predication, and identity relationships), and describe syntactic realization second and less strongly. While it is true that these semantic categories can be expressed using many different syntactic strategies across languages (attributive expressions, predication through juxtaposition, etc.), the rolesets for location, possession and property predication are to be used for *clausal* expressions, rather than *phrasal* expressions, which are covered in UMR with `:place`, `:poss` and `:mod` roles. In fact, the rolesets for nonprototypical predication of location, possession and property serve *as* the reifications of `:place`, `:poss`, and `:mod`. Clausal expressions of location and possession are divided discourse-pragmatically depending on which argument is presented as new information. As for object and identity predication, due to the complexity and structure of the relationships involved, their `-91` rolesets are used for both phrasal and clausal expressions. Appendix A.4 shows the nonprototypical predication rolesets.

In a recent change, all of the above rolesets now follow the argument numbering conventions used for reification rolesets. This means that `have-rel-role` and `have-org-role` have had their argument numbers shifted so that they start with `:ARG1` instead of `:ARG0`. Because of this change, and in the interest of avoiding confusion between versions, the renumbered UMR versions have been given a `-92` suffix.

However, `have-91` and `belong-91` started out as the English have-03 and belong-01. Their arguments have also been shifted to avoid using `:ARG0`. A sticky issue arises when we consider which instances of 'have' and 'belong' in English annotation to retrofit. The rolesets of nonprototypical predication are intended to be used any time the semantic relationship is expressed clausally, and this includes verbal expressions. This suggests that all instances previously annotated as `have-03` in AMR should be converted to `have-91`, and the `have-03` roleset should be retired. But how do we determine when 'the semantic relationship' has been expressed when it comes to verbal rolesets?

For example, `belong-01` has been used for verbal expressions of membership and possession. Should the roleset be retained for instances of membership-belonging, while instances of possessor-focused-possession are represented with `belong-91`? What about verbs expressing location? Some postural verbs can be used in bleached form for generic expressions of location (*'the radio tower lies 10 miles south of town'*), which also seem to fit the criteria for using `have-location-91` or `exist-91`. We doubt annotators would mark postural instance (*'the radio tower lay on its side'*) with a `-91` roleset, but bleached usages need more consideration.

Another interesting issue involves clauses of property predication (`have-mod-91`), often expressed adjectivally in English. English PropBank includes many rolesets for adjectives. Originally, these were limited to predicating adjectives only, but it became apparent that adjectival rolesets were useful in cases where multiple arguments were involved or where multiple senses existed. Over time, single-place adjective rolesets were added even outside of these constraints. AMR did not adopt all of these adjectival rolesets, although they did adopt some. The convention has become to use any roleset that shows up in the editor any time it fits semantically, which means plenty of modifying adjectives have been annotated with adjective rolesets in English AMR. To put it plainly, English AMR has not been consistent on the adjective front. Cross-linguistically, languages express property predication in an even wider variety of ways, including with lexical verbs (Croft, 2022; Heine, 1997). While some linguists may not wish to use language-specific property rolesets for property predication, for languages like Arapaho in which properties are frequently expressed as verbs, it would seem very strange not to. Ultimately, we propose that individual languages make this decision for themselves.

4.3 Other Abstract `-91` Rolesets. AMR has a number of rolesets that are used for other abstract relationships in the graphs. Many of these are `-91` rolesets (`publication-91`, `correlate-91`, etc.) but some are also English-specific rolesets (e.g., `mean-01`, `resemble-01`, `contrast-01`) Appendix A.5 presents a full list of these rolesets and their UMR resolutions. UMR's versions all use a `-91` sufix; argument numbering has been retained.

4.4 Discourse Relations. UMR provides a lattice of categories to annotate relations between clauses in complex sentences. The upper levels represent discourse relations as abstract concepts (which can take a variable number of interchangeable `:opX` arguments, e.g. junction) or abstract rolesets (whose arguments are fixed in number and ordered, e.g. contrast). The bottom level concepts can be expressed roles or their inverses or reifications. Appendix A.6 shows the lattice with AMR concepts overlaying UMR concepts.

The categories are based on typological work by Croft (2022), Malchukov (2004) and Thompson & Longacre (1985). Some of the more coarse-grained categories on the lattice are inherited directly from AMR, as are some of the most fine-grained categories. Most new additions can be found in the intermediate levels. Specifically, UMR maintains the use of coarse-grained AMR `(o/ or)` and `(a/ and)` with their numbered `:opX` arguments, which did the heavy lifting for conjunction and disjunction, and adds finer-grained `(o / or-incl)` and `(o /or-excl)`. As for contrast between clauses, AMR's English-sourced `contrast-01` roleset has been swapped out for a version with a `-91` suffix and no `ARG0`. Given that many languages do not have clearly distinct morphosyntactic strategies for expressing conjunction and contrast, various high- and mid-level values in the UMR lattice combine concepts formerly annotated with `and` and those formerly annotated with `contrast-01`. This is the case for `and-unexpected`, `and-contrast`, and `and-but`. Here, manual reannotation of existing corpora may be necessary if the more fine-grained options are to be used.

On the lowest level of the lattice, UMR uses a number of fine-grained roles to annotate subtypes of conjunction, disjunction, and contrast. Some, like `:concession` and `:manner`, are inherited from AMR and simply placed in the discourse lattice under the appropriate higher-level value (`unexpected-co-occurrence-91` and `consecutive`, respectively). Others are newly introduced (e.g. `:subtraction`, `:pure-addition`, `:apprehensive`). All have inverses and related reified rolesets created as discussed above.

As with other domains where UMR organizes category values in lattices, annotators from individual languages will decide which values are appropriate for (i.e. explicitly expressed in) their language and use only those – the lattice helps make their annotations compatible to those in other languages.

5 Mapping Abstract Concepts

As mentioned in section 2, AMR includes a number of abstract concepts such as `X-entity` and `X-quantity` types, named entity types, mathematical concepts, and other annotation-support concepts like `AMR-unintelligible`. By-and-large, these are unchanged in UMR. Of course those referencing '`AMR-`' have been updated to reference '`UMR-`' (e.g. `UMR-unknown`, etc.). All `X-entities` and `X-quantities` are still in use. See Appendices A.7 and A.8.

When a named entity is identified, UMR assigns a semantic type to it, following the practice of AMR. These types are organized hierarchically, and annotators aim to use the most specific type possible. UMR makes a number of adaptations to the AMR hierarchy in order to make the named entity types more cross-linguistically applicable and practical. Following the general spirit of making UMR ontologies hierarchical so that annotators of each language can select the level of granularity they are comfortable with, UMR arranges the named entity types hierarchically in a lattice. UMR also adds categories that are needed when annotating indigenous languages, as their societies are often organized in such a way that the AMR types did not fit well. For instance, entity types like "clan" are not available in AMR but are added in UMR. The UMR named entity type heierarchy is "backward compatible" in that it is a superset of the AMR entity types, and existing AMR named entity types can be automatically mapped to UMR. See Appendix A.9.

6 Czech and Chinese Corpora

Adapting UMR annotation to other languages need not necessarily mean starting from scratch. In this section, we describe preliminary work planning the use of existing resources for Czech and Chinese to build UMR-annotated corpora. For both languages, there are existing AMR corpora (of varying size), as well as semantically-annotated corpora, for example in the styles used for the shared tasks on Meaning Representation Parsing (Oepen et al., 2019, 2020). Either type of resource can provide a starting point for developing a UMR corpus with less effort.

6.1 Czech Corpora

In addition to Czech's corpus of 100 AMR-annotated sentences (Xue et al., 2014), Czech tectogrammatical (TR) annotation has undergone a preliminary comparison with the current UMR style and guidelines (Oepen et al., 2019, 2020). Xue et al. 2014 describe the relation between Czech TR annotation and AMR, and here we will briefly describe the possibilities for using TR for pre-annotation of Czech to UMR.

The tectogrammatical annotation has been developed for the Prague Dependency Treebank (Hajič et al., 2020) as well as for some of its sibling treebanks, in particular for the Prague Czech English Dependency Treebank (Hajič et al., 2012) which is a parallel treebank based on the WSJ portion of the Penn Treebank. Tectogrammatical annotation focuses on the syntactic-semantic properties of language; while it largely keeps the dependency structure used at the surface-syntactic level, it adds a number of semantic properties relevant to a possible conversion to UMR:

- argument (valency) structure and predicate senses similar to PropBank (Hajič et al., 2003), though the approach to argument labeling is different. Technically, the conversion to the equivalent frame files should be feasible (to allow the UMR annotation tool to be used for Czech structural annotation or conversion);
- elided arguments as separate nodes, with the possibility of linking them by coreference or other relations (see also below);
- removal of function words, replacing them with largely semantic relations similar in number and nature to UMR roles;
- semantic attributes on each node (depending on its type), such as tense (preceding/concurrent), aspect (regardless of lexical vs. syntactic expression), number, modality, etc.;
- coreference relations, both grammatical (wh-clauses, attribute clauses, etc.) and textual (pronominal);
- discourse relations that go beyond sentence boundaries, and paratactic relations within sentences, which can serve as the basis for logical predicates;
- information structure annotation for determining scope in the focus part of sentences; and
- multiword expression annotation for both named entities and terminology.

These features should simplify and automate a large part of the conversion to UMRs. As described in more detail in Xue et al. (2014), about half of the sentences in a parallel Czech-English corpus have the same structure (between the TR annotation and the AMR structure, which is identical or easily convertible into UMR), needing to convert the labels only or do simple structural changes by deterministic rules (such as mapping multiword expressions into a single lexeme if the ontology used requires it). Other algorithmic changes involve TR attributes for modality (some of which will be converted to a structure headed by predicates such as `possible-01`, or to the `:modstr` attribute), TR rhematizer nodes for negation (to be converted to the `:polarity -` attribute), and others.

The other half of the TR structures will have to be checked and possibly corrected by hand; still, most of the annotation contained in the TR-labelled and structured trees will be valid and could remain intact.

6.2 Chinese Corpora

Existing Chinese AMR data sets (Li et al., 2016, 2019) are drawn from the Chinese version of the Little Prince (1562 sentences) as well as the Chinese TreeBank (Xue et al., 2005, 5000 sentences), with semantic roles that are defined in the frame files for the Chinese Propbank (Xue and Palmer, 2009). They generally adopt the AMR annotation style, with adaptations to handle Chinese-specific constructions. The adaptations that are needed to map Chinese AMRs to UMRs are thus very similar to those discussed in previous sections.

Chinese AMR does extend English in a number of ways, and they include the following:

- Chinese AMR adds a few Chinese-specific roles, including :cunit, :tense, and :aspect. :cunit indicates a relation between a noun and a measure word (e.g., 本, a measure word or classifier for books). :tense indicates a relation between a verb and an adverb (e.g., 将 "will"), and :aspect indicates a relation between a verb and an aspect marker (e.g., 着, 了, 过, 正在). The Chinese tense and aspect annotation are thus very superficial. However, when mapping to UMRs, they can be used to help determine the UMR aspect attribute and temporal relations.

- Chinese discourse relations in Chinese AMR are based on discourse relations defined in the Chinese Discourse TreeBank (Zhou and Xue, 2012, 2015). In addition to *and* and *or*, they also include *causation*, *condition*, *contrast*, *temporal*, *concession*, *progression*, *purpose*, *expansion*, and *multi-sentence*. They are annotated as Chinese AMR concepts and can be mapped to UMR discourse relations.

A significant departure from English AMR is that Chinese AMR data sets include concept-to-word alignments, as well as relation-to-word alignments. Since UMR also captures alignment between UMR concepts and word tokens from the source language, the alignment in Chinese AMR data sets will help map Chinese AMRs to UMRs. However, Chinese AMR's alignments are different from UMR's in some ways, so some changes to the alignments are needed to convert between them during AMR-to-UMR conversion. In particular, the relation-to-word alignments will need to be stripped off.

7 Conclusion

As more languages are annotated with UMR, we continue to identify ways the schema can be further refined to support cross-lingual expressivity. However, the process with new languages can be slow. Converting existing AMR corpora to UMR is an efficient way to grow the overall UMR corpus. Also, users with expertise in how AMR categories map to real language conceptual space can help identify the more nuanced areas in which UMR can improve on AMR. We expect the mappings outlined in this paper to be important support for users who wish to be a part of this process.

Acknowledgements

This work is supported in part by a grant from the CNS Division of National Science Foundation (Awards no: 2213804, 2213805) entitled "Building a Broad Infrastructure for Uniform Meaning Representations". It has also been supported by the Czech Science Foundation project "LUSyD", Award No. GX20-16819X, and the by LINDAT/CLARIAH-CZ Large Research Infrastructure, supported by the Czech Ministry of Education, Youth and Sports, Awards No. LM2023062 and LM2018101. All views expressed in this paper are those of the authors and do not necessarily represent the view of the National Science Foundation.

References

Rafael Anchiêta and Thiago Pardo. 2018. Towards AMR-BR: A SemBank for Brazilian Portuguese language. In *Proceedings of the Eleventh International Conference on Language Resources and Evaluation (LREC 2018)*, Miyazaki, Japan. European Language Resources Association (ELRA).

Zahra Azin and Gülşen Eryiğit. 2019. Towards Turkish Abstract Meaning Representation. In *Proceedings of the 57th Annual Meeting of the Association for Computational Linguistics: Student Research Workshop*, pages 43–47, Florence, Italy. Association for Computational Linguistics.

Laura Banarescu, Claire Bonial, Shu Cai, Madalina Georgescu, Kira Griffitt, Ulf Hermjakob, Kevin Knight, Philipp Koehn, Martha Palmer, and Nathan Schneider. 2013. Abstract Meaning Representation for sembanking. In *Proceedings of the 7th Linguistic Annotation Workshop and Interoperability with Discourse*, pages 178–186, Sofia, Bulgaria. Association for Computational Linguistics.

Rexhina Blloshmi, Rocco Tripodi, and Roberto Navigli. 2020. XL-AMR: Enabling cross-lingual AMR parsing with transfer learning techniques. In *Proceedings of the 2020 Conference on Empirical Methods in Natural Language Processing (EMNLP)*, pages 2487–2500.

Claire Bonial, Julia Bonn, Kathryn Conger, Jena D. Hwang, and Martha Palmer. 2014. PropBank: Semantics of new predicate types. In *Proceedings of the Ninth International Conference on Language Resources and Evaluation (LREC'14)*, pages 3013–3019, Reykjavik, Iceland. European Language Resources Association (ELRA).

Claire Bonial, Lucia Donatelli, Mitchell Abrams, Stephanie Lukin, Stephen Tratz, Matthew Marge, Ron Artstein, David Traum, and Clare Voss. 2020. Dialogue-AMR: abstract meaning representation for dialogue. In *Proceedings of the 12th Language Resources and Evaluation Conference*, pages 684–695.

Julia Bonn, Martha Palmer, Jon Cai, and Kristin Wright-Bettner. 2020. Spatial AMR: Expanded spatial annotation in the context of a grounded Minecraft corpus. In *Proceedings of the 12th Conference on Language Resources and Evaluation (LREC 2020)*,.

Marco Antonio Sobrevilla Cabezudo, Rafael Torres Anchiêta, and Thiago Alexandre Salgueiro Pardo. 2022. Comparison of Cross-lingual Strategies for AMR-to-Brazilian Portuguese Generation.

Hyonsu Choe, Jiyoon Han, Hyejin Park, and Hansaem Kim. 2019. Copula and case-stacking annotations for Korean AMR. In *Proceedings of the First International Workshop on Designing Meaning Representations*, pages 128–135, Florence, Italy. Association for Computational Linguistics.

William Croft. 2022. *Morphosyntax: constructions of the world's languages*. Cambridge University Press.

Marco Damonte and Shay Cohen. 2022. Abstract Meaning Representation 2.0-Four Translations.

Marco Damonte and Shay B Cohen. 2017. Cross-lingual abstract meaning representation parsing. *arXiv preprint arXiv:1704.04539*.

Qiankun Fu, Linfeng Song, Wenyu Du, and Yue Zhang. 2021. End-to-end AMR coreference resolution. In *Proceedings of the 59th Annual Meeting of the Association for Computational Linguistics and the 11th International Joint Conference on Natural Language Processing (Volume 1: Long Papers)*, pages 4204–4214.

Jan Hajič, Eduard Bejček, Jaroslava Hlavacova, Marie Mikulová, Milan Straka, Jan Štěpánek, and Barbora Štěpánková. 2020. Prague dependency treebank - consolidated 1.0. In *Proceedings of the Twelfth Language Resources and Evaluation Conference*, pages 5208–5218, Marseille, France. European Language Resources Association.

Jan Hajič, Eva Hajičová, Jarmila Panevová, Petr Sgall, Ondřej Bojar, Silvie Cinková, Eva Fučíková, Marie Mikulová, Petr Pajas, Jan Popelka, Jiří Semecký, Jana Šindlerová, Jan Štěpánek, Josef Toman, Zdeňka Urešová, and Zdeněk Žabokrtský. 2012. Announcing Prague Czech-English Dependency Treebank 2.0. In *Proceedings of the Eighth International Conference on Language Resources and Evaluation (LREC'12)*, pages 3153–3160, Istanbul, Turkey. European Language Resources Association (ELRA).

Jan Hajič, Jarmila Panevová, Zdeňka Urešová, Alevtina Bémová, Veronika Kolářová, and Petr Pajas. 2003. PDT-VALLEX: Creating a Large-coverage Valency Lexicon for Treebank Annotation. In *Proceedings of The Second Workshop on Treebanks and Linguistic Theories*, pages 57–68, Vaxjo, Sweden. Vaxjo University Press.

Iren Hartmann, Martin Haspelmath, and Bradley Taylor, editors. 2013. *The Valency Patterns Leipzig online database*. Max Planck Institute for Evolutionary Anthropology, Leipzig.

Bernd Heine. 1997. *Cognitive foundations of grammar*. Oxford University Press.

Bin Li, Yuan Wen, Lijun Bu, et al. 2017. A comparative analysis of the AMR graphs from English and Chinese corpus of The Little Prince. *Journal of Chinese Information Processing*, 31(1):50–57.

Bin Li, Yuan Wen, Weiguang Qu, Lijun Bu, and Nianwen Xue. 2016. Annotating The Little Prince with chinese AMRs. In *Proceedings of the 10th Linguistic Annotation Workshop held in Conjunction with ACL 2016 (LAW-X 2016)*, pages 7–15.

Bin Li, Yuan Wen, Li Song, Weiguang Qu, and Nianwen Xue. 2019. Building a Chinese AMR bank with concept and relation alignments. *Linguistic Issues in Language Technology*, 18.

Ha Linh and Huyen Nguyen. 2019. A case study on meaning representation for Vietnamese. In *Proceedings of the First International Workshop on Designing Meaning Representations*, pages 148–153, Florence, Italy. Association for Computational Linguistics.

Pengfei Liu, Weizhe Yuan, Jinlan Fu, Zhengbao Jiang, Hiroaki Hayashi, and Graham Neubig. 2021. Pre-train, prompt, and predict: A systematic survey of prompting methods in natural language processing. *arXiv preprint arXiv:2107.13586*.

Andrej L Malchukov. 2004. Towards a semantic typology of adversative and contrast marking. *Journal of semantics*, 21(2):177–198.

Noelia Migueles-Abraira, Rodrigo Agerri, and Arantza Diaz de Ilarraza. 2018. Annotating abstract meaning representations for Spanish. In *Proceedings of the Eleventh International Conference on Language Resources and Evaluation (LREC 2018)*.

Stephan Oepen, Omri Abend, Lasha Abzianidze, Johan Bos, Jan Hajic, Daniel Hershcovich, Bin Li, Tim O'Gorman, Nianwen Xue, and Daniel Zeman. 2020. MRP 2020: The second shared task on cross-framework and cross-lingual meaning representation parsing. In *Proceedings of the CoNLL 2020 Shared Task: Cross-Framework Meaning Representation Parsing*, pages 1–22, Online. Association for Computational Linguistics.

Stephan Oepen, Omri Abend, Jan Hajic, Daniel Hershcovich, Marco Kuhlmann, Tim O'Gorman, Nianwen Xue, Jayeol Chun, Milan Straka, and Zdenka Uresova. 2019. MRP 2019: Cross-framework meaning representation parsing. In *Proceedings of the Shared Task on Cross-Framework Meaning Representation Parsing at the 2019 Conference on Natural Language Learning*, pages 1–27, Hong Kong. Association for Computational Linguistics.

Tim O'Gorman, Sameer Pradhan, Martha Palmer, Julia Bonn, Katie Conger, and James Gung. 2018a. The new Propbank: Aligning Propbank with AMR through POS unification. In *Proceedings of the Eleventh International Conference on Language Resources and Evaluation (LREC 2018)*, Miyazaki, Japan. European Language Resources Association (ELRA).

Tim O'Gorman, Michael Regan, Kira Griffitt, Ulf Hermjakob, Kevin Knight, and Martha Palmer. 2018b.

AMR beyond the sentence: the multi-sentence AMR corpus. In *Proceedings of the 27th International Conference on Computational Linguistics*, pages 3693–3702, Santa Fe, New Mexico, USA. Association for Computational Linguistics.

Elif Oral, Ali Acar, and Gülşen Eryiğit. 2022. Abstract meaning representation of Turkish. *Natural Language Engineering*, pages 1–30.

Tim O'Gorman, Michael Regan, Kira Griffitt, Ulf Hermjakob, Kevin Knight, and Martha Palmer. 2018. AMR beyond the sentence: the multi-sentence AMR corpus. In *Proceedings of the 27th international conference on computational linguistics*, pages 3693–3702.

Martha Palmer, Daniel Gildea, and Paul Kingsbury. 2005. The Proposition Bank: An annotated corpus of semantic roles. *Computational Linguistics*, 31(1):71–106.

Sameer Pradhan, Julia Bonn, Skatje Myers, Kathryn Conger, Tim O'gorman, James Gung, Kristin Wright-bettner, and Martha Palmer. 2022. PropBank comes of Age—Larger, smarter, and more diverse. In *Proceedings of the 11th Joint Conference on Lexical and Computational Semantics*, pages 278–288, Seattle, Washington. Association for Computational Linguistics.

James Pustejovsky, Ken Lai, and Nianwen Xue. 2019. Modeling quantification and scope in Abstract Meaning Representations. In *Proceedings of the first international workshop on designing meaning representations*, pages 28–33.

Alec Radford, Karthik Narasimhan, Tim Salimans, Ilya Sutskever, et al. 2018. Improving language understanding by generative pre-training.

Marco Antonio Sobrevilla Cabezudo and Thiago Pardo. 2019. Towards a general Abstract Meaning Representation corpus for Brazilian Portuguese. In *Proceedings of the 13th Linguistic Annotation Workshop*, pages 236–244, Florence, Italy. Association for Computational Linguistics.

Reza Takhshid, Razieh Shojaei, Zahra Azin, and Mohammad Bahrani. 2022. Persian Abstract Meaning Representation. *arXiv preprint arXiv:2205.07712*.

Sandra A Thompson, Robert E Longacre, and Shin Ja J Hwang. 1985. Adverbial clauses. *Language typology and syntactic description*, 2:171–234.

Sarah Uhrig, Yoalli Rezepka Garcia, Juri Opitz, and Anette Frank. 2021. Translate, then parse! A strong baseline for cross-lingual AMR parsing. *arXiv preprint arXiv:2106.04565*.

Zdeňka Urešová, Alevtina Bémová, Eva Fučíková, Jan Hajič, Veronika Kolářová, Marie Mikulová, Petr Pajas, Jarmila Panevová, and Jan Štěpánek. 2021. PDT-vallex: Czech valency lexicon linked to treebanks 4.0 (PDT-vallex 4.0). LINDAT/CLARIAH-CZ digital library at the Institute of Formal and Applied Linguistics (ÚFAL), Faculty of Mathematics and Physics, Charles University.

Jens EL Van Gysel, Meagan Vigus, Jayeol Chun, Kenneth Lai, Sarah Moeller, Jiarui Yao, Tim O'Gorman, Andrew Cowell, William Croft, Chu-Ren Huang, Jan Hajič, James Martin, Stephan Oepen, Martha Palmer, James Pustejovsky, Rosa Vallejos, and Nianwen Xue. 2021. Designing a uniform meaning representation for natural language processing. *KI-Künstliche Intelligenz*, 35(3):343–360.

Jens EL Van Gysel, Meagan Vigus, Pavlina Kalm, Sook-kyung Lee, Michael Regan, and William Croft. 2019. Cross-linguistic semantic annotation: Reconciling the language-specific and the universal. In *Proceedings of the First International Workshop on Designing Meaning Representations*, pages 1–14.

Ashish Vaswani, Noam Shazeer, Niki Parmar, Jakob Uszkoreit, Llion Jones, Aidan N Gomez, Łukasz Kaiser, and Illia Polosukhin. 2017. Attention is all you need. *Advances in neural information processing systems*, 30.

Meagan Vigus, Jens EL Van Gysel, and William Croft. 2019. A dependency structure annotation for modality. In *Proceedings of the First International Workshop on Designing Meaning Representations*, pages 182–198.

Meagan Vigus, Jens EL Van Gysel, Tim O'Gorman, Andrew Cowell, Rosa Vallejos, and William Croft. 2020. Cross-lingual annotation: a road map for low- and no-resource languages. In *Proceedings of the Second International Workshop on Designing Meaning Representations*, pages 30–40.

Shira Wein, Lucia Donatelli, Ethan Ricker, Calvin Engstrom, Alex Nelson, and Nathan Schneider. 2022a. Spanish Abstract Meaning Representation: Annotation of a General Corpus. *arXiv preprint arXiv:2204.07663*.

Shira Wein, Wai Ching Leung, Yifu Mu, and Nathan Schneider. 2022b. Effect of source language on AMR structure. In *Proceedings of the 16th Linguistic Annotation Workshop (LAW-XVI) within LREC2022*, pages 97–102, Marseille, France. European Language Resources Association.

Shira Wein and Nathan Schneider. 2022. Accounting for language effect in the evaluation of cross-lingual AMR parsers. In *Proceedings of the 29th International Conference on Computational Linguistics*, pages 3824–3834, Gyeongju, Republic of Korea. International Committee on Computational Linguistics.

Kristin Wright-Bettner, Chen Lin, Timothy Miller, Steven Bethard, Dmitriy Dligach, Martha Palmer, James H. Martin, and Guergana Savova. 2020. Defining and learning refined temporal relations in the clinical narrative. In *Proceedings of the 11th International Workshop on Health Text Mining and Information Analysis*, pages 104–114, Online. Association for Computational Linguistics.

Nianwen Xue, Ondřej Bojar, Jan Hajič, Martha Palmer, Zdeňka Urešová, and Xiuhong Zhang. 2014. Not an interlingua, but close: Comparison of English AMRs to Chinese and Czech. In *Proceedings of the Ninth International Conference on Language Resources and Evaluation (LREC'14)*, pages 1765–1772, Reykjavik, Iceland. European Language Resources Association (ELRA).

Nianwen Xue and Martha Palmer. 2009. Adding semantic roles to the Chinese Treebank. *Natural Language Engineering*, 15(1):143–172.

Nianwen Xue, Fei Xia, Fu-Dong Chiou, and Marta Palmer. 2005. The Penn Chinese TreeBank: Phrase structure annotation of a large corpus. *Natural language engineering*, 11(2):207–238.

Zixuan Zhang and Heng Ji. 2021. Abstract meaning representation guided graph encoding and decoding for joint information extraction. In *Proceedings of the 2021 Conference of the North American Chapter of the Association for Computational Linguistics: Human Language Technologies*, pages 39–49.

Jin Zhao, Nianwen Xue, Jens Van Gysel, and Jinho D Choi. 2021. UMR-Writer: A Web Application for Annotating Uniform Meaning Representations. In *Proceedings of the 2021 Conference on Empirical Methods in Natural Language Processing: System Demonstrations*, pages 160–167.

Yuping Zhou and Nianwen Xue. 2012. PDTB-style discourse annotation of Chinese text. In *Proceedings of the 50th Annual Meeting of the Association for Computational Linguistics (Volume 1: Long Papers)*, pages 69–77.

Yuping Zhou and Nianwen Xue. 2015. The Chinese Discourse TreeBank: A Chinese corpus annotated with discourse relations. *Language Resources and Evaluation*, 49(2):397–431.

A Appendices

A.1 Removed Roles

	AMR	UMR
ROLES:	:domain	NonPrototypical predication rolesets
	:subevent	Still available in document-level temporal dependency
	:prep-x	-
	:conj-as-if	-
	:subevent	-
SHORTCUTS:	:cost	:other-role
	:employed-by	have-org-role-92
	:meaning	mean-91
	:role	have-role-91, have-rel-role-92
	:subset	include-91
	:superset	include-91
	:instead-of	instead-of-91

Figure 2: Roles and shortcuts used in AMR but not used in UMR.

A.2 Graph Differences, Arapaho-English, AMR-UMR

ARAPAHO SENTENCE:

Text:	Beni'beebee3sohowuuneti3i' .
Morphological breakdown:	beni'- bee- bee3sohowuuneti -3i'
English glosses:	IC.just- REDUP- do sign language to each other -3PL
Parts of speech:	prefix- prefix- vai.RECIP -infl
English Translation:	*'[They didn't speak.] They were just doing sign language back and forth."*

	Arapaho:	English translation:
AMR:	(b / beni'beebee3sohowuuneti3i'-00)	(s / sign-00 :actor (t / they) :recipient t :mod (j / just) :manner (b / back-and-forth))
UMR:	(b / beebee3sohowuuneti-00 :actor (p / person ***/-3i'/* :refer-person 3rd :refer-number Plural) :recipient p :ARG1-of (c / contrast-91) ***/beni'-/* :Aspect Activity ***/bee-/* :modstr FullAff)	(s / sign-00 :actor (p / person ***they* :refer-person 3rd :refer-number Plural) :recipient p ***back and forth* :ARG1-of (c / contrast-91) ***just* :Aspect Activity ***back and forth* :modstr FullAff)

Figure 3: Comparison of AMR vs UMR graphs for a sentence from Arapaho (a polysynthetic language) and its English translation (non-polysynthetic). Note the disparity between the capturable semantics for Arapaho vs English in AMR. Conversely, UMR's schema allows semantically parallel sentences to appear in structurally-similar graphs. Alignments between tokens and graph elements ensure that tokens not appearing directly in the graph (e.g., 'they') may still be identified with their semantic representations in the graph.

A.3 Reification Roleset Mappings

AMR	+ reification	UMR	+ reification	
:Arg0	-	:actor	have-actor-91	new roles
:Arg1	-	:undergoer	have-undergoer-91	
:Arg1	-	:theme	have-theme-91	
:Arg0/1	-	:experiencer	have-experiencer-91	
:Arg0	-	:force	have-force-91	
:Arg0	-	:causer	have-causer-91	
:Arg0/1	-	:stimulus	have-stimulus-91	
say-01 :ARG2		:vocative	have-vocative-91	
and		:pure-addition	have-pure-addition-91	
or		:apprehensive	have-apprehensive-91	
instead-of-91		:substitute	instead-of-91	
except-91		:subtract	have-subtraction-91	
:location	be-located-at-91	:place	have-location-91	renamed roles
:time	be-temporally-at-91	:temporal	have-temporal-91	
:accompanier	accompany-01	:companion	have-companion-91	
:beneficiary	benefit-01	:affectee	have-affectee-91	
:li	have-li-91	:list-item	have-list-item-91	
:mod	have-mod-91	:mod	have-mod-91	split roles
		:other-role	have-other-role-91	
:cause	cause-01	:cause	have-cause-91	
		:reason	have-reason-91	
:part	have-part-91	:part	have-part-91	
:consist-of	consist-01	:group	have-group-91	
		:material	have-material-91	
:source	be-from-91	:source	have-source-91	
		:start	have-start-91	
:destination	be-destined-for-91	:goal	have-goal-91	
		:recipient	have-recipient-91	
:direction	-	:direction	have-direction-91	unchanged roles
:path	-	:path	have-path-91	
:duration	last-01	:duration	have-duration-91	
:frequency	have-frequency-91	:frequency	have-frequency-91	
:quant	have-quant-91	:quant	have-quant-91	
:degree	have-degree-91	:degree	have-degree-91	
	have-degree-91		have-degree-92	
:poss	have-03, own-01	:poss	have-91	
:topic	concern-02	:topic	have-topic-91	
:medium	-	:medium	have-medium-91	
:age	age-01	:age	have-age-91	
:example	exemplify-01	:example	have-example-91	
:ord	have-ord-91	:ord	have-ord-91	
:range	-	:range		
:polite	be-polite-91	:polite	be-polite-91	
:mode	have-mode-91	:mode	have-mode-91	
:polarity	have-polarity-91	:polarity	have-polarity-91	
:name	have-name-91	:name	have-name-91	
:wiki	-	:wiki	-	
:unit	-	:unit	have-unit-91	
:scale	-	:scale	-	
:value	have-value-91	:value	have-value-91	

Split-role arrows: have-mod-91 → :mod, :other-role; cause-01 → :cause, :reason; have-part-91 → :part; consist-01 → :part, :group, :material; be-from-91 → :material, :source, :start; be-destined-for-91 → :goal, :recipient.

Figure 4: Reification rolesets. *new roleset, renamed roleset, English-sourced roleset.*

A.4 Nonprototypical Predication Mappings

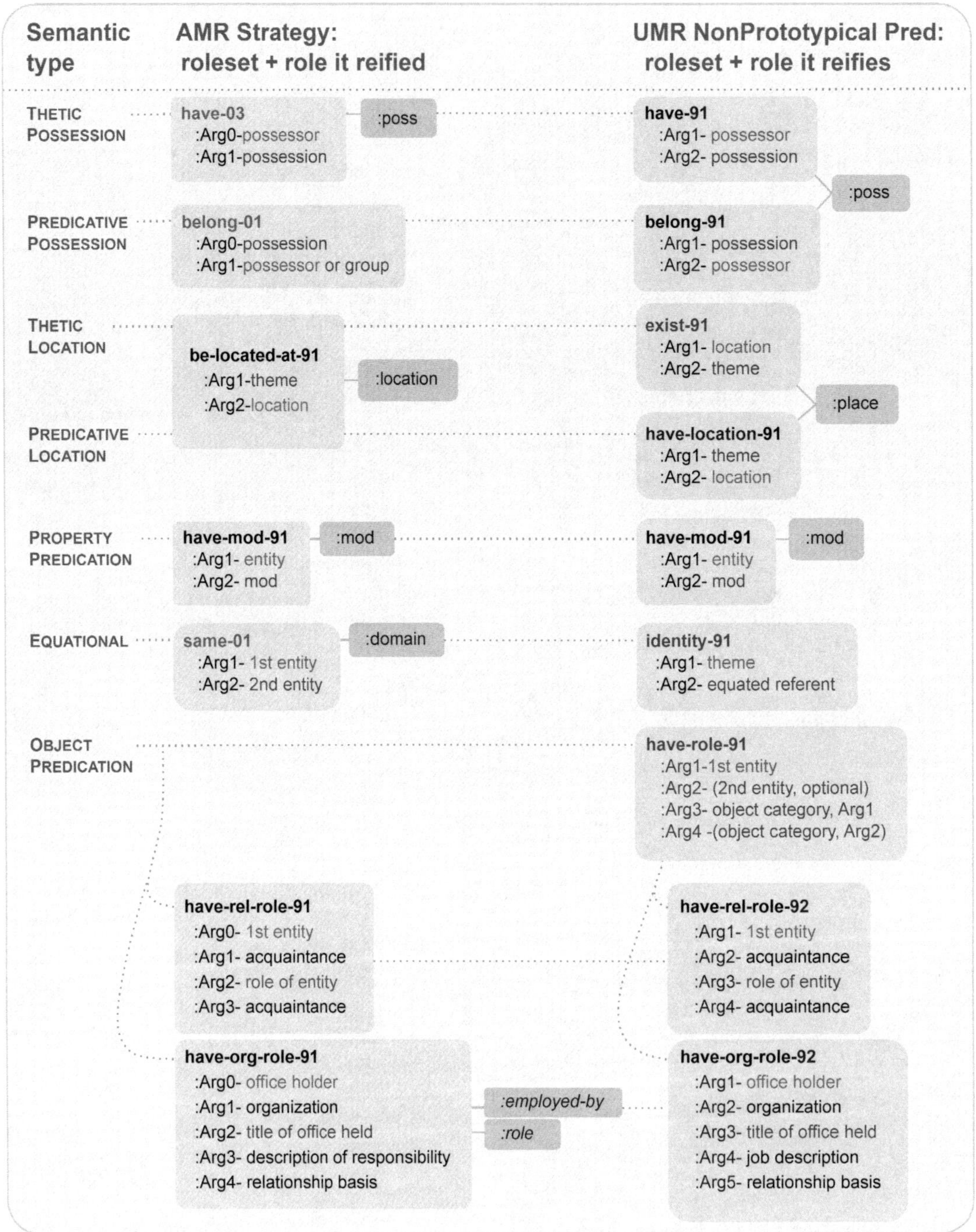

Figure 5: Nonprototypical Predication: *new element, renamed element, English-sourced roleset, topicalized argument, focused argument*

A.5 Other Abstract Roleset Mappings

AMR	UMR
-91 Rolesets:	
byline-91	byline-91
correlate-91	correlate-91
course-91	course-91
distribution-range-91	distribution-range-91
have-degree-of-resemblance-91	- (use: have-degree-91 + resemble-91)
hyperlink-91	hyperlink-91
include-91	include-91
instead-of-91	instead-of-91
publication-91	publication-91
rate-entity-91	rate-entity-91
regardless-91	- (use: :concessive-conditional)
request-confirmation-91	- (investigate further)
request-response-91	- (investigate further)
score-on-scale-91	score-on-scale-91
statistical-test-91	statistical-test-91
street-address-91	street-address-91
English-Sourced Rolesets:	
cite-01	cite-91
cost-01	- (use: :other-role)
counter-01 (for 'anti')	- (investigate further)
infer-01	- (use: infer-91 or :reason, depending on context)
mean-01	mean-91
oppose-01 (for 'anti')	- (investigate further)
protest-01 (for 'anti')	- (investigate further)
resemble-01	resemble-91
Modal Rolesets:	(See Vigus et al. (2019) for full modal dependency annotation guidelines)
obligate-01	:modal PrtAff
possible-01	:modal NeutAff
recommend-01	:modal PrtAff
permit-01	:modal NeutAff
wish-01	:modal NeutAff

Figure 6: Other Abstract Rolesets. Arguments unchanged where rolesets have been retained. *new roleset, renamed roleset, English-sourced roleset, commentary*.

A.6 Discourse Relation Mappings

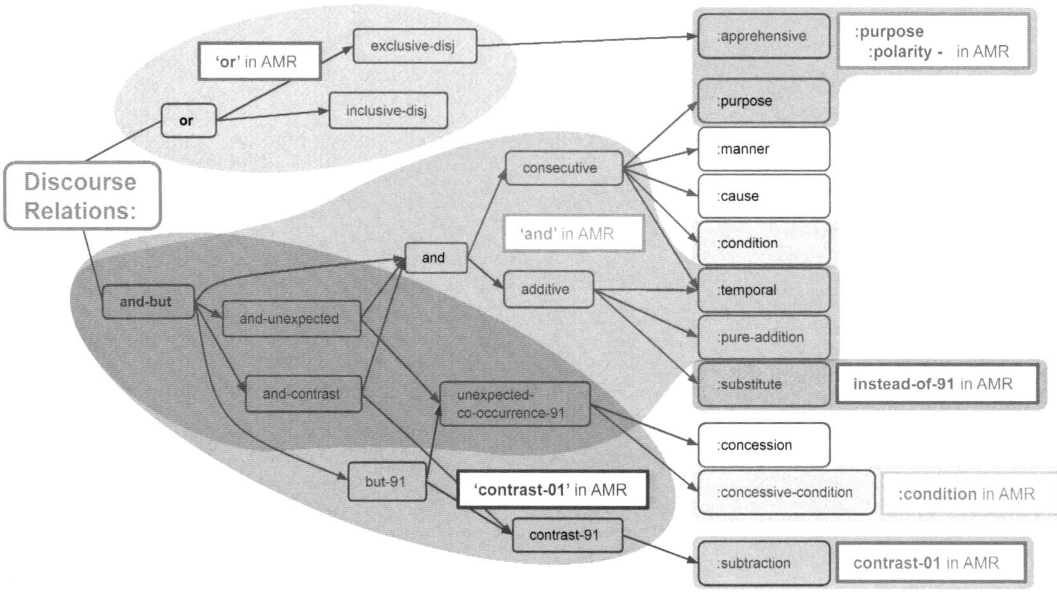

Upper Levels: Abstract Concepts/Rolesets

Meaning	Concept/Roleset	Roles
Disjunctive	or	:op1 :op2 :opX
Exclusive Disjunctive	exclusive-disj	:op1 :op2 :opX
Inclusive Disjunctive	inclusive-dis	:op1 :op2 :opX
And	and	:op1 :op2 :opX
Consecutive	consecutive	:op1 :op2 :opX
Additive	additive	:op1 :op2 :opX
And + But	and-but	:op1 :op2 :opX
And + Unexpected	and-unexpected	:op1 :op2 :opX
And + Contrast	and-contrast	:op1 :op2 :opX
Unexpected Co-Occurrence	unexpected-co-occurrence-91	:ARG1 :ARG2
But	but-91	:ARG1 :ARG2
Pure Contrast	contrast-91	:ARG1 :ARG2

Lower Levels: Roles & Reification Rolesets

Meaning	Relation	Reification	Roles
Apprehensive	:apprehensive	have-apprehensive–91	:ARG1 :ARG2
Purpose	:purpose	have-purpose-91	:ARG1 :ARG2
Means	:manner	have-manner-91	:ARG1 :ARG2
Cause	:cause	have-cause-91	:ARG1 :ARG2
Conditional	:condition	have-condition-91	:ARG1 :ARG2
Posterior Anterior Simultaneous	:temporal	have-temporal-91	:ARG1 :ARG2
Pure-Addition	:pure-addition	have-pure-addition-91	:ARG1 :ARG2
Substitution	:substitute	instead-of-91	:ARG1 :ARG2
Concessive	:concession	have-concession-91	:ARG1 :ARG2
Concessive-Conditional	:concessive-condition	have-concessive-condition-91	:ARG1 :ARG2
Subtraction	:subtraction	have-subtraction-91	:ARG1 :ARG2

Figure 7: Discourse Relations. Above: lattice, with concepts and rolesets in the upper levels and roles in the lower level. AMR concept mappings overlap the lattice. Below: Argument structures. *new relation, renamed relation.*

A.7 Abstract Concepts

AMR	+ Roles	UMR	+ Roles
AMR-/UMR- & Polarity-Related:			
amr-unknown	-	umr-unknown	
amr-choice	:op1 :op2 :opX	umr-choice	:op1 :op2 :opX
amr-empty	-	umr-empty	
amr-unintelligible	-	umr-unintelligible	
truth-value	:Polarity-of	truth-value	:Polarity-of
Entity Types:			
date-entity	(list unchanged, see Figure 1)	date-entity	(list unchanged, see Figure 1)
email-address-entity	:value	email-address-entity	:value
ordinal-entity	:value :range	ordinal-entity	:value :range :range-start
percentage-entity	:value	percentage-entity	:value
phone-number-entity	:value	phone-number-entity	:value
score-entity	:op1 :op2 :opX	score-entity	:op1 :op2 :opX
string-entity	:value	string-entity	:value
url-entity	:value	url-entity	:value
Interval Types:			
value-interval	:op1 :op2	value-interval	:op1 :op2
date-interval	:op1 :op2	date-interval	:op1 :op2
slash	:op1 :op2	slash	:op1 :op2
Other			
name	:op1 :op2 :opX	name	:op1 :op2 :opX
emoticon	:value	emoticon	:value
relative-position	:op1 :direction :quant	relative-position	:op1 :direction :quant
Count & Math			
more-than	:op1	more-than	:op1
less-than	:op1	less-than	:op1
at-most	:op1	at-most	:op1
at-least	:op1	at-least	:op1
sum-of	:op1	sum-of	:op1
product-of	:op1	product-of	:op1
difference-of	:op1	difference-of	:op1
quotient-of	:op1	quotient-of	:op1
power-of	:op1	power-of	:op1
root-of	:op1	root-of	:op1
logarithm-of	:op1	logarithm-of	:op1
ratio-of	:op1	ratio-of	:op1
Generic Concepts for Participant/NonParticipant Roles:			
thing		thing	:refer-number
person		person	:refer-person :refer-number
dummy (Chinese AMR)		dummy	
location		place	:refer-number
manner		manner	:refer-number
quantity		quantity	:Quant-of
event		event	:refer-number
Removed:			
either	:op1 :op2	- (use or/inclusive-disj/exclusive-disj :op1 :op2)	
neither	:op1 :op2	- (use or/inclusive-disj/exclusive-disj :op1 :op2 :polarity -)	
multiple	:op1	- (see mensural constructions, UMR-guidelines)	

Figure 8: Abstract Concepts, not including X-quantities or Named Entities. These are largely unchanged from AMR. *new concept, renamed concept, commentary*.

A.8 Quantity Types

Quantity-type	Arguments + Suggested Values	
monetary-quantity	:unit	dollar, euro, pound, yen, yuan
distance-quantity	:unit	meter, kilometer, inch, foot, yard, mile, light-year, kilo-base-pair
area-quantity	:unit	square-meter, square-kilometer, square-foot, acre, hectare, square-mile
volume-quantity	:unit	liter, cubic-meter, fluid-ounce, pint, gallon, cubic-mile
temporal-quantity	:unit	second, minute, hour, day, week, month, year, decade, century
frequency-quantity	:unit	hertz
speed-quantity	:unit	meter-per-second, mile-per-hour
acceleration-quantity	:unit	meter-per-second-squared
mass-quantity	:unit	kilogram, ounce, pound, ton, atomic-mass-unit, kilodalton
force-quantity	:unit	newton
pressure-quantity	:unit	pascal, bar, psi, atmosphere, torr
energy-quantity	:unit	joule, calorie, kilowatt-hour, btu, electron-volt
power-quantity	:unit	watt, horsepower
charge-quantity	:unit	coulomb
potential-quantity	:unit	volt
resistance-quantity	:unit	ohm
inductance-quantity	:unit	henry
magnetic-field-quantity	:unit	tesla, gauss
magnetic-flux-quantity	:unit	maxwell, weber
radiation-quantity	:unit	becquerel, curie, sievert, rem, gray, rad
fuel-consumption-quantity	:unit	liter-per-100-kilometer, mile-per-gallon
numerical-quantity	:unit	point, mole
information-quantity	:unit	bit, byte, kilobyte, megabyte, terabyte, petabyte, exabyte, zettabyte, yottabyte, nibble
concentration-quantity	:unit	molar (1M = 1 molar = 1 mole/liter), micromolar (μM), kilogram-per-cubic-meter, parts-per-million
catalytic-activity-quantity	:unit	katal (kat), microkatal, nanokatal, enzyme-unit (U)
acidity-quantity	:scale	ph
seismic-quantity	:scale	richter
temperature-quantity	:unit	degree
	:scale	celsius, kelvin, farenheit
angle-quantity	:unit	degree, radian

Figure 9: X-Quantity Types. Unchanged from AMR. More values are possible in UMR than just those listed as suggested.

A.9 UMR Named Entity Types

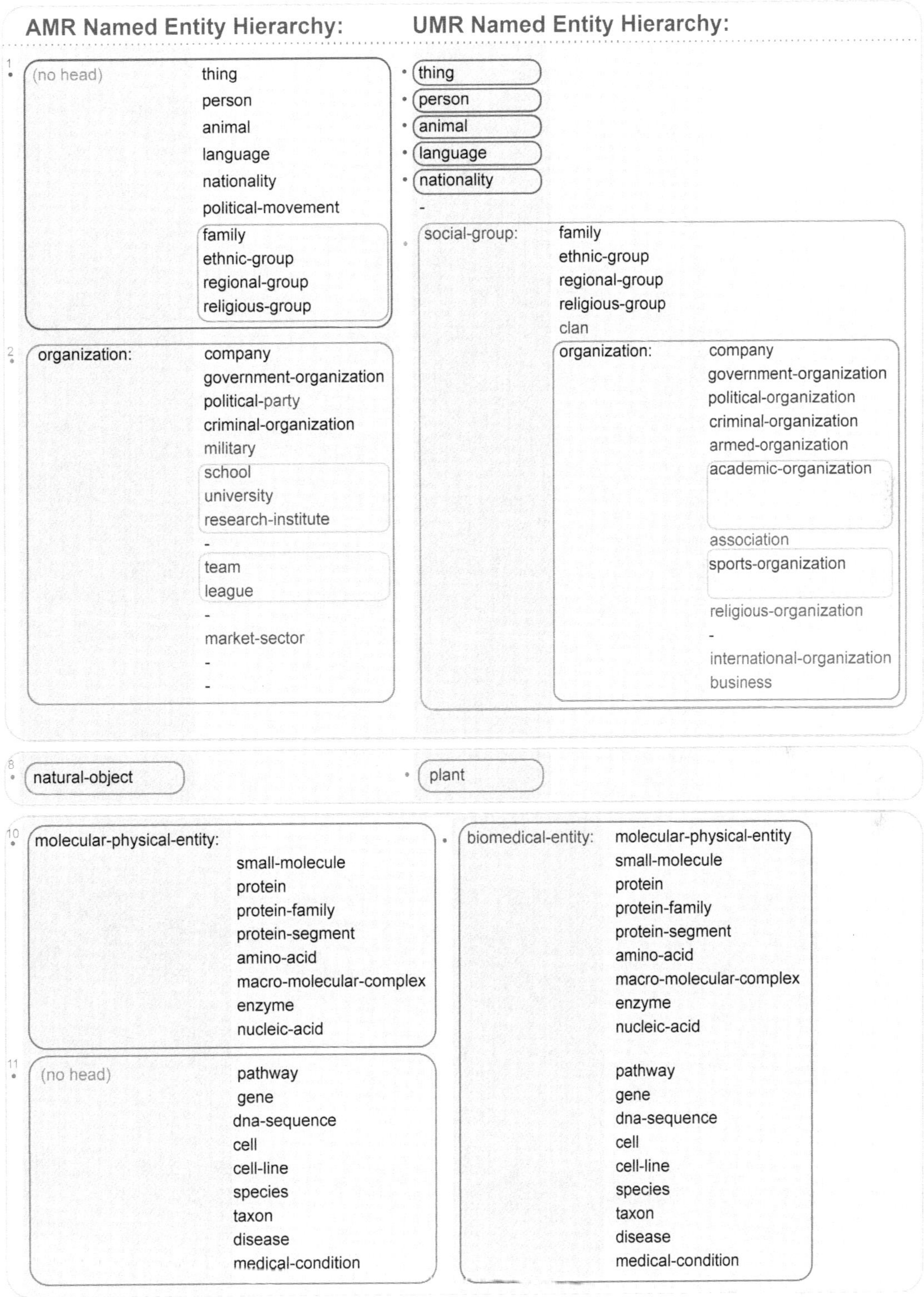

Figure 10: Named Entity Hierarchy Mapping. The far left bullet points on the AMR side are the eleven top-level groupings given in the AMR editor, numbered according to the order in which they appear there. Colored columns distinguish category levels for each hierarchy. *New type, renamed type, old name.*

AMR Named Entity Hierarchy:		UMR Named Entity Hierarchy:	
3 location:	ocean	geographic-entity:	ocean
	sea		sea
	lake		lake
	river		river
	gulf		gulf
	bay		bay
	strait		strait
	canal		- (duplicate)
	peninsula		peninsula
	mountain		mountain
	volcano		volcano
	valley		valley
	canyon		canyon
	island		island
	desert		desert
	forest		forest
	continent		continent
	moon		moon
	planet		planet
	star		star
	constellation		constellation
	local-region	region:	local-region
	country-region		country-region
	world-region		world-region
	city	geo-political-region:	city
	city-district		city-district
	county		county
	state		state
	province		province
	territory		territory
	country		country
4 facility:	airport	facility:	airport
	station		station
	port		port
	tunnel		tunnel
	bridge		bridge
	road		road
	railway-line		railway-line
	canal		canal
	building		building
	theater		theater
	museum		museum
	palace		palace
	hotel		hotel
	worship-place		worship-place
	sports-facility		sports-facility
	market		market
	park		park
	zoo		zoo
	amusement-park		amusement-park

Figure 11: Named Entity Hierarchy Mapping, 3rd, 4th AMR bullet points. *New type, renamed type, old name, commentary*.

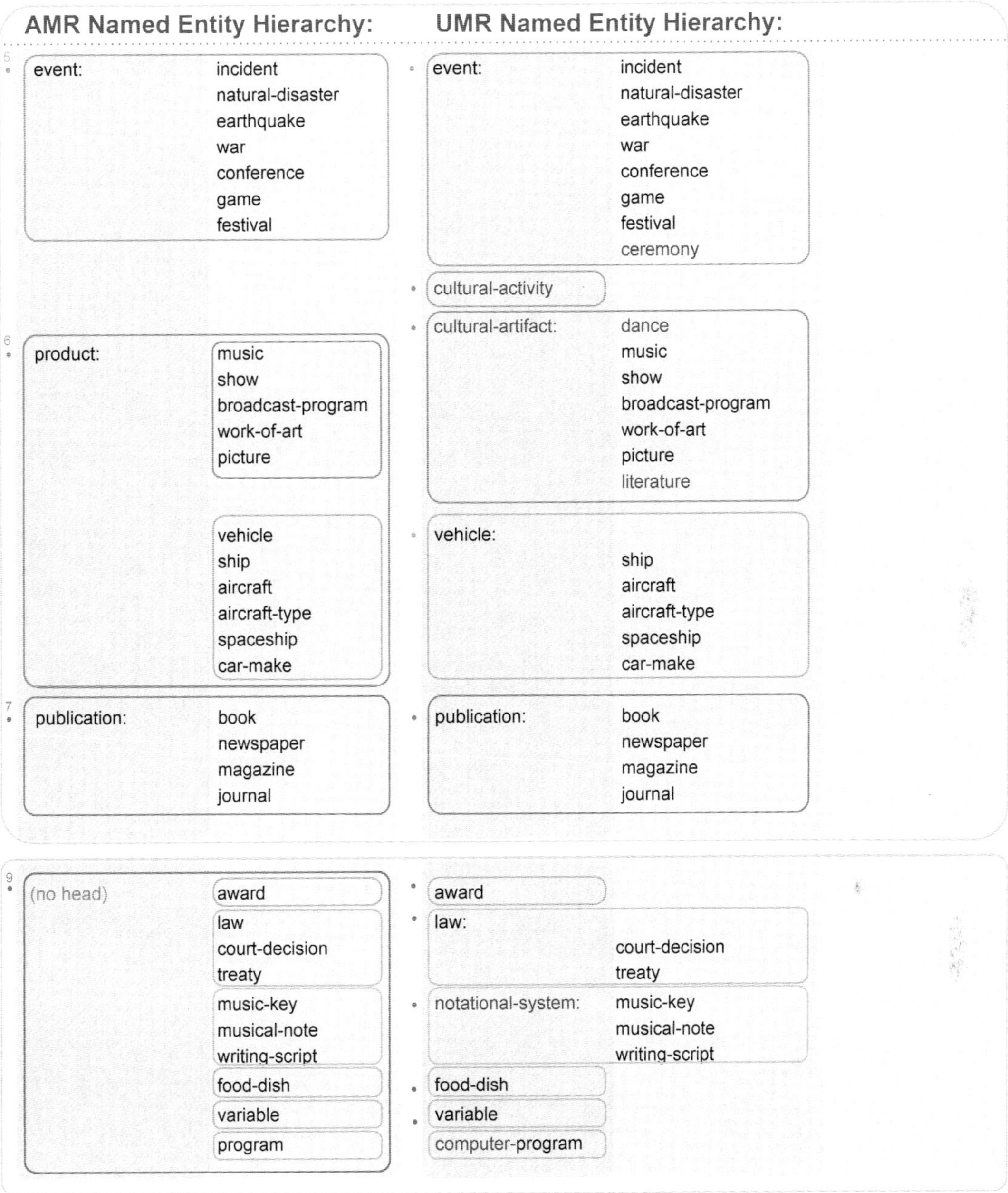

Figure 12: Named Entity Hierarchy Mapping, 5th, 6th, 7th, and 9th AMR bullet points. *New type, renamed type, old name, commentary.*

Author Index

Association for Computational Linguistics
209 N. Eighth Street
Stroudsburg, Pennsylvania 18360

ISBN 978-1-7138-9063-8

CURRAN ASSOCIATES INC.
proceedings.com